A Life of Thomas Becket in Verse

La Vie de saint Thomas Becket
by Guernes de Pont-Sainte-Maxence

Composed in the immediate aftermath of Becket's murder in 1170, and based, in part, on oral testimony gathered at Canterbury and from Becket's sister, Guernes de Pont-Sainte-Maxence's 6180-line narrative poem is the earliest Life of Becket to appear in the French vernacular. Its account of Becket's life and martyrdom, though heavily biased in favour of its saintly protagonist and the cause he embraced, is informative as well as vigorously polemical. It offers a viewpoint different from that of contemporary Latin historians in that it was written to be listened to by lay men and women. It was also recited at the saint's tomb at Canterbury, and provides therefore a picture of events that would have reached a contemporary French-speaking public avid for first-hand knowledge of their new heroic martyr.

Mediaeval Sources in Translation

MEDIAEVAL SOURCES IN TRANSLATION 56

A Life of Thomas Becket in Verse

La Vie de saint Thomas Becket
by Guernes de Pont-Sainte-Maxence

Translated with an introduction and notes by
IAN SHORT

PONTIFICAL INSTITUTE OF MEDIAEVAL STUDIES

Library and Archives Canada Cataloguing in Publication

Guernes, de Pont-Sainte-Maxence, active 12th century
[Vie de saint Thomas le martyr. English]
A life of Thomas Becket in verse = La vie de saint Thomas Becket / by Guernes de Pont-Sainte-Maxence ; translated with an introduction and notes by Ian Short.

(Mediaeval sources in translation ; 56)
Translated from the Old French.
Includes bibliographical references and index.
Issued in print and electronic formats.
ISBN 978-0-88844-306-9 (pbk.). – ISBN 978-1-77110-357-2 (pdf)

1. Thomas, à Becket, Saint, 1118?–1170 – Poetry – Early works to 1800. 2. Great Britain – History – Henry II, 1154–1189 – Biography – Poetry – Early works to 1800. 3. Christian martyrs – England – Canterbury – Biography – Poetry – Early works to 1800. 4. Christian saints – England – Canterbury – Biography – Poetry – Early works to 1800. I. Short, Ian, 1939–, writer of introduction, writer of preface, translator II. Pontifical Institute of Mediaeval Studies, issuing body III. Title. IV. Title: Vie de saint Thomas Becket. V. Vie de saint Thomas le martyr. English. VI. Series: Mediaeval sources in translation ; 56

PQ1477.G45A19913 2013 841'.1 C2013-907069-9
C2013-907070-2

Pontifical Institute of Mediaeval Studies
59 Queen's Park Crescent East
Toronto, Ontario, Canada M5S 2C4
www.pims.ca

MANUFACTURED IN CANADA

Contents

Preface

In 1066, William the Conqueror, known to contemporaries as William the Bastard, brought to Britain, in the words of Gervase of Canterbury, "not only a whole new way of life, but also a new way of speaking." This imported language is what we refer to today as Anglo-Norman or Insular French. It was the idiolect of a powerful Francophone elite, a language of colonialization that was a spoken vernacular as well as a written vehicle of literature, learning and record. Historiography holds pride of place in the literary production of twelfth-century Insular culture, but while its Latin authors, who include Orderic Vitalis, William of Malmesbury, Geoffrey of Monmouth and Henry of Huntingdon, are well known, its French-speaking historians are less so. They include Geoffrey Gaimar, whose *Estoire des Engleis* (1136–37) provides a national narrative from England's mythical Trojan origins down to the start of the twelfth century; Wace, a Norman by birth but an Anglo-Norman by adoption, who between 1155 and 1175 composed histories of Britain (*Brut*) and of the dukes of Normandy (*Rou*); and Jordan Fantosme, author of a contemporary chronicle of the 1174 revolt against Henry II. Some add to this already impressive list a history of the Third Crusade, *Estoire de la guerre sainte*, by Ambroise (1190s), and Benoît de Sainte-Maure's *Histoire des ducs de Normandie*. Guernes de Pont-Sainte-Maxence, though of Continental origin, can also be considered an honorary Anglo-Norman historian, not only by virtue of the subject of his poem, but also because it survives today exclusively in Anglo-Norman copies. Treading the fine and shifting line between historiography and hagiography, Guernes offers us a unique insight into contemporary attitudes to one of the twelfth century's most dramatic political events.

In preparing, over many years, my translation of his poem, I have been fortunate in having John Gillingham as a colleague, and it is a pleasure for me to thank him here for his careful and expert reading of the first draft of this book. The Pontifical Institute's readers' reports also made a significant contribution to improving it. Any persistent errors and other shortcomings are, naturally, to be placed squarely at my door, and mine alone.

IAN SHORT
London
April 2013

Introduction

...from every shires ende
Of Engelond to Caunterbury they wend
The hooly blisful martir for to seke.

Chaucer, *The Canterbury Tales*

In much the same way as the assassination of President Kennedy in Texas in 1963 was destined to become an event of global importance, so news of Becket's murder was, less swiftly but no less momentously, to reverberate across the whole of Western Christendom far beyond the confines of Canterbury. It was here, in his own cathedral, on a cold Tuesday evening, the 29th of December, 1170, that the archbishop of Canterbury was mortally wounded, not far from the high altar, by four heavily armed knights. Though Kennedy was no saint, both men shared a similar fate by virtue of their being among the most supreme politicians of their times, and politics proved to be the undoing of both. But while Kennedy saw himself as a conciliator and a reformer, Becket was, by temperament and action, confrontational and conservative. The circumstances of both their deaths, also, were such as to generate conspiracy theories.

In the case of Becket, the chief suspect was no less a figure than the king of England and head of what looks today very much like an Anglo-French empire, whose borders stretched from Scotland to the Pyrenees. Henry II, formerly a bosom friend and ally of Becket's, latterly his implacable enemy, was a man of notoriously volatile temper. He may well, out of exasperation and impatience more than anything else, have cursed Becket or spoken ill of him within the hearing of some of his more literal-minded subordinates. He acknowledged as much himself, but consistently and vehemently denied having in any way explicitly incited anyone to kill Becket – a man whom he personally had made his chancellor in 1155 and ultimately his archbishop of Canterbury. His personal atonement, after Becket's death, though obviously a political gesture intended for public consumption, struck even his harshest critics as heart-felt and sincere.

How far Becket himself was, as Edward Grim, a clerical eye-witness to his murder, suspected, a willing martyr to the religious cause that he had embraced relatively late in life, is another of the many still unresolved questions raised by the circumstances of his death.[1] Although Becket had accepted Henry's nomination of him to Canterbury with reluctance, he paused only to go through the formalities of ordination as a priest before being consecrated in June 1162. The crucial turning point in his relationship with Henry came when he insisted, against the king's wishes, on resigning the post of chancellor on becoming archbishop. Henry's hopes of having a pliant ecclesiastical ally to help steer through his programme of secular reform were dashed. From having been each other's complement – as Arthur Bryant put it –, the king and his archbishop now became antitheses.[2]

What precipitated the crisis that brought Becket onto such a tragic collision course with his monarch and erstwhile patron were the reforms that Henry was intent on introducing to the country's administrative structures in the aftermath of Stephen's frequently chaotic reign. Part of these reforms entailed the rationalization of legal procedure in the courts. In an effort to re-establish a uniform and equitable framework of justice across the realm, Henry was led to propose some radical changes, and among these were certain aspects of the privileged legal status, within a secular judicial system, that the clergy had come to secure for themselves.

The privileged treatment of clerks charged with serious criminal offences, more specifically the questions of where and by whom they were to be tried, judged and sentenced, was only one of many inequities that Henry set out to reform. It was, however, around this particular issue that state and church (*regnum* and *sacerdotium*) were to enter into a seemingly

1 "... quia ab olim martyrii flagrabat amore, implendi illud occasione, ut videtur, adepta, ne differet ipse ..." ("Having long had his heart set on martyrdom, he now saw that the opportunity to embrace it seemed to be presenting itself"). *Materials for the History of Thomas Becket ...*, ed. James Craigie Robertson and J.B. Sheppard (London, 1875–85), 2: 434.

2 Arthur Bryant, *Makers of the Realm* (London, 1953), p. 239.

irreconcilable series of confrontations, as the principles of secular justice were brought into open conflict with clerical immunity.

Ecclesiastical courts dispensing canon law were operating in parallel to secular courts, and jurisdiction over and punishment of clerks accused of serious crimes lay exclusively with the church. This jurisdiction Henry proposed to transfer to the secular courts, and he enshrined this reform, and others aimed at curtailing the influence of Rome over church matters within his kingdom, in the Constitutions of Clarendon of 1164. The notorious Clause 3 of this document stipulated that all indicted clerks should be answerable to the king's court before appearing before an ecclesiastical court, and that if convicted according to canon law, they should lose their clerical status and then be subject to secular punishment.[3] Despite Becket's principled opposition to such a radical new departure, to everyone's surprise and confusion he first gave his assent, but then on reflection refused to append his seal to the agreement and retracted. Such erratic behaviour did little to increase his fellow bishops' confidence in him as a negotiator, and Becket's position was gradually thereafter to become more and more isolated.

Henry angrily retaliated by indicting the archbishop for a string of secular offences, but he soon lost patience and ordered his arrest. Becket fled to the France of Louis VII in November 1164, and there began a long period of stalemate, during which the archbishop took up residence at the Cistercian abbey of Pontigny in Burgundy. Attempts were made from time to time to bring the parties together: the two met in 1170, the year Henry had his eldest son crowned by the archbishop of York, whom Becket, with papal support, promptly had suspended for infringing Canterbury's long established rights to crown the country's monarchs. By then, however, relations had broken down beyond the point of no return, and Henry and his ex-chancellor were never to be properly reconciled. At a meeting in July 1170,

3 "Clerks cited and accused of any matter shall ... come before the king's court to answer there concerning matters which shall seem to the king's court to be answerable there, and before the ecclesiastical court for what shall seem to be answerable there, but in such a way that the justice of the king shall send to the court of Holy Church to see how the case is there tried. And if the clerk shall be convicted or shall confess, the Church ought no longer to protect him"; *English Historical Documents: 1042–1189*, ed. David C. Douglas and George W. Greenaway, 2nd ed. (London, 1981), pp. 767–68.

however, it was agreed, under papal pressure, that Becket should end his six-year exile and return to Canterbury. No customary kiss of peace was requested, and none was offered, and the Constitutions of Clarendon simply dropped off the agenda. Becket duly returned to Canterbury on December 1st. Before the end of the month he was dead.

It is often argued that responsibility for their tragic confrontation is to be laid at the door of each of the protagonists in turn: that Henry naively misjudged the strength of Becket's commitment to the privileges of the church when he appointed him archbishop; and that Becket on his elevation went native and saw himself as the self-elected champion of a whole raft of ecclesiastical rights that he imagined to be under serious threat. Things were almost certainly more complicated than this.

Personality undoubtedly had a role to play in fuelling the flames of discord. Initially at least, Henry seemed willing to be accommodating both in his original demands and in the negotiations that followed them. He was, however, met with fierce intransigence from a proud, ambitious and somewhat egotistical adversary. Henry's angry and impatient reaction to being thwarted by someone he had raised, as it were, from the dust was certainly a contributory factor to the rapidly deteriorating relations between the two men. Thereafter stubbornness, mistrust and fear of losing face on both sides ensured that what had started off as a rather parochial spat turned into a political and diplomatic drama of international dimensions. That under provocation and in private Henry could have said words to the effect "Who will rid me of this turbulent priest?" – a phrase, incidentally, which no contemporary record ever attributed to him – is not beyond the bounds of probability. That Becket in his turn could have used his privileged personal knowledge of Henry deliberately to provoke, goad or frustrate his former friend and benefactor in his various negotiations with him seems altogether likely. Could, for example, his boldness in confronting Henry have come from knowing that the king's temper tantrums were little more than a means of intimidating those who opposed him? What, on the other hand, Becket is unlikely to have foreseen is that he himself was ultimately to die a victim, albeit indirect, of the king's temper as mediated through a posse of Henry's over-zealous henchmen.

Another argument accuses Henry of over-ambition and of tyrannically forcing the issue at Clarendon (his tactics have even been called Stalinist), but counter-arguments that it was Becket's vanity and lack of moderation rather than royal bullying that destroyed the harmony of Henry's kingdom are defended with no less conviction. However quick-witted, versatile and tireless a worker Becket had been as chancellor, as archbishop he had none of the skill in statesmanship that Henry's experience had inevitably provided him with. Some otherwise sober commentators have gone as far as to categorize Becket as a man of extremes, a hypersensitive self-dramatizer.[4] He certainly did not shun the secular life when he was chancellor, and even as uncritical a biographer as Guernes describes him living a life of ostentatious extravagance interspersed with periods of active military campaigning. As archbishop, however, he became the paragon not only of Christian sobriety but also of severe asceticism. Whatever personality disorders the two protagonists may, or may not, have had, it remains clear that a solution of compromise, memorably defined by Lord Edward Cecil as an agreement between two men to do what both agree is wrong, was something that neither of them seemed willing or able to envisage.

The historian Lewis Warren, in his widely acclaimed study of Henry II, ended a lengthy and insightful chapter on the Becket controversy by concluding that "the story of Henry II and Thomas Becket is indeed a classic tragedy – the story of heroic men with remarkable qualities, undone by equally great flaws of character, flaws of passion and of pride."[5] As far as equitable and fair-minded conclusions go, this is itself a classic, but whether such intellectual impartiality (cynics might be tempted to call it uncomfortable fence-sitting) brings us any the closer to the truth of this unhappy episode is, perhaps, to be doubted. Explicit moral judgements are, in the final analysis, something that historians can quite well do without, unless the thrust of their analyses makes them indispensable or unavoidable. As modern politics (and not just the Kennedy assassination) remind us, events can, for a whole host of seemingly random reasons, sometimes lurch out of control, and no amount of retrospective wisdom can adequately account for everything that happens. Some developments we can begin to understand, others not at all.

The aftermath of the murder strikes the modern reader as much less unpredictable than the series of events that had led up to it. That Becket should have been victorious in death seems to us now more or less inevitable. Within hours of the murder rumours of miracles began circu-

4 Antonia Gransden, *Historical Writing in England, c. 550 to c. 1307* (London, 1974), pp. 302–4; Bryant, *Makers of the Realm*, pp. 240–41, 246–48.

5 W.L. Warren, *Henry II* (Berkeley, 1973), p. 517.

lating among the common people, the poor and the oppressed for whom Becket, the flamboyant populist, had always been a natural champion. The myth had already begun overtaking the man. Collective memory was there to work its magic and transform the sordid banality of contingency into the stuff of heroic legend.

Becket's murder spawned no fewer than nine more or less instant biographies-cum-hagiographies in the language of the church, Latin. Guernes' history, begun in 1171 and completed before September 1174, was the earliest in French, the vernacular of the ruling Anglo-Norman elite of England. This was followed, towards 1185, by an Anglo-Norman French version in tail-rhyme stanzas by a certain Benoît, monk of St Albans. Matthew Paris's illustrated verse life and the Old Icelandic *Thómas Saga* date from the next century.[6] Guernes wrote two versions of his poem, and it is the second, revised version, which is extant today in eight Anglo-Norman manuscripts and fragments, that has become the standard text. The manuscripts are:[7]

London, British Library Add. 59616 (*olim* Phillipps 8113), fols. 27–141 (end 13th c.)
London, British Library Add. 70513 (*olim* Welbeck Abbey I C 1), fols. 9–50v (start 14th c.)
London, British Library Harley 270, fols. 1–122v (end 12th c.)
Paris, Bibiothèque nationale de France, nouv. acq. fr. 13513, fols. 1–98v (start 13th c.)
Wolfenbüttel, Herzog August Bibliothek Cod. Guelf. 34.6 Aug. 2°, fols. 1–83 (12th / 13th c.)

6 *La Vie de Thomas Becket par Beneit*, ed. Börje Schlyter (Lund, 1941); *Fragments d'une Vie de saint Thomas de Cantorbery*, ed. Paul Meyer (Paris, 1885); *Thomas Saga Erkibyskups: A Life of Archbishop Thomas Becket in Icelandic*, ed. and trans. Eiríkr Magnússon (London, 1875–85, repr. Cambridge, 2012); cf. Mary Dominica Legge, *Anglo-Norman Literature and Its Background* (Oxford, 1963), pp. 248–51, 268–69. For an overview see Gransden, *Historical Writing in England*, pp. 297–308.

7 Ruth J. Dean with Maureen Boulton, *Anglo-Norman Literature: A Guide to Texts and Manuscripts* (London, 1999), no. 508; Maria Careri, Christine Ruby, and Ian Short, *Livres et écritures en français et en occitan au XIIe siècle: Catalogue illustré* (Rome, 2011), nos. 37, 48, 64, 97/1. Emmanuel Walberg's base is the Wolfenbüttel manuscript, with recourse to Harley 270 to repair omissions.

The excerpts and fragments are:

London, British Library Cott. Dom. XI, fols. 27–45v (mid-14th c.)
London, Society of Antiquaries 716, fols. 5–6v (Guernes' first draft; ca. 1171–72); fols.1–4v (start 13th c.)
Oxford, Bodleian Rawl. C.641 (12487), fols. 10–13 (end 12th c.)

The standard text was published by Emmanuel Walberg, an experienced textual editor, in 1922 (with the text reissued in 1936). Guernes' first draft from ca. 1171–72 survives only as a fragment of 80 lines (see Appendix). Though the standard version was re-edited by Jacques Thomas at Louvain in 2002, my translation has been made from the more accessible 1936 text as edited by Walberg.

An English translation by Janet Shirley appeared in 1975, and this was followed by two modern French translations, one by Jean-Guy Gouttebroze and Ambroise Queffélec (Paris, 1990), the other by Thomas in his 2002 edition (see Bibliography). While I have of course benefited, and gratefully so, from all three of these translations, and from Thomas's detailed textual commentary in particular, I have deliberately attempted to provide my readers with a fresh and original interpretation of the Medieval French text. In so doing, I have not hesitated tacitly to correct some occasional inaccuracies in the work of my predecessors. My rendering avoids the literal (which Shirley had already attempted), and endeavours to tread the difficult path between textual accuracy, fidelity of tone and overall readability. I will sometimes have strayed from the straight and narrow, and will have disappointed the perfectionists. As my translation is not literal, the order of words and clauses in the original has sometimes been altered according to the requirements of Modern English syntax. An asterisk indicates the presence of a note following the text. Names of persons are, as a general rule, elucidated in the Index.

Despite its glaring pro-clerical partisanship, Guernes' text is that of a conscientious historian and not just a straightforward hagiographer, someone with sufficient critical awareness and scholarly scruple, in fact, to abandon a first version which he had based on purely written sources, and to travel to Canterbury to gather first-hand oral testimony from Becket's friends, colleagues and acquaintances. In addition he went to Barking Abbey, where

Becket's sister was abbess, to pursue his researches.[8] His poem, he also tells us, he frequently read out publicly at the saint's tomb in Canterbury (presumably in instalments or extracts).

An account such as this, written to be listened to collectively in French, was naturally designed to reach a different audience from one written to be read privately in Latin; it catered largely to a secular public. Given, however, the widespread use of the vernacular in convents and monasteries in twelfth-century England, nuns and minimally literate monks might well also have formed part of Guernes' intended audience.[9] It is significant, moreover, that his poem seems not to have been popular outside Britain, even though the author himself was a native of Northern France (Pont-Sainte-Maxence is in the Paris Basin not far from Beauvais). We have no other information on Guernes than what he himself provides in the course of his narrative. Being, as he obviously was, a cleric, his poem almost inevitably becomes a didactic one, and its propagandistic perspective, a tangible and often intrusive presence from the beginning to the end of his work, should come as no surprise.

Guernes' first draft shows him to have become even more entrenched in his personal and professional prejudice when he crossed over to England. From having been willing, initially, to grant the king some benefit of the doubt as far as his complicity in the murder was concerned, once at Canterbury he came to reject the more sober and non-committal account of Edward Grim in favour of a far more critical and negative attitude towards Henry. This anti-Henry, pro-Becket bias is, naturally but no less unfortunately, characteristic of each and every one of the Becket biographies that date from this time. Historians are surely right, in theory, to urge us to see both sides of the story and to look at affairs as they appeared at Westminster rather than as they appeared at Canterbury. They could well be asking for the impossible, however, since no counter-narrative exists, and an impartial version of events remains out of our reach. As Samuel Butler aptly remarked, when it comes to judging between God and the Devil, it is well to remember that God has written all the books.

8 *Barking Abbey and Medieval Literary Culture: Authorship and Authority in a Female Community*, ed. Jennifer N. Brown and Donna Alfano Bussell (Woodbridge, 2012).

9 Mary Dominica Legge, *Anglo-Norman in the Cloisters* (Edinburgh, 1950).

Guernes wrote in Continental French rather than in its Insular or Anglo-Norman counterpart, and he prides himself on the correctness of his particular dialect: "My language is of good quality because I am a native of the Ile-de-France." This would lead us to assume that his Parisian-based French was already at this time enjoying the sort of prestige that would eventually lead to its adoption as the national standard. It also, at least by implication, lays claim to its being in some way superior to Anglo-Norman. But actually more and more Anglo-Norman clerks were at this time using their vernacular rather than Latin as a means of literary and devotional expression, and French in England was in the process of acquiring the sort of linguistic status that would allow it to be used as a functional complement to Latin rather than being considered an inferior substitute for it.[10] It is significant, perhaps, in terms of its linguistic status, that Guernes' vernacular poem was in its turn to become one of the major source texts for Roger de Pontigny's Life of Becket (1176–77), which he wrote in the conventional language of hagiography, that is Latin.

Saints' lives in French verse, based on Latin originals, were particularly popular in twelfth-century Anglo-Norman Britain, which counts no less than a dozen or so examples ranging from St Brendan and St Edward the Confessor to St Catherine of Alexandria and St George.[11] Guernes has, however, adapted the prototypical structure of the Latin saint's life by rebalancing its component parts, with the result that his poem could more accurately be termed a martyrdom narrative. It is different, moreover, from what we might call the standard hagiography in that its protagonist is a contemporary one, which means that the text becomes something of a hybrid and finds a place somewhere along a continuum embracing on the one hand histori-

10 Ian Short, "Patrons and Polyglots: French literature in 12th-century England," *Anglo-Norman Studies* 14 (1992): 229–49; "Language and Literature" (chapter 10) in *A Companion to the Anglo-Norman World*, ed. Christopher Harper-Bill and Elisabeth van Houts (Woodbridge, 2003), pp. 191–213.

11 Françoise Laurent, *Plaire et édifier: les récits hagiographiques composés en Angleterre aux XIIe et XIIIe siècles* (Paris, 1998); Jocelyn Wogan-Browne, "*Clerc u lai, muine u dame*: Women and Anglo-Norman Hagiography in the Twelfth and Thirteenth Centuries," in *Women and Literature in Britain 1150–1500*, ed. C.M. Meale (Cambridge, 1993), pp. 61–85, and the same author's *Saints' Lives and Women's Literary Culture c. 1150–1300* ... (Oxford, 2001). Cf. Duncan Robertson, *The Medieval Saints' Lives: Spiritual Renewal and Old French Literature* (Lexington, KY, 1995).

ography and, on the other hand, hagiography. The factual and the legendary are, of course, rarely if ever water-tight categories in medieval culture. Several modern historians writing on Becket have been ready to lend credence to some of the unique detail Guernes transmits and to treat it as historical documentation. What enhances the text's documentary content and value is the fact that Guernes even takes the trouble to turn the Constitutions of Clarendon into French verse and to translate into vernacular poetry several of the writs and Latin letters that underpin the controversy.

How does Guernes categorize his own text in terms of literary genre? He uses three words: *sermon* (116, 6156), *romanz* (151, 6161, 6167) and *vie* (141, 6171). The primary connotation of *sermon* in Medieval French is 'speech, discourse,' without the moralizing overtones that the term has acquired today. *Romanz*, moreover, in twelfth-century French is used neutrally to refer to any composition in the Romance vernacular as opposed to Latin. The term *romance* in the sense of 'tale of love and chivalry' is a later and secondary development from this.[12] As for *vie*, it might be anachronistic to equate it with our modern biography, since for a medieval audience it would immediately call to mind the *vita* so widely used by Latin hagiographers to describe their lives of the saints.

Though entirely conventional, the truth claims with which Guernes frames his narrative are both unconditional and insistent: "Should it cost me my life or even my soul, I will not stray from the path of truth," "Not a single word has been written here unless it is the truth," "He has not written one word that is not the truth," "Many times I revised what I had first written to remove inaccuracies," "May all those who hear this life know that from beginning to end what they can hear is the unvarnished truth." Guernes is clearly never in any doubt that his personal brand of truth is synonymous with absolute truth. His trust in the oral testimony he gathered in Canterbury and Barking is unconditional, and his commitment to the clerical cause absolute. One suspects that the vast majority of his twelfth-century listeners must have shared his black-and-white view of the world.

Guernes purports to be writing an account of Becket's life, but it quickly becomes apparent that its main focus is on his time as archbishop

12 Peter Damian-Grint, *The New Historians of the 12th-Century Renaissance ...* (Woodbridge, 1999), pp. 211–31, 254–62; cf. M.T. Clanchy, *From Memory to Written Record: England 1066–1307*, 2nd ed. (Oxford, 1993), pp. 215–20.

and the events immediately leading up to his martyrdom. In fact, over nine-tenths of his narrative (lines 741–6180) prove to be devoted to the Becket drama and its sequel.

1 Beginnings

After a typically verbose prologue (1–165) comes a summary account of Becket's birth and childhood (166–229), and his education and early career (230–245) are glossed over with little detail or precision. He joins the household of Archbishop Theobald, where he soon attracts the jealousy of Roger de Pont-l'Evêque, future archbishop of York. But he also comes to the attention of King Henry, who appoints him chancellor (246–275).

2 Chancellor

As the king's closest confidant, he lives a life of secular splendour at the same time as pursuing an active military career, all of which brings him to the pinnacle of worldly success (276–395).

3 Archbishop

It is at this point, in 1162, that Henry has him elected archbishop of Canterbury with only a minimum of opposition (396–530). Thomas is ordained, consecrated and receives the papal pallium (531–640). Whereupon God brings about his instant conversion, and Thomas, putting his former life firmly behind him, becomes the unconditional advocate of God's word (641–730).

4 Disagreements

The storm clouds are, however, not slow to gather. Becket resigns his chancellorship, and has his first quarrel with Henry over payment of the sheriffs' aid. This is quickly followed by a second over the trial and punishment of a canon accused of killing a knight (731–825). There are further confrontations at the council of Westminster in 1163, where Becket opposes Henry's attempts to make the prelates agree to observe the customs of the realm without reservation (826–920).

5 Clarendon

Having agreed, under pressure, to reach a verbal compromise in public at Clarendon, Becket refuses to ratify this in writing by appending his seal to the document (921–1045). Henry sends an embassy to Pope Alexander, but does not succeed in his attempt to bypass Becket and circumvent his opposition (1046–1105).

Hard on the heels of this comes another issue that is to prove even more contentious: that of the legal status of clerks accused of serious crimes. Who has jurisdiction over them, the secular or the ecclesiastical courts? Where and by whom are they to be indicted, then tried, then sentenced? Becket champions the cause of clerical exemption from secular justice, but he gradually becomes more and more isolated as he fails to carry the bishops with him (1106–1190). Guernes' diatribe against the bishops (1191–1235) is followed by a lengthy and laborious discourse on the religious status of clerks (1236–1355).

Sensing danger ahead, Becket attempts to leave the country surreptitiously, but without success (1356–1380).

6 Trial

There follows the longest and most detailed part of the narrative, an account of the council of Northampton in October 1164. It is here that Henry continues to browbeat Becket into withdrawing his opposition, and vindictively brings him to court to answer charges relating to the time of his chancellorship. The archbishop attempts to employ delaying tactics, but is finally obliged to appear, and does so in full regalia and carrying a cross before him (1381–1657). Urged to resign the archbishopric by his fellow prelates, Becket stands his ground (1658–1835). Further charges of financial mismanagement he refuses to answer, at which point he is sentenced to be arrested and imprisoned (1836–2010).

7 Flight

That night, under cover of darkness, he makes good his escape to Lincoln, and from there eventually reaches Sandwich and crosses the Channel (2011–2150). His six-year exile in Capetian France has begun.

8 Exile

A chance encounter with King Louis of France and a meeting with the pope at Sens, both of whose support Becket obtains, lead to Henry's efforts to force the archbishop's return to England being thwarted (2151–2390).

9 Constitutions

The pope places the Constitutions of Clarendon, which Guernes proceeds to translate into French verse (2391–2545), under excommunication. Becket finds refuge at the abbey of Pontigny. Henry meanwhile vents his anger on Becket's kinsfolk, and forbids the bishops to make any appeals to Rome (2546–2680). There follow two royal writs, one outlawing all contact with Rome, the other ordering the retention of Peter's Pence (2681–2745).

The coronation of the Young King by the archbishop of York and two other bishops, in contravention of the traditional rights of Canterbury, leads Guernes to upbraid prelates who bow to royal authority and fail to act as God's servants (2746–2780).

10 Letters
There follows the translated text of two long, somewhat tedious letters sent from Becket to the king (2781–3180), one from the bishops to Becket (3181–3320) and Becket's reply to them (3326–3565). Guernes condemns customs of the realm as a means of constraining Church authority (3566–3610).

11 Pontigny–Sens
After a stay of two years, Becket is obliged to leave Pontigny, and King Louis arranges for him to move to the abbey of Sainte-Colombe near Sens (3611–3800). Henry endeavours to court Louis' friendship in order to have Becket expelled, but to no avail (3801–3850). Becket's exile, we are told, is one of continual self-imposed suffering punctuated by visions and nightmares (3851–3980).

12 Negotiations
After several abortive attempts at reconciliation, each analyzed in detail by Guernes, a meeting at Fréteval in July 1170, instigated by the pope, brings about an agreement of sorts between Henry and his archbishop (3981–4305).

13 Truce
The two meet, have a long conversation, but do not exchange the kiss of peace (4306–4495). Guernes includes the text of two of Henry's writs from this time in his narrative (4496–4516, 4601–4622). Questions over the settlement of debts and restitution give Henry the excuse for further delay (4521–4580).

14 Return
Finally Becket is allowed to leave. He lands at Sandwich, and, warmly welcomed by enthusiastic crowds, returns to Canterbury. His request to see the

Young King at Winchester is refused, and in London he also has a hostile reception from the king's men (4720–4970).

15 Plot

Roger de Pont-l'Evêque and the other excommunicated bishops who had crowned the Young King come to make their complaints to the king in Normandy, and it is here, Guernes tells us, at Henry's court, that the treacherous plot to murder Becket is openly hatched (4971–5100). The four knights set out, urged on by Becket's lifelong enemy the archbishop of York (5126–5127). They meet up at Saltwood Castle and make their way to Canterbury (5101–5161).

16 Hostilities

They enter the hall just as the archbishop has finished eating his evening meal. No greetings are exchanged. The room is emptied so that the knights' message from the king can be delivered in private. Becket, however, quickly recalls his household clerks (5162–5244). The archbishop answers the king's charges by denying any wrongdoing, and it was, he replies, Pope Alexander and not he who suspended the three prelates. To and fro fly the accusations and counter-arguments until finally the knights withdraw (5245–5380). As the four begin to put on their armour, the monks urge Becket to go into the church, which he does only under repeated protest (5381–5465).

17 Murder

Finding their way barred, the knights contrive to force their way first into the cloister, and then into the church, as the monks attempt to get the archbishop to a place of safety under the protection of the holy relics (5346–5492). The knights do their best to drag Becket out of the church, but he, setting his back against a pillar, will not be moved. The knights pounce, but not before Edward Grim, in a desperate effort to protect him, flings his arms around Becket (5493–5575). Knowing his martyrdom to be at hand, Becket commends himself to God and to St Denis. He falls to the ground in silence as the knights' swords rain repeated blows down onto his head (5576–5655).

18 Aftermath

Pausing only to ransack Becket's rooms and to plunder his possessions, the knights make off, leaving the terrified monks to prepare the funeral (5656–5740).

19 Burial
The martyr's blood is collected, and the corpse made ready for burial (5741–5830). The de Brocs, acting on the king's orders, take control of the archbishopric (5831–5855). Not a day passes without God demonstrating his love for Becket by performing miracles, and pilgrims flock from far and wide (5856–5905).

20 Penitence
Four years after the murder in the cathedral, King Henry comes to Canterbury to do penance at Becket's tomb: he is scourged by the assembled monks and receives the kiss of peace from the prior on behalf of the whole house (5906–6060).

Guernes finishes with a prayer for peace in Henry's kingdom and for harmony among his family members (6061–6155). He brings his poem to an end with a short epilogue (6156–6180), to which he adds a postscript thanking the monks of Christ Church Canterbury and the nuns of Barking Abbey for their hospitality and their generosity.

As far as the tone of his poem is concerned, Guernes, in common with so many of his contemporaries, was all too ready to sermonize, moralize and find symbolic meaning behind everyday phenomena. He is not afraid to interrupt the flow of his narrative to insert lengthy pious digressions. His discourse has a vigorous, outspoken quality that is entirely consonant with his unquenchable prejudice and his single-mindedness in defending what he clearly saw as the dire threat posed to the Church by Henry's reforms. Guernes is a poet of the intellect rather than of imagination. Literary embellishment is clearly not high on his list of priorities, and any dramatic or emotional potential in his narrative seems to be studiously ignored as he ploughs resolutely on expounding the rights and wrongs of events, arguing the pros and cons of particular policies and drawing his own moralizing, often self-righteous conclusions. Becket's long and intimate relationship with Henry as the king's chancellor, for example, is casually dismissed in a single line of deliberate indifference (380). Guernes' rare criticism of Becket is confined to his activities in the secular world before his elevation, and only to those actions that brought him into inexcusable contradiction with the teachings of the Church.

Only once does he go as far as to criticize Becket as archbishop, and this on a point of dogma. He condemns the judicial concession that Becket makes which would result in a guilty clerk being stripped of holy orders: who, he asks, can deconsecrate what God himself has consecrated? He is forthright, on the other hand, in his condemnation of those bishops ("Oh, miserable wretches ...") who failed to support Becket and who sided with the king; errant clergy can on occasion find themselves no less firmly rebuked, and even the papal court is not exempt from criticism. Doubt does not dampen the fiery subjectivity of Guernes' discourse, nor does ambiguity divert him from the straight and narrow of his reasoning. His conservatism in observing and promoting Church dogma and teaching is unshakable, his indignation at what appears to him to be injustice heartfelt, his anger at the treatment he sees being meted out to innocent clerics and their persecuted archbishop real and, in its way, moving.

He was clearly a man of considerable learning, entirely at home in the Latinate culture of his time. He had what we might term a scholarly turn of mind, illustrated not only by his commitment to collecting first-hand oral testimony in support of his thesis, but also by incorporating into his poem original documentation such as administrative records and formal letters, which he skilfully contrives to turn from Latin prose into French verse. His command of Scriptural material is impressive. His credulity in matters of the supernatural and the miraculous is essentially that of his age. As august and as widely acclaimed an historian as William of Malmesbury had an equally eager eye for marvels and inconsequential coincidences of all kinds. Women being largely absent from the events which Guernes describes, it would be difficult to charge him with the misogyny one usually associates with medieval clerics.

Guernes' pursuit of grist to the mill of his own prejudice is unrelenting. He marshals his material with efficient thoroughness and presents it lucidly on the whole, with only very occasional lapses in coherence. His skill as a polemicist is perhaps his greatest accomplishment, and in common with many medieval authors he clearly regards repetition as a stylistic virtue. He has an admirable mastery of the standard conventions and commonplaces of rhetoric, including a predilection for sententious expressions and proverbs, though he uses only a restricted gamut of metaphors and similes. His use of wordplay, "especially of figures involving contraries," has been described as "elaborate not to say obsessive."[13] He also makes particularly

13 Sarah Kay, *Courtly Contradictions: The Emergence of the Literary Object in the Twelfth Century* (Stanford, 2001), p. 49.

effective use of recreated direct speech, and has a special liking for apostrophe. He sometimes adopts a spokesman's voice, and when he addresses, for example, Henry in direct discourse, he can convey the impression of speaking on behalf of the clergy as a whole, and of echoing a widely held, if idealistic, view of what the monarchy should be. He is a master of diatribe, and a liberal sprinkling of irony and occasional flashes of humour, together with passages of lively imagined dialogue, are there to illuminate an otherwise unremittingly monochrome narrative.

Descriptive asides are rare: Guernes has no particular eye for the visual or ear for the harmonious, no flights of fancy, and only in such essentially theatrical scenes as the acquisition of Becket's pallium and King Henry's penance does he allow himself some measure of aesthetic embroidery. How far, one wonders, did he succeed in fulfilling the literary expectations of those who listened to him reciting his story in Canterbury Cathedral? The actual scene of the martyrdom, so rich in dramatic potential, is described in a terse, almost matter-of-fact style: to the end Guernes maintains what amounts to an arm's-length historiographic mode of writing – one more or less devoid of literary amplification. This stands in somewhat curious contrast to the poetic form, five-line stanzas of mono-rhymed alexandrines, which he chooses as his medium of narrative expression. The influence of the two major Latin sources which he uses, Edward Grim's (1172) and William of Canterbury's (1173–74) Lives of Becket, may partially account for Guernes' exceptionally sober poetic style, but one suspects that the real reasons lie in the historico-literary context within which he was writing. In the 1170s, French prose had not yet asserted itself as a vehicle for vernacular historiography (it does so only in the early decades of the next century), with the result that the poetic medium was, in practical terms, the only one available to Guernes as he began composing his account of Becket's martyrdom.[14] This accounts for the parallels that have been found between some of his expressions and contemporary epic discourse. Signs of any direct influences from romance diction, on the other hand, are few and far between. A poet as it were despite himself, Guernes was too earnest, too polemical and too committed a writer to permit any

14 Damian-Grint, *The New Historians*, pp. 172–207; cf. Short, review of G.M. Spiegel's *Romancing the Past*, in *Romance Philology* 51 (1997–98): 97–99, and the same author's "Denis Piramus and the Truth of Marie's Lais," *Cultura Neolatina* 67 (2007): 319–40, at 335–36.

concessions to the more innovative aspects of the vernacular literary culture of his day – any diversion, in fact, that would force him to leave the straight and narrow path of truth as he so passionately and single-mindedly conceived it.

Any overall judgement of the value of Guernes' poem is bound to be a modest one. He was certainly an accomplished poet. Judged, however, by the standards of 'historical accuracy' (a notoriously difficult concept to define), his text is not a particularly valuable source of information on the Becket affair, especially as much of its narrative is borrowed directly from Grim and William of Canterbury. Its originality and value lie elsewhere – in the narrator's sense of history, and more particularly in the importance he attaches to first-hand evidence and testimony as historiographic tools. In coming over from France to gather oral evidence from the monks of Canterbury and from Becket's sister, and using this to supplement existing Latin biographies, he shows a critical self-consciousness that is far from usual among contemporary vernacular historians. In incorporating into his poem translations of contemporary political documents, most notably the Constitutions of Clarendon, which he considered important enough to risk disrupting his narrative in order to accommodate, he also shows an attachment to historical documentation which could seem remarkably modern. Despite his presentation being polemical and in places long-winded, the structure of his history is lucid and fluent, and, digressions apart, there is overall sufficient dramatic dynamic to drive the plot forward to its theatrically tragic dénouement.

However prejudiced the author's own viewpoint may seem to its 21st-century readers, his clerical status must surely have lent authority and authenticity to his story in the eyes of his intended audience. The fact that it was read out publicly at the saint's shrine provides us today with a rare insight into how contemporary lay men and women, amongst others, must have seen Becket, how they must have acquired the information that shaped their attitudes to his martyrdom. This in turn can contribute to our own understanding of why and how the saint's cult was able to flourish and spread in such a rapid and unprecedented fashion.

If Guernes' text was representative of the sort of account that people heard when they visited Canterbury just a few years after the event, then we are as close as we are likely to come to witnessing how popular emotions could have been roused, and how attitudes to the martyrdom could have been formed and fostered in French-speaking circles. Guernes has, in other words, left us with a document that is both revealing and significant for the light it sheds on the early development of the cult of St Thomas Becket. It can help us today better understand the wide wave of popular piety which the murder in the cathedral generated in Canterbury, in Anglo-Norman England and Normandy, in France – and well beyond in Europe and even further afield.

GUERNES DE PONT-SAINTE-MAXENCE

The Life of Saint Thomas Becket

Parenthetical references following each paragraph refer to line numbers of Guernes de Pont-Sainte-Maxence, *La Vie de saint Thomas Becket*, ed. Emmanuel Walberg (Paris, 1936, repr. 1964).

The notes following the translation are also keyed to line numbers; in the translation, the presence of a note is indicated by an asterisk.

Prologue

Not all doctors invariably make good practitioners, nor do all clerics know how to sing mass or read correctly.* Some poets quickly show themselves to be incapable of composing good narratives. One author might think that he is selecting the best material but is in fact choosing the least suitable, while another may consider himself better than all other writers but turns out to be the worst.

Anyone wishing to compose or put together a narrative needs to do his utmost to make it a good one, so that no one can make fun of him or find some means or other of discrediting his work. Let him emphasize its moral dimension and avoid any mention of evil. Man improves by contemplating what is good, and no one is any the worse for it.

This is why I have begun what I intend to be an account of the life of St Thomas of Canterbury, if such be the will of Jesus Christ, Lord of us all. St Thomas was killed and died a martyr for his Mother Church, and he is now, beyond any possible doubt, one of the great saints of heaven.*

No one would deny that there are vast differences between people in today's world, differences of attitude as well as in the sort of life they lead. Many are poor, some rich; some behave wisely, many foolishly; some love God, for others Satan is their guide.

My lords, for the love of God and the salvation of your souls, renounce frivolous things and pay attention to what I have to say. There is no one amongst you who is not able to see reason. Reject once and for all the promptings of the Devil: there can be no possible advantage in reaping a benefit that leads to damnation.

Honour God, Holy Church and the clergy; give shelter, food and clothing to the poor; pay your tithes in full accordance with the law; beware of each and every kind of mortal sin. In this way, I tell you truly, you will find God our Lord.

At the outset Holy Church was sorely trampled underfoot and received unjust treatment at the hands of the king. Thanks be to God for having once again turned his attention to the Church! It will, in its turn, be entirely restored through him who, of his own free will, suffered a violent death for it.

The king was in the habit of treating clerics harshly and unjustly. If any of them were caught committing an offence, there would be no other recourse for them but to be sent for sentencing by members of the laity as they saw fit.* Thomas gave such members of the clergy his support; he was their only source of encouragement. He fought for them, and it finally cost him his life.

"If clerks should do wrong, let the appropriate judgement be passed according to God's law. Clerks are your superiors, and you have no right to judge them. They can sin again so grievously that they are stripped of their holy orders, but you are not allowed to inflict any further punishment on them. It is only if they commit yet further offences that you can bring them to trial."

This is the concession that Thomas made, despite it not being in accordance with canon law, in order to restrain the king from any bad-tempered or violent action he might take. But no Church Father ever gave his consent to this, and I for my part do not approve of it either. I fail to understand how a bishop could deprive a clerk of a sacrament that he has received from the King of Heaven.

God answered Elijah's prayer by sending rain onto the earth which had not seen a single drop fall for forty-two months, and where people were on the point of dying because of the drought. The prophet, however, would never have been able to succeed in having this rain sent back up from earth to heaven.

You can have no difficulty in seeing that the king received bad advice. He should not have issued any prohibitions against clerks or the Church nor confiscated what was theirs; on the contrary he ought to have strengthened it. It is from the Church that he receives his crown as well as the authority to make law. May God, the One in Three, make him mend his ways!

It is absolutely clear that St Thomas was right to fight as he did for those clergy who had suffered this sort of harassment. He did so for the love of God, as it was his duty to do. God, ever faithful, has rewarded him amply for it. This no one can deny; it is plain for everyone to see.

Bishops, abbots, nobles and peasants, landed princes – everyone comes flocking to him at Canterbury. No one sends for them; all come of their own accord. Anyone who has never been there is in a great hurry to go. Even little children are carried there in their cradles.

There the dumb speak, the deaf hear, many are cured of leprosy and dropsy, cripples stand upright again, the dead live again, the blind see light again. St Thomas is quick to help anyone who, provided he acts with complete sincerity, goes on a pilgrimage to his shrine and prays to him.

One extraordinary phenomenon that we witness – and there is proof that it is absolutely genuine – concerns the water in which his blood-stained clothes are washed: it cures diseases both on the body and internally. A thousand people have been cured either by drinking or washing in it, and several dead people have been brought back to life again in this way.

It is rare to see kings, earls or dukes become saints. God rejects them because they are unwilling to serve him. Greed often makes them stray from the straight and narrow. They do as they please, and only what they want to do. They legislate to their own advantage, and they have no fear of dying.

God does not choose kings or accept them among the elect, nor dukes nor high-placed individuals. But people who live honest lives in the fear of God, be they of high-born lineage or low-born folk, these are the ones whom God raises and glorifies – provided they set their minds on serving him.

Saul, first king of the Jews, came from a low-born family, and he was one of God's elect; that much is certain. He waged a long war against the enemies of God until he finally broke his commandment. This he did out of greed, and God took his vengeance for it.

God then chose David, son of Jesse, to take his place, a red-haired shepherd boy from a very low-born family. He was anointed by the prophet and reigned as an exceedingly brave, wise and powerful king for the whole of his lifetime. When he did wrong, he acted with humility and made amends.

Only a fool is willing to wallow long in sin. Let him beg God's mercy and not fall into a sinful sleep. It is easy to cut one's life short by spending it in sin, and when it comes to the moment of death, many are so taken by surprise that they cannot open their mouths to speak to a priest.

God loves the humble, and the poor as well, for they live by the sweat of their brows in constant suffering. They love Holy Church, the clergy and the poor like themselves. They pay their tithes as the law requires, and they live clean and honest lives. These are the sort of people whom God will glorify in all eternity.

Peter and Andrew also, true brothers, were fishing from their boat with their nets when God called on them to leave their lowly drudgery. They were subsequently crucified for love of God. They are now in heaven, lords of glory and apostles.

This is why I have begun to compose this account for you of the glorious lord and martyr St Thomas, to whose holy house everyone flocks as pilgrims, the church of the Holy Trinity Canterbury,* where he suffered his passion in the cause of upholding truth and justice. (120)

Ah, wretches! Why did you kill this most holy of archbishops? You gained nothing by it. He had done no wrong, and you made a most grievous mistake. Make haste and repent! Do you wish to be caught out unshriven? You have to make amends for however long you live – forever, even. (125)

Do you wish to lose your souls on account of your foul bodies, which will be dead and gone before you even realize it? The glory of this world lies neither in property nor in inheritance. You will leave all that behind you, whether you like it or not. No fortifications, no stronghold will keep you safe from God. (130)

God, merciful and true, had a particular affection for St Thomas, who was killed in a very special place – in a sacred church. Nevertheless some nobles, valiant knights, killed him, and thereby forfeited their reputation. Can they not recover it? It is certainly possible for them, if only they are willing, to be reconciled with God. (135)

No sinner's sin is so foul but that, as soon as he puts it behind him once and for all and repents, God forgives him and gives him renewed strength. The reason why God suffered death for sinners is so that he can bring them to safety when they place themselves in his hands. (140)

* * *

If you would like to listen to the life of the holy martyr, you can hear my full and complete version of it here. I will not knowingly omit anything and will steer clear of inaccuracies. I have needed the best part of four years to complete the writing of it, during which time I have taken great pains both cutting down my material and adding to it. (145)

My first draft was based on hearsay,* which resulted in frequent inaccuracies. I then went to Canterbury where I heard the truth from the lips of St Thomas's friends and those who had attended him from an early age. I laboured patiently to revise my account by inserting some things and removing others. (150)

This first poem, however, was stolen from me by copyists before I had completely finished improving it. I had no time to make it more palatable by sweetening what was bitter and diluting what was sweet, to eliminate what was superfluous, or even make any erasures or additions. (155)

Although it is in some places misleading and incomplete, it is nevertheless accurate for the most part. Several prominent people paid for copies of this work, but others pirated it and for this deserve only reproach. The version which I now present, however, is an improved and complete revision.

In all of the other vernacular lives of the martyr that I have heard, whether written by members of the Church or the laity, monk or lady, I have found a great deal of inaccuracy and omission. But my own account, as you will be able to hear for yourselves, is both truthful and complete. Even at the risk of death or perdition, I will not stray from the path of truth.

1 Beginnings

Archbishop St Thomas, the object of the account that you are about to hear, was actually born in the city of London. He belonged to a family of honourable citizens* who were responsible for his upbringing. His father was called Gilbert Becket, and his mother Matilda. They were honest and respectable people.

As soon as she conceived her child, his mother had a dream in which the water of the river Thames poured into her womb. A learned man to whom she revealed her dream interpreted it for her and said: "This heir of yours will exert authority over many different peoples." How I personally interpret it is that she was carrying springs of pure running water in her womb.*

In another highly appropriate dream that God revealed to her, she saw herself arriving at the church of the Holy Trinity, but when she was about to enter, she found her stomach so swollen that she could not get through the door. My own understanding of this is that the whole of Jerusalem could not contain his goodness.

On another occasion, when she was about to give birth, she dreamt that the twelve great stars of heaven fell down before her. This is highly significant: the twelve tribes of Israel are here all bowing down to him, and he will be one of the twelve who will judge them.

After the birth of her child, she had yet another dream – that the baby was lying uncovered in his cradle. Feeling very sorry for him, the lady asked the nurse to cover the child, to which she replied that he was already well covered with a large folded length of silk brocade.

They both got up and hurriedly began to unfold the silk sheet, which was coloured red. The room proved to be too small, so they moved into the rest of the house, which they also found not wide enough, so they went out into the street, only to find that much too narrow also. They ended up by going into Smithfield. (195)

But even Smithfield turned out to be too small for the sheet. They then heard a voice from on high which said to them that the size of the sheet was such that the whole of England was too small to contain it. We can surely read into this that the saint's blood is to spread over the whole of the world. (200)

Thomas was sent to school at a very young age, and when he had finished learning his psalter, he went on to Latin grammar and then, when he had finished song school, he studied the seven liberal arts. He was a conscientious pupil and worked extremely hard, but he did not stay for very long at the various schools. (205)

A frequent lodger at his father's house was one Richier de l'Aigle, and Thomas got into the habit of going hunting with him in the woods and along the river banks. They went around together for as much as six months at a time, or so I have heard. Thomas's great love for hounds and hunting hawks dates from this time. (210)

One day the boy went water-fowling with Richier with the aim of learning how to handle hunting hawks and seeing how they behaved. They came to a wide water course where there was no bridge or ferry, only some planks for people on foot to cross by. Richier went first, with the boy following behind. (215)

When the knight had crossed over the planks, Thomas followed him, all huddled in his cape. But one of his horse's legs slipped, and both he and the horse fell into the water. Thomas tumbled out of the saddle and went floating off downstream. (220)

Not far from the crossing place there was a water mill; it was working at that time, and its wheel turning at a furious pace. Up floated Thomas, and the boy was on the point of falling headfirst under the wheel when the miller, having decided that he had finished milling, suddenly shut the sluice gate. On this occasion God saved the boy from certain death. (225)

The reason why God was willing to preserve his life and protect him was because his intention was to accomplish great things through Thomas. God allows some people to survive and live so that they may be instruments of great evil, while others in their turn are destined to do much good. (230)

Thomas was, reputedly, twenty-one years of age or more when he finished his education. A set of unfortunate circumstances resulted in him being deprived of his financial support, and he had very little to live on, for his father and mother's money had all sunk without trace, and never again did they recoup their loss or manage to regain stability. (235)

But before this his father had been a very rich man, his wife a beautiful and attractive lady, and they came from a good family and had been materially very successful. But fire had severely affected them and then brought them down. So often were they the victims of fires that they came very close to getting into dire straits. (240)

Thomas went to live with a relative, a wealthy Londoner called Osbern Huit-Deniers, who immediately took him into his employment. Osbern was well known in both French and English circles, and Thomas was his secretary for something like two or three years. It was from this time that he began to show his wisdom and good manners. (245)

Thomas kept himself busy to-ing and fro-ing, and he ended up in the employment of Archbishop Theobald through the intermediary of one of his marshals, who was a frequent lodger at Thomas's father's house. Thomas arrived as a very well turned-out young man with a fine horse, aided and abetted, as he clearly was, by the King of Heaven. (250)

Thomas was clever, and God saw to it that he prospered through the intelligence he deployed and the judgements he made. He worked day and night and took the greatest possible pains to serve his lord. He seized every opportunity to make himself available to his council meetings, with the result that the archbishop frequently asked him to be in attendance. (255)

Roger of Pont-l'Evêque grew resentful of him, and did his utmost, either by himself or by using others, to have him marginalized, and often used to refer to him as Clerk Baille-hache,* after the person who had first introduced him into the archbishop's court. Thomas, however, was clever enough to outmanoeuvre Roger. (260)

Archbishop Theobald took Thomas to Rome with him, after which Thomas often went there on missions for him. There, and indeed everywhere, Thomas gave such satisfaction in serving him that the archbishop kept him close at hand, and finally took him unconditionally into his confidence. (265)

When William archbishop of York died, Archbishop Theobald went to considerable lengths to secure the appointment of his archdeacon Roger of Pont-l'Evêque to the post. He installed and consecrated him, and then appointed his clerk Thomas as his own archdeacon. (270)

He secured for him the post of provost of Beverley, as well as income and church benefices in several places, for he had never found anyone who served him so well and gave such satisfaction. God, from whose inspiration Thomas had benefitted, saw to his success, and Thomas strove constantly to act with honour, wisdom and kindness.

2 Chancellor

Thomas was very fond of such secular pastimes as hunting with hounds and hawks. He was extremely generous and highly esteemed, with a quick, lucid intelligence. Nor did he refuse to accept gifts himself if any were offered him, just as people do if they are in a position to hinder or help others, and wish to get on in the world by using their wealth.

Archbishop Theobald did not neglect to see to Thomas's future, and he arranged for him to be introduced to the court of Henry II, whose employment he immediately entered as chancellor. By this means Thomas's honour and wealth went from strength to strength, though he remained in everything he did assiduous in the king's service.

He was extremely happy to serve the king in whatever way he could, and gave himself over to the task exclusively in both thought and deed. He gave away to the knights whatever came into his possession: silver, money, gold, clothes and horses. He was exceedingly meek in heart, but had a very proud, even fierce demeanour.

He was humble to the poor, but showed a proud face to the mighty: a lamb on the inside, a leopard on the outside. He took great pleasure in serving the king, and never stopped from morning till night. Whatever his behaviour, there was no trace of malice in him, while his innermost self he always kept for God.

However arrogant and frivolous he may have been in his everyday dealings and outward appearance, he remained chaste in body and healthy in spirit. And even though he devoted all of his time to serving the king, he was, as far as he was able, the right hand of Holy Church.

It was during this time that King Henry II, lord of England, was in Staffordshire, where he had fallen in love with a lady, the most beautiful of all the empire, whose name, or so I have heard, was Avice of Stafford.* She could, however, see that the king's love was now on the wane.

The royal flame was already beginning to cool, which caused the lady, who was very fond of the king, great distress. Chancellor Thomas was at that time in Stoke, and this lady sent frequent messengers to him there. Thomas's landlord, a very shallow sort of person, interpreted this in quite the wrong way. (310)

The house where Thomas was staying belonged to one Vivien, a clerk. On one particular night, seeing that Thomas's bed had been made up with fine, expensive sheets and a coverlet of silk, Vivien imagined that the lady had come and that Thomas was sleeping with her. This is what someone had told him. (315)

When he thought that Thomas would have finished making love with the lady and fallen asleep, he wanted to make sure that Thomas had indeed betrayed the king. So he took a lantern and went to where the bed was. He was quite amazed to find nobody there. (320)

Not a single sheet on the bed had been disturbed; everything was just as it had been earlier that evening when the bed had been made up. Vivien then imagined that Thomas had gone off to the lady's house. To be certain he brought the candle closer – and discovered Thomas lying innocently on the ground next to the bed. (325)

He was covered in a cloak of fine woollen twill, except that his legs and feet were protruding. He had exhausted himself praying and was so tired that that he had simply laid down on the ground, and, because he had gone without sleep for so long, fallen fast asleep. (330)

The more Thomas grew in stature and rose to prominence in the secular world, the more meek he was in his heart, however different he might have appeared in society. In the interests of the king he was frequently guilty of different sorts of wrongdoing, but at night he would make amends in private to God. It was because he was such a solid foundation that God built so much on Thomas. (335)

Not one of his closest advisers, clerk or colleague, no chamberlain or servant, steward or groom, no one who had served in his house for any length of time, would be able to maintain or prove that they had at any time witnessed Thomas committing this sort of misdemeanour. (340)

He cut a fine figure of a clerk, and one who lived a life of ostentatious extravagance. Even as powerful a king as Henry, who ruled over so much of the world, did not live more extravagantly, believe me. Nor could you find a cleverer man than Thomas even if you were to search for a whole year.

In actual fact he suffered a great deal of pain and discomfort in the king's service. (345).

He maintained a large retinue of valiant knights to whom he would give generous gifts and daily rations, and in his service he retained mercenaries, archers and men-at-arms. He led them off the straight and narrow and committed grievous crimes, but at the same time inflicted great damage on the king's enemies. (350)

Castles, baileys and strongholds he stormed, towns he burned, walled cities he attacked. So long did he spend in the saddle on his war-horse that the trusty hauberk with which he armed himself often caused him great discomfort, but he wore it to protect himself from being wounded by arrows. (355)

He spent a long time fighting wars in Gascony, and the Gascons were obliged to yield certain of their castles to him. In Normandy he was once again extremely useful to his lord, and I myself saw him ride out against the French on several occasions. He did a great deal to assist the king in his military campaigns. (360)

This world is a place of corruption, as you can see for yourselves. The more possessions a man has, the less he strives to live wisely, and the more powerful he is in the world, the less worthy he can be in the eyes of God, for he neglects and is indifferent to him. He wishes to embrace the world, but actually it is the world which is gripping him in its clutches. (365)

What is more, the Devil is constantly on the look-out for the Christian in order to entrap him, and the more he sees him to be good, honourable and charitable, the harder he tries to turn him into a sinner so as to be able to drag him down into Hell with him. (370)

Thomas, the subject of my story, was at that time at the height of his power. Before becoming chancellor, he had not been in the habit of behaving badly. He was kind to everyone, both great and small. Now, however, he became exceedingly enterprising in advancing the interests of his lord. Everything he did, his every effort, was directed at pleasing him. (375)

As chancellor he served to the king's complete satisfaction, and everything he did met with his approval. He was privy to his most intimate secrets; the king hid nothing from him, and in whatever he did, he acted on Thomas's advice. At that particular time there was no one whom the king loved more than Thomas. (380)

He even entrusted him with his eldest son Henry, to see to it that all the barons swore him the oath of loyalty. And if there was anyone in the entire kingdom who had the temerity to refuse, Thomas had orders immediately to lay siege to his castle. (385)

No one could get the better of Thomas in any way whatsoever. When the king had reason to complain about some powerful knight, earl or baron, and would have liked to exact vengeance, never did the king notice that his chancellor was ready in any way to defend such a person. (390)

Thomas would say: "So he has done you wrong, has he? It was rash of him even to have thought such a thing, that's for certain." Or he would say: "He's a powerful and influential person," or "He's served you well, and he will make proper amends. What is needed now is a little patience so you can get at the truth." (395)

3 Archbishop

When Archbishop Theobald died, the king had the appointment conferred on his chancellor, so close was the relationship between them. In the whole kingdom Henry knew of no other clerk of similar ability, and he believed that Thomas would carry out his wishes in all circumstances. (400)

At that particular time King Henry was in Normandy, as was Thomas also, pursuing glory and renown. In his service Thomas had the most prominent knights in the kingdom to wage war on Louis, king of France. He was doing his utmost to serve the king as well as he could. (405)

There was no one in the whole of the realm, however mighty or powerful, who could have been capable, had he wished, either of damaging Thomas or offering him any assistance. Whoever was granted an audience with the king, and whatever his business might be, the king would immediately refer him to his chancellor, and whatever Thomas decided to do or not to do, Henry would give his approval. (410)

Thomas had effective control over the whole of England as well as the whole of Normandy, and other countries also, and whatever the decisions he took, they were invariably confirmed by the king. Thomas was always accompanied by a large retinue of knights, and on many occasions his assistance was of great help to the king in the conduct of his wars. (415)

There was no one in the land more generous than he when it came to hospitality. There was a constant stream of lords and knights coming to eat and drink at his table – the dissolute, even, and prostitutes. His hospitality often left the king's tables empty, so much so that Henry began to feel annoyed by it. (420)

When Thomas was archdeacon, then provost, then chancellor, he treated widows, orphans and the poor with great kindness. None of his servants or almoners had to arrange special sittings: Thomas fed them whenever they came along, and he was very pleased to do so. On feast days, the holier the occasion, the more copious his hospitality was. (425)

From Normandy the king sent Thomas to England, placing him in charge of all his business there, and on this occasion also he advanced the king's cause with great efficiency, knowing him, as he did, from top to toe. His sole desire was to preserve the king's friendship. (430)

Thereafter the king sent three bishops, all well informed as to what he had in mind, to Holy Trinity at Canterbury, along with Richard de Lucy, a magnate of considerable intelligence. They went into the chapter house together with the monks, and Richard de Lucy acted as spokesman. (435)

"King Henry," he said, "whom we all acknowledge as our lord, lets it be known, through us, to the monks and prior that, seeing that the church has for some time now been without a shepherd, the king's wish is that you should now have a father and a superior – one who will act both to your advantage and to the king's honour." (440)

"May God grant us," they replied, "a shepherd pleasing to the king, able to defend Holy Church and us, the monks! Blessed be the king for being willing to allow us to elect a shepherd for our church!" "He has no intention," replied the bishops, "of depriving you of your rights. (445)

"You need, however, to take very careful counsel amongst yourselves and see to it that you elect someone capable of serving your interests in all matters concerning the king, for as you are well aware, electing someone against his wishes could result in grave damage to your church and put its future at risk. (450)

"You would forfeit for evermore the king's peace and his favour, and there would be everlasting discord and division between you. It is not in your interest to rouse the king's anger. If, on the other hand, it were possible for you to elect someone for whom he had great affection, you could get over all your difficulties." (455)

The monks then consulted their advisers. They summoned Hilary bishop of Chichester to join them, and they included also Bartholomew bishop of Exeter, as well as Richard de Lucy, who held a fief and some inherited property from them, asking them to act as advisers to the church of Holy Trinity. (460)

They advised them to follow what they themselves judged to be the best course of action. But then, so insistently did the advisers recommend their own view to the meeting that everyone, young and old, gave their consent to electing Thomas to this position of honour. This decision met with the approval of the king's envoys. (465)

Their opinion was that the king would be willing to endorse their choice; no one could have chosen a more honest clerk, nor anyone better able to advance the interests of their church, nor anyone who enjoyed better relations with the king. By doing what the king wanted, the church would be in a position to derive considerable benefit for itself. (470)

Thus the monks gave their full and formal approval to the appointment, and the envoys made their way to London, where they summoned the whole of the country's magnates. All the many bishops and abbots were there also, as was prior Wibert of Holy Trinity. (475)

It was then that they formally elected Thomas as their lord and protector. There were no dissenting voices of any sort, either lay or clerical, save only from Gilbert Foliot, now bishop of London. He mumbled some sort of protest,* maintaining that Thomas had in fact been a persecutor of Holy Church, and it would be very wrong if he were to have the honour of such an appointment. (480)

Thomas had himself, against everyone else's wishes, refused election: he was not worthy, he claimed, to wear an archbishop's vestments. He had taken part in the destruction of Holy Church, failed to observe its laws and constantly persecuted it. It was not right that he should have been elected. With tears in his eyes, he begged for a stay on proceedings and a delay. (485)

"But yes, my son, you will be archbishop," said Henry of Blois, bishop of Winchester, to Thomas.* "However misguided you were when serving in the secular world, serve now the Lord of Heaven better and even more devotedly. In the past you were as a wolf to the sheep; now may you be their pastor and priest! From having been called Saul the persecutor, you will now become, as you should, Paul." (490)

With great rejoicing, now that all the assembled clergy had nominated and elected him, they proceeded to elevate him to the archbishopric. The king, however, had sent word, by letter, to the justices and to the clergy that they should defer the decision.* But they did not reveal the existence of this letter, and instead rushed the appointment through. (495)

I have no idea why the king wished to back down so suddenly. My belief is that he understood that, Thomas's situation having so completely changed, he would no longer be able to get his own way with him, and that as archbishop he would not allow the rights of the church to be taken away. Whatever God has willed, however, no man can undo. (500)

Alternatively, understanding that Thomas had in all circumstances served him well and with loyalty, and that he would never again find anyone else to serve him in that way, the king now regretted that he was no longer in his service. In any event, Thomas had already been presented to Henry's son as archbishop. (505)

King Henry had already made over the realm to his son so that, whatever might happen to him, the future Young King's succession would be secured, and he had accepted everyone's homage and oath of loyalty.* In the king's letter to his justiciars he let it be known that he would ratify whatever decision they might come to. (510)

This is the reason why the election decision was presented to the king's son and to those to whom the king had delegated his authority in the matter; all gave their assent and confirmed the decision. The bishop of Winchester, who was very skilled in the law, did not want them to lay themselves open to any legal proceedings for whatever reason. (515)

So he addressed the king's son and the barons in the following terms: "My lords," he said, "pay attention for a moment to what I have to say. This man has been one of the king's officers of state as well as a close friend of his. This is the person we have elected, and you have confirmed this choice. Our wish is now for you to grant him, in the interest of us all, immunity from any future claims against him. (520)

"He has been an officer of state and a justice in the land. He has had all the royal revenues at his disposal. His Church requires him to be exempt and immune from any claim regarding the rendering of accounts, or anything else to do with his activities as a servant of the crown, so that, whatever may happen in the future, there is no detriment to the Church." (525)

The royal justices, whose every decision the king had formally undertaken to ratify, together with Henry's son, declared Thomas entirely immune from any matter relating to the rendering of financial accounts. He was then admitted to holy orders, and was thereafter, amid great rejoicing, elevated to the supreme office of archbishop.* (530)

* * *

Shortly after this, they led him in joyous procession to Canterbury, where he was welcomed with great honour and consecrated. He did not immediately, however, change the way he dressed. He wished to use the clothes he wore to disguise something his heart was particularly set on. (535)

The monks often grumbled about the way he came into the choir with his tunic trailing down to his feet. But they had no idea of what God had been building up in his heart. Someone who was a close friend of his alerted him to this, and told him about a dream that a particular monk had had. (540)

God had appeared to this monk as he slept and said: "Go immediately to the chancellor and tell him that I order him to start wearing a monk's habit, and let him do this without any delay! Should he fail to do so, I will always stand in the way of whatever he does, and for the rest of his days he will suffer the consequences." (545)

On hearing this, the archbishop gave a knowing smile, thus giving his friend some indication of what he had been thinking. His innermost thoughts, however, he showed only to God who, before he was even born, had called him to be one of his elect. He was now an entirely different person from what he had been previously. (550)

No sooner had he taken office than he gave up his former bad habits and ceased serving any secular interests. He ruled over the clergy and Holy Church with a rod of iron, and was ever ready to strike with the sword of justice. Neither fear nor greed for wealth would cause him to act otherwise. (555)

Everything it was his duty to love, he loved and firmly upheld, and what he had to hate he abandoned and cast aside. He kept his distance from anything that brought service to the king into conflict with service to God. The poor he clothed, fed and gave sustenance to. He strove in whatever way he could to serve our Lord God. (560)

The monks said that since he was their master, their leader and their father, he should also be their abbot. And as their abbot, he should dress and act accordingly. His new calling should lead to his being born again. Honouring the divine was incompatible with wearing secular dress. (565)

The regular canons were opposed to bishops or archbishops wearing monastic dress. The monk, as befits a man dead to the secular world, is given an over-garment of black, they said – a robe that is not suitable for any prelate. The canons' point of view has considerable authority behind it. (570)

Thomas's own clerks, on the other hand, had a different point of view. According to them, if he had been a monk and found himself in the particular situation he was now in, he would have given up monastic life and renounced the order. Living as he did with clerks, he would have to dress as clerks do, for he would not be wielding his episcopal power in the capacity of a monk. (575)

Feeling harassed from three different sides by these sorts of arguments, Thomas consulted a very well-respected man on the matter, Richard prior of Kenilworth.* He had some clothes cut for the archbishop. Thomas gave up wearing secular clothing and adopted that of the regular canons. Though a canon to the outside world, inwardly for himself he was something different. (580)

He did not wish to make any sort of display and appear too religious. What he actually wanted was to wear both orders at the same time and on the same body. He wore a monk's cowl, the order he wished to conceal, underneath his canon's robes, but with the skirts and sleeves specially shortened. He wore a hair-shirt next to his skin for greater self-mortification. (585)

There were two reasons why he did not wish to give up the idea of becoming a monk: because of the dream from God that had been passed on to him, and because none of the laymen who had been willing to take on the high office of archbishop had ever managed to make a success of it. There were in fact two examples of God bringing such people low in a most humbling fashion. (590)

Stigand was deposed from his see by the pope, who had him finish his life in suffering in prison. God had Ælfsige lose his life in the St Bernard Pass in the Alps. He had his mare's stomach cut open and then pushed his feet in, but he failed to get warm and died of exposure inside the animal.* (595)

Thomas next summoned the abbot of Evesham, Master Adam of Senlis, a highly esteemed and well-known man, and gave him orders to go and bring back his pallium. He was accompanied by two well-qualified clerks and a monk, and they found Pope Alexander in Montpellier. (600)

The clerks were learned men, well versed in the arts and in both canon and secular law. Each of them spoke in turn and made their formal request. All three spoke well, as befitted learned men, and Pope Alexander listened carefully to them, I am sure, but did not grant their petition for the pallium on this occasion. (605)

They went several times to consult the cardinals, who kept asking what they had brought for them and for the pope, since they had been expelled and ejected from Rome and had not received a single penny from their incomes. (610)

The envoys straightaway replied that they had come there from a distant country, and that they had spent almost everything that they had brought with them. They had come to seek the pallium according to church law – and with no strings attached. One thing they would never be accused of is simony. (615)

Despite all their entreaties, they obtained nothing more. When the abbot saw that he had a favourable opportunity to speak, with the cardinals standing grouped around the pope, he began to make his case with great eloquence, while at the same time steering clear of any mention of canon law. (620)

"My lord," he said, "this is what the God of truth has to say – and you who are his representative can only confirm it at every opportunity: 'Ask what is legitimate and you shall receive; seek righteously and you shall find; knock at the door of truth and it shall be opened unto you.' (625)

"We have come from afar and are weary. It is legitimate for us to ask for what we have come for. It is here that we should find what we are seeking. You will open the door to us, since we knock righteously. You are the representative of God, and we will find God in you." (630)

When the abbot had finished speaking, the pope replied: "Brother in God, what you seek here you shall receive. Your request is legitimate, and you shall be granted it. We shall now open the door to you, since you have knocked." The pallium was thereupon brought out. (635)

The pope gave it over into their safekeeping and, taking it, they returned home. In this way Thomas was successful without resorting to bribery or sin. He gave no gold or silver or money for his pallium, and his successors to the see would do well to follow his example. (640)

* * *

How mighty, powerful and bountiful is God in so quickly bringing about a change in Thomas's heart in the way he did, for there is no king on earth powerful enough to change anyone's heart or mind against his will. (645)

God, however, since it was his will and pleasure to do so, rapidly changed Thomas's mind for him, and caused him to hate what he used previously to love. From bad God makes him good, welcoming him into the company of the virtuous, if he duly repents and is truly contrite for his previous misdeeds. Such penitence smells sweet to God. (650)

No one, be he clerk or layman, should find it surprising, or be foolish enough to consider God to be unjust, if he is willing to bring certain people out of sin and raise them up, while others he casts down and lets perish. He has no love for the wicked, but cherishes the good man. (655)

It is not man that God hates but man's folly. He knows only too well what is in men's hearts and how they are going to live the whole of their lives. He is well aware that one will make a good death while another will end his life in wickedness. God comes to the aid of such a man the moment he repents and gives up his evil ways. (660)

God knows for certain all those who are to be saved, and these alone are destined to enjoy everlasting life. God knows equally well those who are to be damned. He has no desire to deter them from their iniquity. Their fate is everlasting death, for they shall end their lives in wickedness. (665)

Those who are damned are destined for everlasting death. Their damnation is without recourse, and were God to save them, he would be cheating the Devil. They will end their lives in sin and not reach a safe haven: they will sink into the fetid pit of Hell from which no one ever returns. (670)

God does not force anyone to do right or to do wrong. Each individual is endowed with the same free will, enabling each and every person to do as they wish, right or otherwise. God loves and saves those he finds to be obeying his commandments, and hates and damns those he finds to be too involved with worldly matters. (675)

When the eagle has hatched its chicks in the nest, it makes them open their eyes straight into the sun. Any chick which cannot bear to look into the sun's rays the eagle throws out and ejects from the nest. God is not willing to nurture anyone who is not willing to love him. (680)

God has endowed us all with intelligence, strength and willpower, and then allows each of us to act according to how we see fit. When a man neglects God in order to do wrong, and wastes his strength and wisdom committing sin, is it in your judgement right for God then to find his behaviour acceptable? (685)

The sentinel, perched high on top of yonder mountain, sees the bandits in the valley below setting an ambush to capture those travelling along the path. The travellers are well aware of them too, and know that they will be caught in the trap, but they nevertheless deliberately allow themselves to be captured. (690)

And if we deliberately seek damnation, do you think that God is going to force us to be saved? He is up there in heaven, watching what we do. On the day of judgement he will come to judge both the good and the evil-doers, and he will let the demons carry off all those who have served them. (695)

And if God were to save any of those destined for damnation, he would be acting unjustly to the others who are to die an everlasting death. Were he to force a single one to be saved, then he would by rights save every one. But the good and the evil-doers will be judged equitably and rewarded each according to their merits. (700)

And if anyone asks me why someone destined for damnation should do good, since it would not save him, I reply that he is certainly mistaken. The greatest evil-doer in the world could save himself if only he would give up doing wrong and turn to God. (705)

God in his goodness calls us all to his Kingdom, Saracens* and pagans, Christians and Jews. Some people are clear-sighted, others blind. Some are satisfied with little, others seek vast possessions. Each person's place is made ready for the moment when he is overtaken by death. (710)

Some men love their wives more than they love themselves, and they neglect the Lord God in order to increase their children's well-being. They break God's laws repeatedly to acquire wealth; they disinherit other people, steal, break their word, perjure themselves, practice usury and live thoroughly lawless lives. (715)

Nevertheless, no one should hesitate to do good. In so doing everyone can get some relief from their suffering, and even those who are condemned to Hell with no recourse might possibly alleviate their fate through any good they may have done. This is why everyone must work for their own salvation. (720)

I tell you, therefore, my lords, leave evil well alone; turn your thoughts to making amends for the wrong you have done. Do not wallow in sin. Set about preparing yourselves so that when God comes for you, you will be in a position to go with him and, with your lamps lighted, ascend to Paradise. (725)

Even if you do not fear God, fear the fire of Hell; no one who enters there can ever leave again, whatever means they employ. Take note of the good folk who are no longer with us, of all the many sinners whom God has taken to his bosom, and of the holy martyr Thomas who so recently died. (730)

4 Disagreements

You have heard in detail what sort of person Thomas was formerly: he would bite like the wolf swooping on the lamb. He was aggressive and did wrong, he sought glory and renown. Then he became humble and kind-hearted: he despised ermine and miniver furs. The more he loved God, the worse his relationship was with the king. (735)

As soon as he had been consecrated archbishop, he became a preacher of God's word, turning all his energy to serving his sovereign Lord. This may, for all I know, have been why the king took such a strong dislike to him, but it was from that moment on that he withdrew his affection from him. (740)

I can tell you all about how he first provoked Henry's anger. Thomas sent Master Ernulf over the Channel to announce to the king that he was returning his chancellor's seal to him. Upon which Henry flew into a violent rage: "God's eyes!" he said, "Is he then unwilling to keep it for any longer? (745)

"I have written permission and full authorization for him to be archbishop and chancellor at the same time." "He won't do it," replied Master Ernulf. "He's adamant about returning the seal because of all the heavy responsibilities he has as archbishop." "If you want my opinion," said the king, "he's not at all interested in serving me." (750)

The second time the king's anger flared up was at Woodstock. This time the reason for his violent outburst was the sheriff's aid. The established custom in England was for this tax to be collected in each county at the rate of two shillings per hide of land.* (755)

The country's major landholders used to pay it to those who had the responsibility for the security of each county and for protecting their lands and their vassals without having recourse to the law courts or imposing penalties. The king now wished this to be paid directly into the royal revenues. (760)

"Sire," said the archbishop, "you should not take the aid for yourself. It cannot be reallocated and turned into crown revenue, for if we want to, we will simply refuse to pay it. The sheriffs actually give us such good value that it would not be right for us to stop paying them the aid." (765)

"God's eyes!" replied the king, "each and every one will be recorded on the Exchequer rolls. It is your duty, what is more, to do as I request in this matter, since whatever belongs to you and yours will be disposed of precisely as we see fit." "By the eyes you swear by," said Thomas, "as far as my own land is concerned, not a single payment will ever come your way!" (770)

After that there was another violent confrontation in London concerning a canon, a resident of Bedford called Philip de Broi, who was wrongly accused of having caused the death of a particular knight by killing him. It was the king's wish that he be shipped off to a place of no return. (775)

Why I say that Philip was wrongly accused and badly treated is because he had already had a lengthy trial in the bishop's court, after which all his accusers had dropped their case against him, and he had therefore been judged legally cleared of the charge. And lo and behold! Now the judge had reopened the case against him. (780)

Simon fitz Peter had been the judge appointed for the trial, and if he had had his own way, he would have sentenced Philip to death. Philip became very irate and grossly insulted him. The king was of the opinion that Philip's offensive behaviour to the judge was tantamount to his having insulted the king himself. (785)

The king had his say, but those who put Jesus to death were obviously guilty of a greater crime than those who later killed St Peter or St Vincent. Henry swore that he would be the one to pass sentence on the cleric, but Archbishop Thomas took on the case in his own court. (790)

He asserted that it would be here, in his court, that the reparations Philip would have to make would be set. Whether he liked it or not, Henry was obliged to send bishops and secular officers there to bring charges against the clerk. Henry's orders were that, if they valued their eyes, they should see to it that full and proper justice was done. The first charge they brought was that he had caused the death of the knight. (795)

The clerk, unwilling to submit himself to a retrial, replied simply by denying the charge of murder, since he had not committed any murder. He had, indeed, been acquitted of this accusation; he had cleared himself, and the matter had been settled. He was not willing to be re-tried, be it by defending himself or by retracting. (800)

The judges then asked him to answer the charge of insulting the judge and to enter a plea. Being a gentleman, the clerk made no attempt to deny the facts, and declared that he was quite ready to make good the offence, and would be only too happy to make Simon fitz Peter reparations. The judges reply: "Since he does not deny the charge, we need to come to a judgement." (805)

Their judgement was that he should be deprived of his living for a period of two years, and that the income from it should in the meantime revert to the king, for him to donate to churches, the poor, bridge-building and other charitable causes, as he saw fit. As far as almoners go, Philip could now claim to have a truly powerful one! (810)

They sentenced him in addition to appear before Simon fitz Peter, should he give his permission, without clerical dress and, in the presence of his friends and allies, to offer him arms.* On these, in accordance with the custom of the country, Philip would swear that he would be willing to accept from Simon, for the same offence, the sort of reparation that he was now offering. (815)

When the sentence was reported to the king, he said that the judges had not done the right thing by him, and that they had spared the clerk because of his clerical status. He had wanted them to go as far as to impose the death sentence. They replied that they had reached a decision that was entirely fair according to the law. (820)

"God's eyes!" said Henry, "I'll have you swear to me here and now that the sentence you passed was a faithful one as far as my own interests are concerned." "Sire," the bishops replied, "we are quite ready to do so, but our sentence is already a very severe one for Philip." They offered to swear the oath, whereupon the king flew into a rage. (825)

* * *

Henry then summoned all the prelates to his presence and demanded that they promise to observe and maintain the customs of the realm over which he had to rule – customs which his grandfather had established in the kingdom. They were, they said, willing to obey "saving their order."*

The king wanted them to agree "saving their order" or not, and he added that he would not have a single syllable of that particular phrase mentioned again. Unanimously they replied that without "saving their order" they would not on any account agree. At which the king became very hostile towards them.

He would not, he said, let them get away with this for any reason, for in his grandfather's day archbishops and bishops who had subsequently become saints used to observe these customs. The archbishop's response to this was: "I am not willing to do without 'saving our order,' nor would any of the bishops agree to omitting the phrase.

St Thomas addressed the assembled bishops in the following terms: "Just see," he said, "how oppressively King Henry is acting towards us. What he wants is for bad customs to be imposed on Holy Church. If I agree to them being established, this brings shame on Holy Church. I cannot, however, stand alone in this against the whole country.

"I would like now to hear from each of you to see what you think about it." To a man, they told him to stand his ground resolutely, and said they would support him in everything he did. They swore an oath to this effect. Roger of Pont-l'Evêque also promised to support him and not in any way ever to let him down.

What happened next was that Arnulf bishop of Lisieux came to Salisbury. Relations between him and the king had been somewhat acrimonious, but he subsequently behaved in such a way that the king's affection for him was plain to see. He gave the king the sort of advice that would deceive his brother in Christ. From this man sprang the inspiration and the wherewithal to ensure the archbishop's defeat.

"Sire," he said to the king, "if you wish to defeat Thomas, get a number of the bishops on your side. As long as he enjoys their support, you will never get the better of him." Hilary of Chichester was then sent for, and the king treated him in such a way that he retained his close friendship.

He then won over Roger of Pont-l'Evêque to his side, and he converted Robert de Chesney bishop of Lincoln to his point of view. At that time the king was at Colchester,* and it was there that these bishops agreed to observe the king's customs, and Henry swore to them that there would henceforth never again be any talk of his acting against their order.

Hilary bishop of Chichester then went to Teynham to see the archbishop. He wanted him to be grazing in the same meadow as he was. He ought, he said, to be on good terms with his secular lord, he should agree to the king's customs, and it would still be possible for him to enjoy the king's friendship. "You will never succeed," replied the good priest, "in getting me to change my mind. (870)

"The king has won you and Archbishop Roger over to his side, with the result that you are now going to keep his laws. You want to enlist me as well, but you will never succeed." "But why ever not?" asked the bishop. "For God's sake, explain to me why you won't do it, and what your thoughts are about this whole business." (875)

"The king has promised you that he will make no demands on you that would be contrary to your order. He'll keep his word, but only if he wants to, and if he doesn't want to, no one is going to gainsay him. You, on the other hand, will have no choice but to carry out your promise, for you are his vassals, and he will force you to keep your word." (880)

Robert of Melun – such was the name of the bishop who at that time occupied the see of Hereford – then went to see the archbishop at Harrow. He took Count Jean de Vendôme along with him, a man for whom Archbishop Thomas had had much respect in the past. (885)

Present also was an abbot by the name of Philippe de l'Aumône, who had come from across the Channel with the task of making peace between archbishop and king. The pope, he said, had sent him over, and he came equipped with the appropriate papal letters. (890)

He assured the archbishop under oath that he was indeed an envoy of Pope Alexander, whose wish it was that Thomas should come to an agreement with the king and comply with his wishes. He was recommending this course of action even though it might place Thomas's duty to his order in jeopardy, and he accepted full responsibility for any error that Thomas might make. (895)

The abbot also brought with him letters from the cardinals, and swore that the king had given them assurances that all he was seeking was for Thomas to show him due respect by verbally complying with his request before an assembly of all of his magnates. (900)

He would never be asked to observe any custom which was contrary to his order or to do anything against his will. The king had no intention of letting himself be thwarted in this. He called upon Thomas simply to grant what he was asking for, in which case all bad feeling on both sides would be forgiven, and the king would make the archbishop the most powerful force in the kingdom. (905)

In the past the king had had more affection for him than for anyone else, and Thomas had been an extremely faithful servant to him. The abbot, who spoke with an authority that impressed Thomas, succeeded in so beguiling him with sweet talk that he persuaded him to go along to Woodstock with him. (910)

There he was made to give his consent and to promise the king that he was willing to observe his customs in all good faith and loyalty. He thought that that would be the end of the matter, but by way of reply the king added: "If you are willing to agree, you need to acknowledge as much publicly in the presence of all of my magnates. (915)

"Everyone has heard how you have been defying me. If it is your intention to respect the understanding you have entered into, summon all your clergy, and I for my part will summon all of my magnates without delay. Then declare openly in front of everyone what agreement you have come to with me." (920)

5 Clarendon

The magnates assembled at Clarendon, and there was a full complement of bishops also. The king's wish was that what the archbishop had conceded to him should be publicly announced to all those present. The archbishop, on the other hand, already regretted having gone as far as he had. (925)

He was profoundly distressed that he had consented to observe the customs, because it had been improper of him to do so, and he preferred to be taken to task by the king rather than cause such turmoil in Holy Church. He was more afraid of God than he was of threats or imprisonment. (930)

Seeing that he could not get the better of him, Henry could only rant and rave. He even threatened to mutilate men who had received ordination from God. If it were in his power, he would bring Holy Church to its knees. But whatever the king might threaten him with, the archbishop was unwilling to yield. (935)

I have no idea what plans the king and his cronies were devising, but two bishops went direct to the archbishop, Jocelin bishop of Salisbury, whom the king hated, and William Turbo bishop of Norwich, whom he had never liked. This is what they had to say to Thomas: (940)

"My lord," they said, "for God's sake have mercy on yourself, on the whole of Holy Church, its clerks and ourselves! The king is so incensed and furious with you that, if you do not make a lasting peace with him this very day, we tell you that we'll both of us lose our heads!" (945)

None of this caused the archbishop in any way to deviate from the course he had previously set his heart on. Then two English earls came to see him: Robert earl of Leicester, widely renowned for his intelligence, and Reginald earl of Cornwall, a particular friend of the king's. (950)

They begged him to have mercy on those under him and on himself, and to look to the interests of Holy Church and its clerks, for if that very day he did not do as the king wanted, they would feel obliged to take matters into their own hands and do something so reckless that both the king and they would be put to shame just as if they had been common outlaws. (955)

Not even as horrendous a threat as this could shake Thomas's resolve. Two Templars then came from across the Channel, Master Richard of Hastings, Master of the Temple, and Otto of Saint-Omer, both well-known figures. They stood before the archbishop with tears in their eyes. (960)

"My lord," they said, "for the sake of God, ever truthful, why do you show no mercy on the whole of Holy Church? Do as King Henry wishes and agree to his customs. Then you will be good friends once again. Otherwise Holy Church and its clerks will be in for some very bad treatment." (965)

They were absolutely convinced that if the archbishop agreed to the king's demands, then Henry would do whatever Thomas wanted, and that there would never again be any talk of him acting contrary to his order. To this they pledged themselves and their word. (970)

May they die an everlasting death in damnation, they conceded, if the king was seeking to set a trap for him or to deceive him, as long as Thomas showed him due respect in the presence of all of his magnates, and that he now agreed to what he had previously refused to accept. Henry had no wish to be thwarted in this, or for people to consider him to have acted in a manner unbecoming to a king. (975)

The archbishop now understood just how hard they were pressing him; he understood just how prone the king and his followers were to sin; how he, the clergy and the whole of Holy Church were in such dire trouble; and how he could, or so he believed, immediately recover the king's friendship, especially since those advising him to do so enjoyed such a high reputation. (980)

"My lords," he replied, "I shall follow your advice. Since this is what you recommend, I shall agree to the king's demands." Having brought their meeting to a close, Thomas, in the presence of Henry's assembled magnates, promised the king to observe, sincerely and, he added, in good faith, both the customs and the laws.

"My lords," replied the king, "you have all heard clearly how the archbishop has been good enough to promise me that he will observe the laws of the time of the first King Henry. I now wish him to give the same undertaking in the presence of all the bishops assembled here."

"Sire," said the archbishop, "this is what I hereby order to happen." All then rose to indicate their agreement. The bishop of Salisbury, however, rising to his feet, asked the archbishop to confirm whether he personally agreed with all the others. "Yes, I do," declared the archbishop. "Then I also agree," replied the bishop of Salisbury.

"Yet you," said the king to Thomas, "are the one person who has consistently opposed me." He continued: "My lords, now that the bishops have agreed to observe the laws of our kingdom, you must make provision and take special precautions to ensure that in future there is no dispute between us about these laws.

"Go now, therefore, and make a record for me of the laws of the first King Henry and set them down in writing. When this is done, read the written version out to me." The king entrusted this task to the most learned of his men. They drew up the written version and brought it before the king.

The document was read out to the whole assembly. Then the king said: "I am anxious that there be no further dispute and now require the archbishop to affix his seal." To this the archbishop replied: "By the faith I owe the God of virtue, this I will not do as long as my soul remains alive in my body!"

The understanding with his advisers – and those close to the king confirmed this – had been that if Thomas showed due respect to the king by verbally agreeing to his demands before the assembled magnates, nothing would ever be written down or placed on record.

It had further been agreed that the king would respect Thomas's wishes, and that all bad feeling between the two of them would be set aside. Now Henry's side had completely failed to honour this agreement. Thomas would refuse henceforth to take any further steps. He has already gone further than he wanted and he regretted having gone as far as he had.

Then the king's supporters thought up another plan. They had a chirograph* prepared and cut in two. They gave one half to the archbishop, who accepted it in the belief that it was a means of defending the clergy. "My lords," he said, "this will enable us to see just how evil-minded they are. (1025)

"Now we can clearly see the trap that we should be on our guard against. They intended Holy Church simply to fall into their trap." The archbishop then left, angry with himself for having agreed to their malicious scheme and for not having been able to obtain the king's friendship. (1030)

His own behaviour led Thomas to suspend himself, and he did not celebrate mass again until he had informed the pope of what had happened. The pope lifted the suspension when he realized why the archbishop had acted as he did – he had done so to protect both the king and the clergy: to spare the one from death and further wrong-doing, and to prevent the other from sinning. (1035)

* * *

The next thing to happen was that the bishop of Evreux, who went by the name of Rotrou, came to Porchester to make peace between Henry and Thomas. The king said that he could well go on discussing the matter for ever and ever unless the archbishop could get the pope himself to endorse the laws with his own personal seal. (1040)

On the insistent advice of Bishop Rotrou, Thomas sent letters to the pope begging him to confirm the king's laws by affixing the papal seal. The pope, however, knowing full well that Thomas had made the request under compulsion, refused. (1045)

Finding himself thoroughly snubbed, Henry grew exceedingly angry with the archbishop and sought advice on how Thomas might be brought to heel. The advice he received was reinforced by some additional evil scheming. If it had been possible, he would have had great pleasure in taking revenge. (1050)

Both his closest advisers and his magnates proposed that, if he were able to get the pope to invest the archbishop of York with the powers of papal legate, he would have no difficulty in taming archbishop Thomas. Whether he wanted to or not, he would come grovelling at the king's feet. (1055)

Accordingly he dispatched two of his clerks to the pope: John of Oxford, who put a great deal of effort into the mission, and Master Geoffrey Ridel, who had taken all the necessary steps for preparing the message that had been entrusted to them. They went off to the pope. The pope rebuffed them. (1060)

The church of Holy Trinity, declared the pope, always had been, and still was – as was only right – an establishment of great authority. The church of York had never had any power over it, and he would ensure it never would as long as he lived. And their two prelates had, in any case, never been on friendly terms. (1065)

But one of the messengers was a very devious fellow. On bended knee he swore to the pope on holy relics that if the king were not happy with the outcome of his legation request, as soon as the envoys returned to England the archbishop would find his stature diminished by the loss of his head. (1070)

The pope, who was a man of great wisdom, understood that it was sometimes necessary to do wrong in order to avoid an even greater wrong. He agreed to the king's legation request, but on condition that such powers would not cause harm to anyone, and that the present archbishop of York would not be installed as legate. (1075)

His intention was to immediately write another letter and send it to a close associate of his in England. If Henry was going to use the legation powers to harm anyone, then this person would prevent him from doing so. His legation, in other words, would never be of any use to him. (1080)

The king's envoys were clever enough to see that they had got more or less nowhere, so they said to Pope Alexander: "My lord, the king has been a good friend of yours, and you should have no objection to granting his request. (1085)

The king's idea is not to depose anyone, and he is seeking simply to curb the archbishop and see whether he might be able to get him to do what he wants him to do. He wants also to be able to show Thomas and all his clergy just how easily he could, if he so wished, do him harm." (1090)

"You will get no other sort of legation from me," the pope replied. He had his letter drawn up and handed it to them. On their return to England, they showed it to the king. When he understood that he would not be able to get his own way, Henry attached very little importance to the letter, considering it more or less useless. (1095)

This did not prevent him, however, from frequently showing it off so that bishops, earls and magnates could all see it. "Look!" he said to them, "I have legation powers. Now I can really put the archbishop in his place!" But he could not, in fact, do him any more harm than this. (1100)

It was a source of great annoyance to him that he could make no other use of the letter. He accordingly sent letters back to Pope Alexander, and declared all-out war on Holy Church and its clergy. On every occasion he could find, he treated clerks with great harshness, and went into a deadly huff whenever he saw the archbishop. (1105)

* * *

Another violent quarrel erupted between Thomas and the king over those wayward clerks who had the misfortune to be thieves, murderers and secret law-breakers. The king wanted them to be subjected to the law of the land, but this law was one that Thomas rejected. (1110)

Throughout the whole world, in Christendom and even in pagan lands, there is a legally established law that anyone caught stealing or committing a similar crime should feel the full, unmitigated weight of the law and not be spared, whatever his family connections might be. (1115)

This is why not only King Henry but his barons also wanted any clerk caught committing a crime such as theft, murder or treason to be unfrocked as a result and then subjected to mutilation and death.* (1120)

A number of priests and deacons had in fact been apprehended for theft and murder and put into the king's prisons. Often they were placed in open carts and transported across country. They were taken to courts of law where they were sentenced either to mutilation or hanging or execution. (1125)

Archbishop Thomas fought on their behalf and insisted that the Lord's servants be handed over to him. Even if they had committed an offence, this was no reason for him to abandon them, and if anyone took them to court, he maintained in all cases that it was his right to have them brought to trial in the Lord God's court. (1130)

The king was unwilling to accept any of this. He would not tolerate them getting away with it in this way. He wanted them first stripped of their orders then handed over, at his command, to secular justice to be hanged, burned or dismembered. (1135)

In his grandfather's day, clerks committing such heinous offences were sentenced to mutilation, and Henry's wish now was for the customs and usages of his ancestor to be maintained in their entirety and not in any way encroached upon. Woe betide the archbishop if he should carry on arguing about it! (1140)

The archbishop's reply was that he would never let such a state of affairs come about, and would never hand over clerks to secular justice. He would, on the contrary, defend them in all circumstances according to God's law and the requirements of justice. He would pass judgement in accordance with canon law. He for one would not allow Holy Church to be belittled. (1145)

"Clerks should not," Thomas declared, "obey your secular laws, nor should they be punished twice for the same offence by being deprived first of their holy orders and then of their lives. That is why I am justified in defending them in all circumstances. You will never see me give way on this, whatever the reason. (1150)

"I readily admit that any clerk found committing such serious crimes should be deprived of holy orders, but thereafter he should be granted immunity from any physical punishment. If any are subsequently found guilty of a further crime, let them suffer blinding, flaying or hanging, as you deem appropriate. (1155)

"Those who are answerable only to themselves in everything they undertake should not be taken as models of justice, nor should those who were at one time, or still are, living in the secular world. Our models should be those to whom God has granted his Holy Spirit, otherwise man will be out of consonance with God. (1160)

"When King David, who had certainly received the Holy Spirit, decreed that his son Solomon would be king, the majority of people opposed his choice and instead elected his son Adonijah king. Abiathar was willing to consecrate him in defiance of God. (1165)

"Because of this act of rebellion against God and contrary to reason, Abiathar was brought before Solomon to be judged. Solomon, however, was unwilling to subject him to any physical punishment, so he ordered him to be suspended from all his duties and to go and remain in his own house. (1170)

"No man should be placed in jeopardy twice for one offence. Once a clerk has been deprived of holy orders, no greater disgrace can be inflicted on him. It is my duty to defend Holy Church and its clerks, and I shall always do so for the sake of God, whom I am here to serve. Never will you see my resolve weaken even if it should cost me my life."

When Henry saw that he was incapable of defeating the archbishop, and that Thomas would not allow clerical criminals to suffer mutilation, he exploded with anger. He swore that he would humiliate him and bring him back down to where he had raised him from.

This conflict between the two men lasted for a long time. King Henry was incapable of making the archbishop yield. Thomas continued to offer protection to wayward and recalcitrant clerks. He struggled alone and had few allies, for almost all the bishops had gone over to the king's side.

The others left him in the lurch to battle on single-handed. They had handed victory to the sinner,* so afraid were they to dare draw the sword of God. They feared their secular lord much more than they did Jesus, the almighty Creator.

Alas! Miserable wretches that you are! Tell me what you are frightened of. Are you afraid that the king will take your power away from you? If you are brave enough to hold on to it, he will not, I swear. You are not real bishops, you only call yourselves bishops. You fail to fulfill a single one of your responsibilities.

Your duty is to be leaders of men and set them on the right path, and all you do is let them fall over and crash to the ground. You even lead the king of the country astray. You have no business telling him exactly what he wants to hear. What you ought to do is keep criticizing and reprimanding him.

God has assigned you the task of looking after his flock, and if the king is one of your sheep, your duty is to be his guide. The shepherd must always bring home the stray and carry the ailing sheep over his shoulder – not let the thief wring its neck.

You are not real shepherds – such people are rare –, you're hired hands. The king understands this all too well and will despise you even more for it. It was God who placed him in his kingdom, and God will ask you to account for what he does since he is in your safe-keeping. And when the king finally mends his ways, he will hate everyone who gave him bad advice.

The king has to govern the people of his realm, and to do so needs the sort of laws that suit him best. Lay people want to keep their laws and customs exactly as their parents before them had done. God is the God of Heaven, and his law is divine. (1215)

What I now want to know from the king and his clerks is which laws it is better for Christians to observe: those instituted by Saracens, Slavs and other people all over the world with the aim of curbing criminals, or those which the Church Fathers have set down in writing. (1220)

Do not believe bad advice, king, but think things out better for yourself. The bishops whom you have caught in your snare are false bishops, more pliant than the reed buffeted by the wind. If they cheat their own Lord, they are hardly likely to be faithful to you. Do not put your trust in the night; let the sun shine on you! (1225)

Permit Holy Church to have its own rights and its own laws. The Church is the bride of God, and God is Lord of kings. His anger will be roused if you in any way diminish his Church. He will tolerate you for a year or two perhaps, or three, for thirty or twenty or ten – for a month, a week, a day. (1230)

Had Nero been alive today, he would have had no difficulty in finding Simon Magus, the one who hoodwinked the whole world by his words and his magic gifts. Rome was once the house of God; today it is a den of thieves. Moses is quite alone in Pharaoh's kingdom, for he can find no trace of his brother Aaron.* (1235)

Clerks are God's servants, and he elects them by drawing lots from amongst the saints – hence their name [*clerks* from *kleros* meaning 'lot']. Whatever they are, they are servants in God's house. You have no business laying a finger on them, not even the most insignificant little cleric who is, if you look at it in the right way, God's creature. (1240)

Being an anointed king and wearing a crown of gold, you should be a shining example of virtue, not pride. You ought to be both leader and guardian of your people. Your crown will not always be on your head, and you were certainly not born with it. The glory of this world is short-lived. (1245)

The clerk always wears his badge of office on top of his head. It does not weigh on him heavily as far as his body is concerned, but it does weigh on his soul. Everywhere he goes, near or far, his tonsure makes him look like a court jester.* He ought not to be arrogant or act violently to anyone, but he must be humble to all and bring peace wherever he is. (1250)

The clerk is a throne for God, and God is to reside in him. He should never stop learning, as there is so much he needs to know. In all circumstances he needs to be discerning as well as wise. God has not, however, granted him, as a human being, the power not to be a dupe to sin. (1255)

Clerks should protect lay people and keep their souls safe. No one should condemn those in authority over them, whether clerk or lay. This is why there are different levels of authority. Anyone committing an offence is to be handed over to his immediate superior, and should be treated in accordance with the law by which he lives. (1260)

Clerks who have done wrong will be handed over to the bishop. How and by what means are they to be deprived of their orders? How is it possible for the words of the sacrament to be retracted? And who can deconsecrate what God has consecrated? This is not, in my view, justice; it is arbitrary law. (1265)

If a defrocked cleric can go to Rome, be granted the pope's forgiveness and seek permission to say mass by himself, you will not see the pope ordaining him all over again. The clerk simply proceeds to celebrate mass without further ado. (1270)

What God has consecrated no man can deconsecrate, nor can anyone unbaptize a baptized Christian, except that it is always possible for someone to be expelled from Holy Church. I am not for a moment maintaining that, when a criminal cleric is apprehended, he should be let go and allowed to continue behaving as he did previously. (1275)

The criminal cleric is not afraid of losing his clerical status. Someone who murders other people, steals the possessions of others or robs them has little love or respect for holy orders. He has no fear of shame, the gallows, torture or death. Woe betide anyone who would let such a person off once he has been caught! (1280)

There is much in common between a criminal and the wild boar that you have heard about in Avianus.* This animal was in the habit of ravaging the rich man's cornfields. It was captured twice and then released, but not before having its ears clipped. (1285)

After it had been captured the second time, the landowner told the boar never to come back again. If it were to come back, he promised it would pay dearly for it. After which he marked it, then let it go. But the animal took no notice, and was captured for a third time. (1290)

This time it was killed and handed over to the cook. The cook ate the boar's heart, and when the lord asked for it, the cook gave him to understand that the boar had been born without one. Had it had a heart, then it would have thought twice before coming back yet again. A criminal will always be a criminal and will never act as a wise man does. (1295)

This is why I think it reasonable to draw the following conclusion and make this assertion: if the clerk's crime is such that he loses his livelihood, let his bishop throw him into prison and never again let him out. He can, if he so wishes, make amends for his crimes there in prison. (1300)

When Adam was created by God and placed in Paradise, he was not put to death for the wrong he did, but cast into the prison of our vale of tears. He lived the rest of his life in torment and grief to atone for his earlier error. (1305)

Both Adam and the clerk have only one master, and that is God, hence my comparison is, I believe, a valid one. If the clerk is caught again committing the same sort of offence, let the bishop have him thrown into prison. King Henry can have complete confidence in my reasoning. (1310)

Whereas man-made law should spare no one in order to curb criminals and punish them, God's mercy is not such as to reject anyone. God wants the sinner to live so that he might cleanse himself, renounce sin and then turn to God once more. (1315)

This is clearly the case with Adam, the first man ever to do wrong. God dressed him in animal skins and made him, and us all with him, mortal. Because of what Adam did, God cursed our land from which our sins sprout up and from which so little good comes. The soul, however, he did not curse, so as not to deny its heavenly heritage. (1320)

God exiled Cain for killing his brother, and with him separated those who are to be excommunicated from the virtuous. God cursed the earth which swallowed up the blood from the murderer's hand, but spared the soul. He excommunicated those who spill the blood of their neighbour. (1325)

Nebuchadnezzar had a huge gold and silver statue made of himself and had it worshipped by everyone throughout his kingdom. If they did not do so, he had them tortured or killed. Then God turned him into an ox fit only for grazing and eating grass. (1330)

After seven years, however, God turned him back into a man. We often see the worst sort of sinner become humble, good-natured and entirely repentant, an example of virtue for all, great and small, to follow. God reinstates him in the glory of Heaven which he had previously lost. (1335)

There were seven demons living inside Mary Magdalene. She washed away her sins when she washed Jesus's feet with her tears and wiped and dried them with her hair. At whatever time the penitent is judged, the love of God and of his neighbour brings about his salvation. (1340)

St Peter the apostle, powerful here on earth and in Heaven, denied God three times saying that he did not know him. He eradicated his sin, wept bitter tears, and God forgave him. Everyone who begs for forgiveness in all sincerity will obtain it. (1345)

No one has ever heard or read in Scripture of a sinner who prays for mercy not obtaining it. But if he despairs, drowns or kills himself, his sin against the Holy Spirit will prevent him from obtaining mercy. God values mercy beyond everything else. (1350)

It was because God loves merciful justice and prefers forgiveness to sacrifice that the good archbishop undertook his struggle to defend Holy Church and its clerks. He clearly understood that no secular hand should interfere in this. (1355)

When the archbishop came to realize that he was not able to regain the king's friendship, that the king hated him to the point of threatening his life, and that once Henry came to hate someone, he would never again offer them the hand of friendship, he prepared to leave the country. He put to sea in the vicinity of New Romney and set sail. (1360)

When the wind had taken them well out into the Channel, the sailors spoke among themselves. It was sheer madness for them, they informed Adam of Charing, to be aiding the king's enemy to flee the country, and they feared that they and all their families would lose all their possessions.* (1365)

Together they spoke to the archbishop and explained to him how it was impossible for them to sail against the wind. No one could possibly cross the Channel in a wind like that. "If we really must turn back on account of the gale," said Thomas, "head for whichever harbour God leads you to." (1370)

This is how the archbishop often told the story afterwards, and this was, as far as he knew, the reason why they turned back. God was not yet ready to let him cross the Channel, and he had not yet entered the lists for the battle ahead, or embarked on the great struggle into which God was to thrust him. (1375)

But when the king heard that Thomas had intended crossing the Channel, he was very unhappy and also worried. Being afraid of such an intelligent man, he assumed that he would have been going to see the pope, and that the whole kingdom would be placed under interdict. (1380)

6 Trial

But even Thomas's failure to leave the country did not enable the king to force the slightest concession from him. Henry therefore arranged for his council to meet at Northampton, and he issued a proclamation summoning all the bishops and magnates to attend, all those, that is, who enjoyed the right of holding their land directly from him.

Without distinction earls, magnates, bishops and abbots all attended this council. Archbishop Thomas did not refuse to join the other dignitaries, but wisely he came with a modest retinue.

The king's men, who were well aware of what had been planned, had had their horses stabled where Thomas was due to lodge. So the archbishop announced to the king that he would not come to plead in his court until Henry had had the whole of his lodgings cleared. Horses and squires were accordingly ejected.

The archbishop was summoned to attend on a specific day so that he would be present in person and ready to answer the charges. The king had implemented a statute in the kingdom which was proving very detrimental to the country's barons, since it was now possible for an individual baron to lose the right to hold a court by someone swearing a false oath.

If anyone brought a case concerning land at his lord's court, he was to present himself, along with his associates, on the first day that had been set for the hearing. If the proceedings were delayed in any way, he was to go to the justice to register his complaint. He was then to return to his lord's court accompanied by two oath-takers.

There he was to swear, together with the two of them, that his full rights to justice had been denied him by the court. By use of this oath, be it genuine or false, the plaintiff would be able to go to the court of the next lord in rank above the last, and so on, one after the other, until eventually he reached the king's court.

John the Marshal's case was one such. He was claiming a particular property in a plea before St Thomas's court. As his case was getting nowhere and he was still waiting for justice to be done, he swore an oath that justice was being denied him in the archbishop's court. He brought his complaint before the king, who was always looking for ways of harassing Thomas.

Thereupon the king had Becket summoned to answer the charge that he had denied John full justice. Let the archbishop be ready to defend himself on the day set for the hearing! It so happened, however, that Thomas was ill on the appointed day and unable to travel, so he sent two of his men to ask for his absence to be excused. (1420)

The king refused to accept his non-appearance, and this is why he had the archbishop come to Northampton. Anxious not to cause another postponement, Thomas wisely agreed to come. He lodged with the monks of St Andrews in Northampton. The next day he was to have a heavy burden to bear. (1425)

He went to the king to seek permission to go overseas to see the pope. The reason was that Roger archbishop of York was in the habit of having his cross paraded throughout the area under Thomas's jurisdiction, something that Thomas could not tolerate. They had both appealed to the pope, so he simply had to go. (1430)

This is why the next day Thomas appeared before King Henry and sought his urgent permission to go to Rome. No, said the king, he could not go; he must immediately explain his failure to appear earlier. Thomas replied that he had been ill and that he had sent his apologies. (1435)

But no illness, no apologies were of any possible use to him. The king insisted on bringing the matter to judgement. Accordingly they proceeded to pass judgement, but in fact they closed their eyes to justice and ignorantly condemned the archbishop to a fine of £300, to be paid in cash.* (1440)

Thomas wanted to challenge the verdict, but everyone without exception begged him earnestly not to react angrily and not to make a formal challenge. Let him do as the king wished, and let Henry have his own way! In that way it would be possible for Thomas to make peace with him. (1445)

This is how they got him to accept the verdict and to provide the king with sureties for the £300, which he had no difficulty in finding since there was no alternative. No sooner had he found them than they brought another charge against him, this time concerning the accusation made by John the Marshal. (1450)

He had no intention of answering this charge there and then, replied Thomas. This John had indeed been in his court, but had not been able to show that any wrong had been done to him. And when the time came for him to leave, he was not willing to swear his oath on any other book than a troper* that he had brought along with him. (1455)

It is not the custom in this country to use a book of tropes on which to swear an oath; it should be done on bended knee with a book of the

Gospels. John had intended to deceive God by swearing in the way he did, but within the year worms were able to eat into his corpse and those of his two beloved sons.*

Unwilling to let matters rest there, the king demanded that he provide accounts of all the business he had managed when he was chancellor. The archbishop replied that he was not willing to address this matter now, as no date had been set by which he had to produce his accounts.

The king instructed him to be ready the next day to answer the charge and to present his accounts in full. The archbishop's reply was courageous: one day was not reasonable notice for him to plead on such a specific matter. God's eyes, the king retorted, Thomas must absolutely appear the following day.

When the archbishop realized that he would never win back Henry's affection, he threw himself at his feet and appealed for clemency. He fully recognized that the king had raised him up from nothing and made him what he was. This much he admitted. Let him not now undo all the good he had done him! "God's eyes," said Henry, "what you are doing at present has put me to shame!"

The king, pale with anger, his brow beaded with rage, went off into another room and summoned all the bishops to his presence, leaving the archbishop all on his own like a lost soul. "God's eyes," he said, "tell me what advice you have to give me.

"Archbishop Thomas used to be my servant, and for several years he was in charge of collecting all of my revenue. Because he is now archbishop, he is unwilling to produce accounts for this or for anything else. I want to hear what you think about this." He found that they all fell silent: not one of them uttered a single word.

When he saw them reduced to silence, he flared up in a rage: "God's eyes," he said, "have you nothing to say to me?" Turning to the bishop of Winchester, he said: "My lord and father, what do you advise me to do? You are the most senior, and it is your duty to give me your advice."

"Sire," replied the bishop, "since you ask me, I'll tell you exactly what my view is. From the time he was consecrated, he has not been subject to your laws. Despite his having been your agent, he will not provide you with any accounts. Take great care before having him arrested on this score!"

The king then flew into a mighty rage on seeing that they did not come to the decision he wanted. He stormed back into the room. The archbishop rose to meet him, and, just like a serving lad, prostrated himself at the king's feet. (1500)

All the other bishops likewise fell at his feet, but in an attitude of prayer for the archbishop. The king's mood, however, did not soften in the least. Seeing them all lined up together round him, he said: "God's eyes! Why are you putting me to shame in this way? No man ever received more ignoble treatment at the hands of his own vassals!" (1505)

Thomas understood that this was as far as he would get. As evening fell, he went off to his lodgings. The pain in his side flared up, and it lasted the rest of the day and all night. This was something he was prone to suffer from, and it caused him frequent distress. The violent emotions to which he had been subjected had brought it on again. (1510)

But early the next day the king sent for him, swearing by God's eyes that he would have his accounts. Thomas said that he could not come: the pain was giving him a fever. If it pleased God, he said, the pain would pass, and he would come to court just as soon as he was able. (1515)

The king swore by God's eyes that come he must and, whether he like it or not, produce the accounts. The more unwell he was, the harder Henry pushed him. Archbishop Thomas replied that, for the love of God the Creator, he should be patient with him. (1520)

When Henry saw that he was not going to get him to come, he thought he was just pretending to be ill in order to mislead him. He sent two earls to verify whether or not Thomas was ill, the earl of Leicester, whose intelligence was widely recognized, and the earl of Cornwall. Their task it was to bring back the truth to the king. (1525)

Once there, they saw that he was in fact ill. They informed him that they were acting on the king's behalf and that he was summoned to appear in court. Thomas replied by pointing out that he had been suffering from his pain all night and that it was still hurting now. He was, moreover, still feverish. (1530)

He begged them for God's sake to let him stay in bed. If Henry were willing to be patient with him until the next day, he would come to court to listen to what the king wanted to be done. Even if it were to cost him his life, he would not fail to come. He would even have himself hoisted on a bier and carried there! (1535)

On behalf of the king they granted Thomas the delay he requested, adding that the king absolutely insisted on hearing him give his accounts the next day, and nothing would make him change his mind. Thomas undertook to go. The two earls went back to the king and reported on what they had discovered.

Then, the same day, Thomas received further news from two highly influential magnates. They assured him that if he went to court, this was what was in store for him: he would be thrown into such a dark prison that he would never again be able to see his own feet; either that or he would be killed without further ado.

On hearing this, the archbishop began shaking all over. He went to disclose all this to a certain holy man who told him that, at the following day's service, he should celebrate the mass of the first martyr St Stephen. This would ensure that his enemies were incapable of harming him.

The pain from his illness having abated, Thomas rose at dawn the next day and celebrated the mass of St Stephen with great devotion. He divulged his predicament to God, and prayed that he be spared a disastrous outcome.

Nevertheless, the bishop of London, when speaking later on behalf of the king in the presence of the pope, accused Thomas of having celebrated this mass for the purposes of sorcery and in order to spite the king. This is a distortion of the truth.

Once the mass was finished, the archbishop did not disrobe but sat there in his vestments. He sent his people to fetch the bishops, and when they came, he calmly made the following speech to them: "My lords," he said, "in God's name give me your advice!

"The king has become so violently angry with me that no one could say or explain what great harm he is seeking to do me, he and the empire's great and good.* You can all see for yourselves what direction he is going in, and no one, unless it be the Lord God, can find me a remedy.

"For this reason I am very much afraid and greatly alarmed, since I am privy to the king's plans and to what he has secretly decided to do. Some of his closest associates have faithfully reported this to me, and that is why I wish to go to court dressed in my vestments, cross in hand, to ensure my personal safety."

One of the bishops, who was not at all happy with the idea since he approved of the king's policy and wished to drive it forward, replied: "My lord, what are you seeking to do? You surely don't want to cause an uproar by going to the king's court with a drawn sword in your hand, because if you did that, the quarrel would never be settled.

"If that's how you intend to go to court, with sword drawn, hauberk on, lance in hand, the result will be anger and hatred welling up between you and the king. No one will ever be able to bring about peace between the two of you, and there will never be a day when Holy Church will not shed a tear.

"You are already on bad terms with the king and have quarrelled bitterly with him. If you go to court as you intend, it will be a grave insult to him. If you go there bearing arms, you'll be looking for a fight! Your blade is blunted, his sharpened. If he draws his sword against you, you won't be able to withstand the blow.

"Lay down your cross, leave your vestments to one side, and have someone else carry your cross before you! You ought to go to court humbly, so that no one will be in a position to criticize or blame you. It will be that much easier, also, for people to talk peace with the king."

The good archbishop's reply was a measured one:* "I have not drawn my sword, nor am I lashing out at him. And I won't have my cross carried for me by someone else, whoever might put himself forward for the task. I am looking for peace, and it saddens me that anyone should withhold it from me, and I will be far sadder still if Holy Church were to shed tears over it.

"I have no desire to do the king any wrong or bring dishonour on him. There is no one in the whole world who wishes to see him honoured more than I do, and I am extremely upset to be the object of his hatred. If his is a sharp sword, mine is an inflexible one, and I must of necessity obey only the Lord of Heaven.

"I now beg and command you to give me such advice as will prevent me from disgracing myself in the eyes of God and of the world." "My lord," said one of the bishops, "be submissive! Surrender the archbishopric into the king's mercy! You can be sure that this is the only way that you will have peace."

"That is bad advice you give me," said Thomas, "and I will never do that. Go now to the court, and I will get ready. So please God, I will follow the truest possible advice." He immediately then took off his alb, leaving on his cope and surplice – this I know for certain.

He went off to court in response to the summons he had been issued with. Over his surplice he put on the armour of the stole, and a canon's cope over this, knowing, as he did, how bitterly he had quarrelled with the king. Commending himself to God, he mounted his horse.

He was extremely frightened of the king and of the ferocity of his temper. Having worked closely with him for so long, Thomas knew him, and all his little secrets, only too well. He was well aware just how violently the king hated him. He also knew that he would have very few allies when the meeting reconvened. (1625)

I am at a loss to know why the king hated him as much as he did, unless it was because he had left his service, thus depriving him utterly of the advice he used to give, or because he dared defy him in whatever way. He was not even a member of the nobility, and his friends lacked any sort of influence. (1630)

Considering how much the king had done to promote his interests, and how he had shown him so much affection on different occasions that he had taken him unreservedly into his confidence, Henry had never encountered anyone who could make him so angry. It seemed to him despicable of Thomas ever to have started the quarrel. (1635)

A king's anger is not something to be trifled with.* Once he begins to hate someone, for whatever reason, petty or otherwise, he will never again like them for the rest of his life. According to some, a king's will is law, and everyone obeys their temporal lord. (1640)

God's vassal had abandoned his temporal lord to become the unconditional vassal of God his Creator, whom he desired to serve with fidelity and love. He realized that a particularly harsh struggle lay ahead of him. He feared losing his freedom more than losing his estates. (1645)

The good priest St Thomas went to court dressed for his personal safety in God's armour. He had his archbishop's cross carried on his right, and held the horse's bridle himself in his left hand. For advocate he chose his master Jesus Christ. (1650)

He dismounted directly in front of the great hall and, leaving his horse to be looked after, went inside. There he found a large number of people, young and old. Once inside he took hold of the cross himself. The king was in his apartments with his closest associates. (1655)

Thomas went in, accompanied by only a small number of companions. Our understanding is that he took few attendants in with him. There he found the king surrounded by his close advisers, bishops, abbots, earls and magnates. Like a doughty champion, he entered the field of combat alone. (1660)

As he approached, the bishops rose to their feet, remonstrating with him for carrying the cross and reproaching him with grossly insulting his lord the king and with calling down further enmity onto his head. Let him hand the cross over to someone else – that was their advice to him. (1665)

Robert bishop of Hereford asked for the cross to be given to him: as a bishop he was the right person to be entrusted with it. The bishop of London then came forward to claim it as his entitlement. As dean of the Canterbury chapter, he said, it was only right that he should carry it. He attempted to use force and to snatch it out of Thomas's hand. (1670)

"You always were foolish," he said, "you're acting foolishly now and you always will – marching up like this to the king with a drawn sword. If he draws his sword against you, how can you possibly defend yourself? It's a very disrespectful thing to do, coming into the king's court as if you were spitting fire and flames and using your cross as a weapon. (1675)

"Put it down and hand it over to someone else. Don't provoke our lord the king's anger." Roger bishop of Worcester joined in: "My lord bishops, pray desist! Let his cross be! Don't lay a finger on it! It is not the act of a virtuous person to carry this particular cross." (1680)

They struggled hard to take the cross off him, but he refused to let any of them have it. You should have seen him clinging on to it with both hands! Hardly any of the bishops were willing to support him, but Roger of Worcester was unwilling to forsake him. (1685)

Archbishop Thomas went straight ahead, carrying his episcopal cross himself. So great was his fear that he would not hand it over to anyone. He sat down on a bench, leaning on God for support. He held the cross in his hand, but he was carrying it in his heart. (1690)

The king was sitting in a separate room with his close attendants, consulting with the most prominent amongst them. The archbishop did not go up to him, knowing that Henry was infuriated with him. All their exchanges that day were done by means of intermediaries. (1695)

Bad feeling and bad advice misled the king into being so incensed against the holy man. The king had had an excellent understanding of Thomas in the old days, and thought that he was still the same person now. But he had turned into a completely different person now that the Holy Spirit was in him. (1700)

The king next wanted to open proceedings against Thomas on the question of the criminal clerks, but the magnates managed to get him to drop this particular matter: if he sought to start any action against the clergy, he would find all the bishops joining forces, and he would then not be able to make the archbishop give ground. (1705)

There was much to-ing and fro-ing by the magnates, two or three at a time, between the king and Thomas, who remained sitting on his bench. He was told, in the greatest secrecy, by those advisers closest to the king to look to his own personal safety, since preparations were afoot to kill him. Several of them had sworn and pledged their word to this effect. (1710)

I have no idea whether it was the king himself who had arranged to have the archbishop thrown into chains or killed, but people kept telling him all day that his life was in danger. The king was perhaps attempting to intimidate him, thinking that by threatening him he would find it easier to make him yield. (1715)

King Henry next summoned the bishops to his presence and told them in no uncertain terms that he now required them to keep the promise that they had earlier made him, namely that they would observe the customs and laws of the realm, and that the archbishop would be no exception. (1720)

The bishops went off to confer with the archbishop, and explained that they were under an obligation to observe the king's laws, since it was Thomas himself who, in the name of obedience, had made them agree to these laws and then formally to confirm them *in veritatis verbo*.* They had no desire to break their word to him in any way. (1725)

He himself, they added, also had to observe the laws, for he had agreed to them and ought not to renege; he had sworn an oath and could not go back on his word. And now the king wished to find out whether his intention was not to respect the fealty that Thomas owed him. (1730)

St Thomas listened carefully to everything they had to say and then made a measured reply: God, he said, is in the person who loves the truth, and the person who does not love loyalty is no lover of God, for God hates deceit and all manner of iniquity. (1735)

"The laws," he said, "to which you say the king is so attached, have nothing to do with loyalty but are laws of wickedness, contrary to God and unlawful, and are designed to destroy the clergy. I for one will not observe them for anything in the world. In the name of holy obedience, I forbid you to observe them. (1740)

"A wise man is one who gets to his feet again if he falls down, and it is far better to get up immediately than to take one's time about it. Seeing that this court is bent on causing me such great harm – and you also who should, as reason demands, stand by me – I intend to appeal to Rome, since I am unwilling to proceed with something that is unlawful." (1745)

*When the archbishop had first understood what was happening, he had considered appealing to the papal court to see whether this might be a way out of his predicament. He now saw the bishops standing all around him, not one of them willing to say a single word because of the king. (1750)

He saw clearly now and understood that his life was in danger. Seeing the bishops standing all around him in silence, he said: “Lords, I am lodging an appeal, for my need to do so is urgent. This court is doing me such great harm.” “My lord,” said the bishop of London, “spare me from any blame in this!” (1755)

“Spare me from any blame, my lord,” said the bishop of London. “No,” replied Thomas, “I will not. But if anyone lays a finger on me, I request all of you to see to it that justice is done. You should spare no one for any reason.” The bishop of Winchester was greatly dismayed when he heard this. (1760)

“My lord,” he said, “in God’s name listen to what I have to say. Surrender the archbishopric into the king’s mercy. It is the only way you will have peace. That much is clear to me.” He did not speak out of malice; his advice was given in good faith. He could see grave danger looming and a deadly act of violence. (1765)

“No, I won’t do it,” Thomas replied. “Never in my life will I hand over divine authority to a layman. To do so would be an act of illegality and a crime against God.” Then Hilary bishop of Chichester said: “If I had my way, you would relinquish the power you have and be just plain Thomas.” (1770)

Most of the bishops, on hearing that Archbishop Thomas was being put in danger, felt profound grief. They immediately called out to Archbishop Roger, to the bishop of London, who had an intense hatred of Thomas, and to Hilary bishop of Chichester, who never had any love lost for him: (1775)

“For the love of God, my lords, this is not the way to do things. If anyone kills the archbishop, you will be considered responsible, since everyone in the country knows that you have always hated him. Unless you can save his life, we are all in deep trouble. The king, Holy Church and all of us will be put to shame.” (1780)

Then the bishops went off to speak together and confer to see how they might save Thomas. They decided to go and talk to King Henry, and to explain that, if the bishops were to bring their own charge against him before the pope, they might well get Thomas deposed from his see. (1785)

They went to explain this to the king and to beg him to show mercy. "Sire," they said, "for the sake of God, this is not the way to do things. Drop this trial you have begun. It will always be a stain on your reputation, and we ourselves will be disgraced and suspended from our posts. (1790)

"Sire," they said to the king, "let us try our hand at solving this. As well you know, he made us confirm your laws and now he is wanting us all to go back on our word. This is a reason for us now, collectively, to bring a charge against him. In this way we will most likely be able to get him deposed from his see." (1795)

To this King Henry replied: "I approve." "Let us go ahead, then," they said, "and we'll do everything we can to put an end to this disorder, whether it's to the archbishop's liking or not." Some of them acted out of malice, others out of loyalty to him. Then they all came, with much trepidation, to see the archbishop. (1800)

"We are to bring a charge against you," they said, "for we are being grossly mistreated. The promise we recently made to the king and which, in the name of obedience, you had ordered us to make, you are now forbidding us to carry out. You have forced us into a position of having to break our word, and this is why we are bringing the charge." (1805)

King Henry's advisers had informed him of what was happening. When he learned that Thomas was persisting in going totally against his wishes, and that he was to make an appeal, what his thoughts or feelings were I cannot tell, but he did not keep these from his advisers. (1810)

The bishops had said to him: "Sire, you must not go ahead with what you are doing. If you follow our advice, Thomas will lose the archbishopric. We will make him give way on everything. He wants to make us perjure ourselves and betray you, and that is what we intend to accuse him of before the pope." (1815)

"Go to it straightaway," he had replied. "See to it." And then they had come to Thomas who had heard them out. "My lord," they had told him, "given the way you are behaving towards us, making us and you yourself break our word to the king, we are bringing a charge against you, for you are grossly mistreating us." (1820)

The bishops' decision to appeal to the pope greatly reassured the king and did much to soothe his anger for the moment. He believed that, if they could prove in God's court that Thomas was now reneging on what he had earlier promised, this would mean that he should lose his crozier and be stripped of his office. (1825)

It is my belief that the archbishop of York and the bishop of London both advised him secretly not to inflict further suffering on Thomas in public. Henry should summon him the following day when there would be no one there and take him into custody without any fuss. (1830)

This had the effect of allowing the king to curb his anger considerably, and of ensuring that the evil plot that had been set up failed to materialize. Their malicious ruse thus turned out finally to have a positive result. Whatever a man may think of doing, his power to carry it out is feeble, for God is there to bring powerful people low and thwarts evil intentions. (1835)

Then the king sent some of his knights to Thomas. His wish was for him to provide full accounts of everything he was in control of as chancellor – in the order of £30,000 cash. The answer he gave to the messengers was an apposite one: (1840)

"My lords," he told them, "I have no intention of entering into any proceedings. My lord the king has no right to demand accounts from me, for I used and allocated this huge sum that I hear you mention for the king's business, and he regularly heard it accounted for. (1845)

"And when I was elected and raised to the dignity of archbishop in London, I was declared exempt – on the king's own orders, as well you know – from having to give accounts among several other things. This is why I have no intention of reopening this case, which I consider as over and done with." (1850)

When they relayed these words to the king, he flushed with anger, redder than hot coals on cinders. "God's eyes," he said, "even though he's my liege man, he refuses to provide me with accounts. I'll have him sentenced!" They replied: "Yes, sire, but for another reason, an even greater wrong that he is committing. (1855)

"Being your liege man, he is required to be faithful to you, to preserve and protect your honour in all circumstances. Since he is now denying the competence and validity of your court and appealing to some other court, you can use this to make trouble for him, since in doing this he is deliberately bringing great dishonour on you. (1860)

"This is a charge you can lay against him," explained his magnates. "Let him be sentenced for that, then," the king replied, "and see to it immediately!" Nero's henchmen gave their verdict: evil fools that they were, they condemned their spiritual father to arrest and imprisonment by the king. (1865)

Archbishop Roger came out of the meeting and said to Thomas: "Have mercy on yourself, and on all of us as well, because if you do not do exactly what King Henry wants you to do, we are in extremely serious trouble." St Thomas replied: "Get you behind me, Satan!"

Once the sentence had been drawn up and agreed to, it was read out and repeated in front of the king. Henry sent two of his closest advisers to Thomas, Reginald earl of Cornwall and the earl of Leicester, a very wise man.

Both of them came straight to the archbishop and stood in front of him. The earl of Leicester spoke first: "My lord," he said, "the king commands you, through us, to hear what sentence has been given and passed on you." Glaring at him fiercely, the good priest replied:

"I am not ready to hear any sentence today," said the good archbishop, "because I have lodged an appeal." "But how," replied the earl, "since you owe the king fealty, homage and allegiance, can the sentence be avoided? You hold vast fiefs and estates from him in baronial tenure.

"Seeing that you hold vast fiefs from him in this way, you must abide by the sentence of his court and the justice it dispenses." "I hold no fiefs, no property from him as his tenant. All the lands I have are charitable donations or held in perpetual alms.*

"Everything that his ancestors have donated to Holy Church was granted in perpetual alms, and there was never any question of baronial tenure. These are the very terms which the king has confirmed in his charters: the land was granted in alms in perpetuity.

"And this is why," he continued, "in the name of God and the Christian values which you embrace through us, I forbid you to pass any sentence on me today." The earl replied: "Given the defence you have put forward, I have no wish to get involved, and I personally consider you exempt."

Then Earl Robert added: "But it is up to you, Earl Reginald, to pronounce sentence. I dare not do so in view of such a forceful defence." "So help me God, I won't do it either," said Earl Reginald. "That was not my remit, and I shall not be so bold. You pronounce it if you wish, since this Reginald will not be of any assistance to you."

"My lord," said Earl Robert, "by St Denis, wait until the king has heard what your answer is to the judgement." "What," archbishop Thomas asked, "am I under arrest, then?" "No, by St Lazarus, you are not," said the esteemed earl. "Then I'm leaving here and now," said God's ally.

The two mighty vassals then went off to the king, and the holy archbishop got up from where he had been sitting. He hurried out of the royal chamber, taking no one with him except God of Heaven. He was still holding the episcopal cross in his right hand. (1915)

When he came out of the king's chamber, certain justices and barons, whom I should not name, shouted loudly at him, violently raising their voices against him: "The traitor's making off, just look at him, look!" Thomas continued walking without uttering a single word. (1920)

Even Earl Hamelin failed to keep quiet. When he saw Archbishop Thomas leaving, he heckled him, raising his voice to a shout: "You foul traitor, you're slinking off just like a common criminal!" And Hugh Wake as well yelled at him until he was fit to drop. (1925)

Thomas was in a great hurry to get out of the chamber. When he reached the middle of the hall, he stumbled over some wood and almost fell. Whereupon Ranulf de Broc shouted out at him: "The traitor's sneaking away!" The holy man did not say a word but kept walking. (1930)

The hall was filled with shouts of "traitor!" and from every direction came loud cries. The shouting would not have been louder if the whole town had suddenly collapsed. They even threw handfuls of straw at him as he passed.* He had no wish to start a discussion with them and went on his way. (1935)

The Jews acted in the same way when Jesus was condemned to death: they shouted vile insults at him, struck and pummelled him, spat in his face. Jesus was willing to suffer all this for the sins of man, as was Thomas to save the clergy from degradation. (1940)

Evil men, menials and sluts, who thought they were doing what the king wanted, hurled abuse at St Thomas and threw fistfuls of straw at him, just as Ranulf had told them to. But those who feared God and had always loved Thomas sighed deep sighs and shed secret tears. (1945)

The king was informed of how Thomas was being showered with insults and how people wanted to injure, even to kill him. If it were not stopped, it would be a cause of shame for the king, so he gave orders by proclamation that Thomas and his men should be free to leave. (1950)

Thomas leapt onto his horse and came galloping up to the gate. To his great consternation he found it locked, and he feared he would be arrested and taken prisoner. God, however, worked a miracle and extricated him from his predicament. (1955)

The archbishop was accompanied by his squire, a certain Tronchet, who turned out to be extremely useful to him. From afar he spotted the keys to the gate hanging on a branch. He did not lose a moment, but took them down and unlocked the gate without having to call the gate-keeper. (1960)

God had no intention of abandoning the archbishop. There were two good handfuls of keys, but with the first key he tried, the squire found the right one. The gate-keeper was busy giving a hiding to some poor wretch or other, so the holy man, beloved of God, was able to get away. (1965)

The earl of Leicester, who had heard all the commotion, had told the king how people were hounding the archbishop. It was shameful, he had said, to insult such a venerable man, and he should not allow it. People would blame him for it. The king had then ordered that Thomas should be left alone. (1970)

When Thomas dismounted, back at the monastery, he went into the church and enquired whether it was time to sing nones.* But since the time for this was past, he celebrated nones and vespers together. Whatever the time of day was, he never forgot divine service. He took great pleasure in serving God, and God rewarded him for it. (1975)

And when he came back out of the church, he called his servants and asked for his meal. All his clerks and knights had run away, and had he needed them, he would not even have found half a dozen left. They had scattered in all directions for fear of the king. (1980)

He then asked for the poor to be brought in, and he had the rest of the refectory tables filled up with them. He had other things on his mind besides filling his stomach, I should think, but he ate a good, leisurely meal and put on a cheerful face to keep his men happy. (1985)

* * *

Before he had finished eating, night had fallen and it was dark. His bed was carried into the church in full view and made up behind the high altar. His lambskin nightcap was placed on his pillow, over which his blanket was folded back a little. (1990)

When the monks came in to sing compline, they actually thought that the good archbishop was asleep, so they sang quietly in order not to disturb him. They gestured to one another to keep back, pointing out that he was tired and that they should leave him in peace. (1995)

He had detailed one of his men to guard the bed, and if anyone came close, he was told to go away and to let his lord rest. No one would have gone up to look in the bed after this, and everyone expected him still to be there the next morning. (2000)

In the meantime all preparations were underway for his journey, though he was willing to tell only very few of his men about it. He did not want to take even one of his own horses with him. Instead he had four strong warhorses brought and placed outside, as if they belonged to some guests who were on the point of leaving. (2005)

At that time the majority of people were still eating, and the man of God saw that this was the opportunity for him to leave. It was raining heavily with little prospect of it letting up. At one stage during the night he had to have his cape cut shorter, for it was so heavy with rain that it was almost impossible to wear. (2010)

7 Flight

After dusk and when night had fallen, Archbishop Thomas got ready to leave. He did so in secret, informing no one, close adviser or cleric, relation or friend, except three people who had been in his service previously. (2015)

The good priest took with him two white Gilbertine canons: one was called Robert of Cave, so I have heard, and the other brother Scaiman. He did not omit, either, to take along with him one of his squires, Roger de Bray, a fine, dark-haired young man. (2020)

He had taken the two brethren, who had come to him from Sempringham, into his confidence in addition to his squire, one of his closest associates. They left by the north gate under the cover of darkness. None of them was seen, and they encountered no one. (2025)

All the gates of the town, however, were being watched. I have no idea why, but in the circumstances we can easily guess. The good archbishop had sent people to reconnoitre the gates, and the north gate was the only one they found without a watchman or gate-keeper. (2030)

Archbishop Thomas had no desire to dawdle. He had been told in no uncertain terms that if he waited until it was light, he would be thrown into prison, and he was very much afraid of this happening. Out under the stars and through the gloom they went, commending themselves to our Lord God. (2035)

They would travel all night until dawn, and during the daytime they would stay concealed until dusk, hiding either in monasteries or convents or in the woods. They ignored the main roads and the direct route, and in this way finally reached the coast. (2040)

The next day, the king's messenger came three times in the early morning to hurry him up to come to court. The person guarding the door would not let him in, telling him to allow the archbishop to continue resting. The messenger kept insisting more and more, so it became impossible to keep up the pretence. (2045)

Then Master William de Capes, Thomas's marshal, went to King Henry to beg for pity on behalf of the archbishop's men, to protect them from being molested: almost all of them had run away and left as a result of the hostility of the de Brocs. (2050)

The king had Ranulf de Broc issue a proclamation throughout Northampton that the archbishop's men were to be allowed to leave freely in broad daylight: no one should be bold enough to lay a finger on any of them. Ranulf complied grudgingly and dared not refuse. (2055)

On the second day following the night of his escape, Thomas came via the main road to Lincoln where, together with his men, he found lodgings with Master Jacob. Thomas took to wearing a Cistercian's grey habit for a better disguise. Now Thomas is no longer Thomas: he is Christian. (2060)

Before daybreak St Thomas, accompanied only by Robert of Cave, took a boat. Passing directly under Lincoln Bridge, he made his way to the Hermitage in the direction of Sempringham, and there he stayed in a monk's cell for eight days or more. (2065)

Scaiman and Roger went by land as far as Sempringham, where they stayed. Here in secret they prepared the archbishop's journey, not revealing their intention to a soul, high-born or low. When they saw the opportunity, they set out by night. (2070)

Anyone who saw the holy man, when Robert was away, sitting down to eat without any clerk or knight to keep him company, without friend or stranger, steward or groom, cook or butler, would have been moved to pity, and tears would have streamed down his face. (2075)

They stayed at the Hermitage long enough for the king to think that they had crossed the Channel, then they headed for the sea, travelling by night. They even passed through Canterbury at night. Everywhere they went, their lodgings had been arranged in advance. (2080)

On reaching the coast the good archbishop embarked at Sandwich and late in the evening landed between Gravelines and Marck. Travelling by foot was impossible, since it quickly tired Thomas. All he had was a big pair of shoes that a brother had lent him and which he had tied on round the ankle and knotted. (2085)

In trying to make haste he fell over on the beach. He got to his feet again and examined his hands. They then arranged to hire a mare for him, but it had no saddle, and they were unable to find another at that particular time. The halter that the owner had provided the animal with was even made of hay. (2090)

They had come across a young man on the beach and had hired the horse from him for eight pence. But he took a long time fetching it, and they thought they were going to be denounced or taken prisoner. But he did finally bring the mare, and they set Christian on it. (2095)

They got him to ride two leagues without a saddle, with just a cape folded under him. Then together they took a boat to Clairmarais and from there, without losing any time, they made their way to St Omer. Whenever they stopped to take lodgings, they stayed well hidden. (2100)

Lord Richard Lucy, on his way to St James of Compostela by way of Flanders, arrived in St Omer and, having heard people talking about the archbishop, came to see him. If Thomas would go back with him, he said, he would arrange for him to make peace with King Henry on all counts. But it was to no avail. (2105)

The archbishop replied that he did not want to go back, since it would simply not be possible for Richard to bring about peace, and he was not willing to place himself in his hands in this way. His intention was to go straight to the pope, whose advice he would follow on all matters. (2110)

Richard's reply was both irate and arrogant: "Since you don't want to come back to the king with me, I hereby withdraw my fealty from you and that of my men." The archbishop answered him with calm and composure: "Richard, you are my man, and it is your duty to give me your fealty." (2115)

Richard replied: "I also give back my homage to you." "That is not something I lent you in the first place," was Thomas's immediate rejoinder. "But from now on what is certain is that you will not hold any land from me." "I'm not giving you back any fief or land holding," said Richard, "but in future do not count on me for anything." (2120)

The good archbishop then sent two abbots to Count Philippe of Flanders to ask for safe conduct so that he could cross Flanders: he had landed there, he said, having left England surreptitiously on account of a quarrel he had with his lord the king. (2125)

The count replied that he would consider the matter, but added that he was a man of sufficient means to be able to retain an archbishop within his territory. On hearing this, Thomas conferred with Bishop Milon of Thérouanne who, that same night, took him away with him. (2130)

The archbishop feared for his safety when he heard the count's answer, and he paid particular attention to the terms he had used in his reply, given that the count was King Henry's cousin and that they were very close and intimate friends. He had disclosed his plan to Bishop Milon. (2135)

He had come to visit the archbishop that day, and when the time came for him to leave, as evening turned into night, Archbishop Thomas, ever clever, went out with him. So as not to be seen or noticed by anyone, he had the candles put out. (2140)

"Put out those lighted candles," he told them, "and let the bishop leave in God's keeping!" This is how he got away. They stepped back into the dark, and Thomas climbed onto a large white horse that had been brought for him from the bishop's palace. This is how he contrived to leave. (2145)

Thanks to Bishop Milon, who accompanied him that night, he slipped away from his own men under the cover of darkness. He left Flanders and went to Soissons. The next day he sent word back to his men that he was going to Soissons and that they were to join him there. (2150)

8 Exile

Something very much to his advantage happened to Thomas then, and many people afterwards considered it to have been a miracle. Master Henry of Pisa, one of the cardinals, and King Louis of France had come separately to Soissons, and they all happened to meet up in the street there. (2155)

Thomas explained to them the cause he was fighting for and the reason for his exile. Good King Louis took pity on him and in the friendliest possible way offered him hospitality. Master Henry of Pisa likewise undertook to do everything he could to help him. And this is what he did, without stint. (2160)

King Henry next dispatched his messengers to Louis king of France at Compiègne. He reminded him that, in the agreement they had reached after they had made peace again, they had agreed and made a promise to each other that was explicitly mentioned in their treaty. (2165)

This stipulated that, if any of their men should leave their country and were found to be anywhere in the other's country, they should immediately be arrested and detained, then handed back without hindrance to their lord. And lo and behold! The most prominent person in the whole kingdom had now left the country. (2170)

Gilbert Foliot was a member of this embassy. He was a very learned man, a servant of Ashtoreth.* He came, however, to rue the day he ever spoke a word against the holy man. He left Sodom and followed in the footsteps of Lot. (2175)

Another of the messengers was Richard of Ilchester, one of King Henry's privy councillors, master and justiciar of the whole country. He brought along two sparrow hawks for Louis. Now that he has abandoned the side roads, he is following the straight and narrow. (2180)

William d'Aubigny, the good earl of Arundel, was another: wise, brave and courtly, without a stain on his character. But then he contributed to the casting of the Golden Calf and put himself in the wrong by trying to throw Daniel into the lions' den. He eventually found grace at the saint's tomb. (2185)

They gave their message in fine, well-turned phrases. "I have no idea what you're talking about," said King Louis. "Sire," they replied, "King Henry is making a formal complaint to you regarding one of the most prominent men of the whole of England, who has fled the country by night. (2190)

"Archbishop Thomas has done the king wrong. He was in control of the entire realm and collected all the revenue for years on end. Now he is unwilling to provide accounts for everything he has helped himself to. Nor will he accept the sentence that has been passed on him. He has become a person of ill repute. (2195)

"In view of his refusal to provide his lord with an account of what he has taken for himself, and since he will not submit to his sentence, our view is that his departure is clearly of criminal intent. The king also asks you to be so kind as to ensure that he finds no asylum in your country." (2200)

"I have indeed seen Archbishop Thomas," said the king. "He was the chancellor who served King Henry so well. The king has hounded him out of the country, and now hates him so much that he can find no refuge anywhere at all. A fine recompense for such fine service! (2205)

"Yes, I am indeed acquainted with Archbishop Thomas. The reason that France is called free – I swear by the saints whose tombs I have just been to visit – is so that those who need refuge can come and find it here. Let the archbishop be welcomed! He can find support here. If I knew where he was, I would go and greet him myself." (2210)

The earl of Arundel replied: "King Louis, sire, King Henry, through us, would have you know that Thomas has in the past been your deadly enemy: he has ravaged your land and captured your castles. He is the one who was responsible for the king continually quarrelling with you." (2215)

"My lord earl," replied Louis, "what I know for certain is that, seeing with what great loyalty he served his lord, if he had been my man, he would have served me exactly as I would have wished. And since he conquered castles and lands for him, the king should have had all the more reason to cherish him." (2220)

"Sire," said the messengers to Louis, "in the name of the love you owe our king, send word to the pope and ask him not to listen to such a deceitful fugitive as Archbishop Thomas, nor to support or befriend him, nor to listen to or believe any of his lies." (2225)

Thereupon Louis summoned the almoner, Brother Franc: "Don't lose a moment," he said, "go at once to the pope and tell him that, if he wishes to have my support in any matter, he should help the archbishop, support him and treat him kindly. May he let absolutely nothing deflect him from this!" (2230)

Brother Franc happened to be a very close associate of the pope's. He was a member of the papal almonry and ever ready to serve him night and day. This was the reason why he enjoyed such a high reputation everywhere. At that particular time he had come to pay a visit to Louis. (2235)

* * *

The messengers left Compiègne. Brother Franc delivered his message very efficiently, relaying it to the pope, who listened most carefully. Archbishop Thomas then continued his journey as far as Sens and there he found the pope. (2240)

Before, however, God's ally reached Sens, King Henry had already dispatched his own messengers, bishops, magnates and knights of renown, to the pope. At that time the pope had fled from Rome and had been staying at Sens for a matter of months. (2245)

The messengers were: the archbishop who presided at York, Guy Rufus, Roger bishop of Worcester, the earl of Arundel, Richard of Ilchester, John of Oxford, the bishop of Exeter, Hugh de Gundeville, Hilary of Chichester, (2250)

Renaud de Saint-Valéry, Henry fitz Gerold, who was a close friend of the king's, Gilbert Foliot, who made his voice heard, and many others both young and old. Someone, however, made himself look a fool when he spoke. (2255)

King Henry's messengers came and stood before the pope. Several of them spoke well, but many badly: certain spoke in Latin, some correctly or some somewhat ungrammatically. One person in particular made an impersonal verb into a personal one, and could not tell his singulars from his plurals. (2260)

One of the messengers spoke with such bitterness that the pope said to him: "Tone down your language, frater. I will not allow him to be slandered."* I do not have access to the precise wording they used, but I will tell you as much as I know of what they requested of the pope. (2265)

"My lord," said the messengers, "King Henry begs and requests you, his beloved father, to send him two cardinals empowered both to bind and to unbind, and whose decisions cannot be appealed against by anyone. (2270)

"They should be strong-willed and granted such authority that whatever decision they come to cannot be overturned, appealed against or in any way thwarted. If King Henry has acted at all wrongly in relation to the archbishop, let it be rectified by them. (2275)

"And if the archbishop has committed any offence against the king, let it be put right and let judgement be passed once and for all." This seemed to be in every way a fair and just procedure, but there was not a word of truth in it. Everything was consummate trickery and deception. (2280)

Henry, powerful, clever and cunning as he was, was well aware that cardinals are mercenary extortionists, even greedier for money than a peasant is for newly cleared land. The king had two close friends, Masters Gold and Silver, adept at turning a good man into a bad one in the twinkling of an eye, and a brave man into a coward. (2285)

This stratagem did not deceive the pope. He replied to them like the wise man he was: "No cardinal can have such power. None of them will be granted illegal authority by me, and I do not intend to invest anyone else with papal powers." (2290)

At the time when the king's messengers were on their way to see the pope, Archdeacon Reginald fitz Jocelyn happened to be living at Corbeil. He went as far as Paris in order to meet up with the messengers, and asked them in the friendliest terms if they would do him the honour of staying with him. He would be extremely grateful to them. (2295)

He came, he told them, from a good family back in England, but had left in solidarity with the archbishop. If they did him the honour he was seeking from them, good King Louis, who had appointed him abbot of Corbeil at that time, would be all the more appreciative of him. (2300)

They replied: "We are unwilling to eat at your table on account of King Henry, who is no friend of yours and who would certainly not be pleased with us." "You won't be successful in all your dealings with the pope," Renaud replied, "but if you were to accept my hospitality, at my expense, you would enable the king to take vengeance on one of his enemies." (2305)

Then the messengers continued on their way to Sens to see the pope. As he was unable to meet their demands, the pope did make them one concession, namely that Roger archbishop of York should be papal legate in England. The documents were drawn up but not sent off. (2310)

But Reginald fitz Jocelyn, alias the Lombard, was a privileged member of the papal court, and on learning how things had turned out, went secretly and by night to the court. He had no desire to be denounced, since during the daytime the presence of the king of England's men made people very fearful. (2315)

He said to the pope: "My lord, please do not do this. If Roger of York has the legation, he will depose all the bishops the king hates." At Renaud's intervention the pope had all the documents that had been prepared earlier torn up, and he sent others off instead. (2320)

Henry's envoys did everything in their power to obtain what they wanted, but they got nothing more. They mounted their horses and set off home. Renaud de Saint-Valéry had friends in the region, otherwise they would have been in for some rough treatment there. (2325)

There was no question of their waiting for their archbishop to arrive, for they were incapable of proving anything against him. He would lose no time in giving the pope information about them that would put them at an immediate disadvantage, and they would not be able to offer a defence on all of the points that he would raise. (2330)

* * *

Three or four days later, St Thomas arrived at Sens. Being tired from the journey, he went immediately to where he was staying. There he conferred with his clerks to see which one of them would plead his cause. They were entirely open with him: they just sat there passively, for none of them was ready to plead, whether they were prevailed upon or actually ordered to do so. (2335)

It was because of King Henry that none of them dared speak up. They would lose his goodwill, they explained, for ever and a day. So the archbishop, with God as his ally, undertook to do it himself. The next day, after divine service, he went to the pope and fell at his feet. (2340)

The custom is for people entering the pope's presence to offer him a gift and to lay at his feet some precious object, gold or silver, rich plate or costly clothing. The archbishop took hold of King Henry's chirograph and opened it out with both hands at the pope's feet. (2345)

"This," he said, "is the reason for me having to endure exile. See, here it is, my lord, just listen to what it contains! These are the laws that the king wishes to establish in his kingdom and which he intends to force on Holy Church. I, however, am unwilling to consent to something that goes against God. (2350)

"This, my lord, is what I came here to show you." The pope then asked him to rise and instructed him to read out the laws, and everyone to listen. The saint began to demonstrate, point by point, what end the king actually had in mind with these laws. (2355)

There was present a cardinal, one William of Pavia, or so he was called, I believe, who was a great supporter of King Henry. Henry had contrived to win over all the cardinals by giving them money and, therefore, a reason to support his cause, be it openly or surreptitiously. (2360)

When the archbishop began speaking and started explaining his case elegantly in Latin, William kept interrupting him at the slightest opportunity. He believed that someone else had written the speech for Thomas to learn by heart, and that if he were to be heckled, he would be unable to reach the end. (2365)

But St Thomas was a very intelligent man, and the Holy Spirit was with him. He understood perfectly well what William was saying, and was able to reply point by point, elucidating each issue in consistently elegant Latin.* William contrived to keep him discussing his case for half the day. (2370)

When he had dealt with each of William's questions, Thomas would return to his own argument as if he were Solomon, and continue pleading his cause with highly sophisticated reasoning. Their debate lasted half a day and more, with William defiantly bearding him point by point at every conceivable opportunity. (2375)

By the time the archbishop had brought his speech to a fitting conclusion, having demolished the laws by virtue of sound reasoning and logic, and by providing proof positive, everyone, clerk and layman, was listening to what he was saying, and the pope was taking in every point he made. (2380)

The pope immediately invited Thomas to come and sit beside him, and kept telling him how welcome he was. He was extremely grateful to him for taking on the onerous task of defending Holy Church against a temporal king. He would help him in every way he could – within the bounds of reason. (2385)

Archbishop Thomas thanked him repeatedly for his kind welcome and for the honour he was doing him. The pope proceeded to excommunicate the laws and anyone, whoever they might be, who observed them. He then confirmed that they would always remain under anathema. (2390)

9 Constitutions

If you wish to hear the laws that King Henry wished to impose and establish in his kingdom, and that he wanted to oblige Holy Church to observe and keep, you can learn about them here, for I have no wish to mislead anyone regarding them. The fact that St Thomas detested them is reason enough for everyone else to detest them.* (2395)

"If a dispute should arise between laymen or between clerks as to which of the laymen should be the patron of a particular church, or as to which of the clerks should be endowed with the church's living, the dispute was to be tried and concluded in the king's court." The rights of Holy Church were ignored here. (2400)

"No one should transfer the benefice of any church within the whole of the king's fief without the king's consent." As you can clearly see for yourselves, the whole of the kingdom is his, so he should control it in its entirety! This law would have enabled him to bring the patronage of all churches into his gift by tricking everyone with sophistry. (2405)

"Clerks were to answer all accusations made against them firstly in the king's court and thereafter they were to be brought before the court of Holy

Church, where the king's justice would be present at the trial. Those convicted would be stripped of holy orders and subject to mutilation." It is wrong for a man to be punished twice for one offence. (2410)

"No prelate or beneficed clergy were to leave England without the king's permission. If granted permission, he was to swear that he would not seek to harm either the king or the kingdom." If this were to be the case, no one without power would ever be able to obtain justice. King Henry would be granting himself the same power as St Peter. (2415)

"Individuals who have been excommunicated should not give pledges to Holy Church as caution against future wrongdoing,* but only in order to obtain absolution for the gravity of their sin." Most people would feel entirely free to commit more sins if the clergy were not able to impose further restraints on them. (2420)

"In an episcopal court no one, clerk or layman, was to bring an accusation against any layman, nor would the person accused need to answer the charge, unless the accused heard legitimate witnesses bring evidence against him* – as long, that is, as the archdeacon did not lose his rights in the process." According to this law, however, the parties would never reach any settlement at all! (2425)

"If this person were such that no one dared bring a charge against him, the bishop would have to inform the sheriff. The latter would then have the truth ascertained by twelve men able to swear that they would do so to the best of their knowledge." So henceforth God is to make his appeal to St Peter! (2430)

"No one holding his land directly from the king, nor any of the king's officials, nor their lands, were to be excommunicated or placed under interdict unless the king's opinion had been sought, provided always that he was present in the country or within his kingdom. (2435)

"If the king were not to be found in the country at that time, the bishop would have to go to the justiciar so that the king's business could be concluded in the king's court, and the bishop's business in his own court." Surely someone who passes judgement on other persons' sins may just as well hear their confession also! (2440)

"Appeals should be heard in the first instance by the archdeacon; thereafter they had to be made before the bishop, and then before the archbishop. If the archbishop were unable to reach a decision, the king would then see to it that the matter was brought to a conclusion in God's court, and the appeals were not to be transferred to any other court without his permission." (2445)

That would be making King Henry's court supreme in the extreme if it were placed even above the court of Rome! The whole of England would then be deprived of God's justice, nor would the country be counted as one of the twelve tribes unless Moses were supreme judge.* (2450)

"If a clerk were to wish to start proceedings against a layman regarding a holding that the clerk intended to change from a lay fee into a free-alms fee, or if a lay person intended to change a free-alms fee into a lay fee, the justice would get twelve men to adjudicate whether the holding should continue to be a lay fee or a free-alms fee.* (2455)

"If both parties should claim that they held the land from the same lord, both, whether clerk or lay, should take the matter to the lord's court. But should they acknowledge two different lordships for the holding, they would both have to make their plea in King Henry's court. They were not, however, to lose possession of the land as a result of any verdict." (2460)

This article is unacceptable to both the clerk and the lay person. It can lead to Holy Church losing its rights and be the ruination of clergy and laity alike. It is quite possible for the oath sworn by the twelve jurors to lead to the lord losing his fief in the case of his having to hand it over to his tenant. (2465)

"If anyone living in a castle, borough, fortified city or manor belonging directly to the king were to be accused of any crime before his local prelates, and if he should refuse deliberately to respond to their lawful summons, the matter should then be referred to King Henry's officer. (2470)

"If the officer were to be unable to obtain full redress, he himself was to be discharged and placed at the king's mercy, and after this the bishop would be able to pass judgement. No one should have dared excommunicate the accused before this, although he could possibly have been expelled from the Church. (2475)

"Beneficed clergy and prelates of the country who held land and property from the king should hold them, just like other barons, directly from the king, and should be present in his court, just like the king's other close associates, until sentences of death or mutilation were passed." (2480)

A clerk has no right to pass judgement on a lay person, nor a lay person on a clerk. No one should hold land alms-free from anyone but God. If it is possible for the king to claim equality with God, he has it in his power to drive all the saints out of heaven. I wonder, however, whether he would be good enough to leave God somewhere to stay! (2485)

"If any institution in the kingdom such as a priory, abbey, bishopric or archbishopric were to fall vacant, the king would take possession of its revenues and profits, and would have the income from it and retain it for his own use until such time as the institution had the benefit of a pastor." (2490)

I have been to several places that have been seized by the king. No guests and none of the poor were made welcome. I was turned away by the doorkeeper from outside the door. I understood from what he said that charity was not in residence. The king had removed everything except the fittings. (2495)

Monk, cook, servant, squire and groom, each had their allotted ration of bread, for the king's servants were still running the house. When they left, they wrought such havoc that you would not have found even the scrawniest capon by way of provisions. (2500)

This is a great wrong on the part of the king, a wrong to God, to the institution and to the barons whose fathers had founded its church. They carry out all the duties of service they owe in return for the fief, but the king confiscates their alms and then transfers them to his treasury instead of distributing them to the poor and other good causes. (2505)

"When the time comes for the king to provide the church with a pastor – for everything must be done according to the king's wishes –, he will summon three of the church's beneficed clergy and call a meeting in his chapel of those members of the clergy and those magnates whom he chooses to invite." (2510)

If a church is to be given the benefit of a pastor in accordance with God's wishes, knowledge and noble status have to be eliminated from the appointment, for intelligence would be kept busy outsmarting the barons, and nobility would be in bitter conflict with merit. Simony might, in such circumstances, give the advantage to a mediocre candidate. (2515)

"The person elected was to do homage to the king there and then, swearing fealty and allegiance as if to his liege lord for his life and limb and for his temporal estate." In this way the Saviour's servants would have to do homage, even though, if it had not been for the crozier, none of them would ever have done so as long as they lived. (2520)

"If anyone should seek, by force, to prevent prelates from dispensing justice, the king, either himself or through an intermediary, would see to it that the prelates' rights were restored. If, by any chance, someone were able to obstruct the king in such a way as to deny him justice, the prelates should pass judgement on him to the advantage of the king." (2525)

The king's duty is to protect Holy Church and its clergy. Clerks should not bear arms or wage full-scale wars. Their task, whoever they may be, is to serve God night and day. They are not to harm the king's enemies for him or alienate in this way the French or the Welsh from God. (2530)

"If anyone were to have fallen under forfeiture to King Henry, his goods were not to be stored in a cemetery or a church after the justice had made his visitation." I am well aware that, if some thief or robber or some other unfortunate wretch were to turn up, the church and its cemetery ought properly to provide him with protection. (2535)

"Pleas relating to debt, whether entered into under oath or not, should all be heard in the king's court." Legally I am not required to plead in a lay court on any criminal matter. Clerks will have their own court and their own law for debt and other matters, as will all those whose living and sustenance derive from almsgiving. (2540)

"No peasant's son was under any circumstances to be ordained without the consent of the lord on whose land the peasant was born." And this despite the fact that God has called us all to his service! Better by far a villein's son who is worthy and wise than a nobleman who is a faithless reprobate. (2545)

Such were the articles of King Henry's laws. I tell you for certain that good Pope Alexander excommunicated them, as did also St Thomas, and all those who from that day forward might keep them. Those who love God should not observe them. (2550)

This sort of law was very much to the liking of fools and felons. Every person of faith should oppose it, for in every respect it was antipathetic to the King of Heaven. His champion, I see, has been greatly exalted for battling to overcome this wickedness. (2555)

For a month or more the archbishop stayed at Sens in the company of the pope, who then instructed him to go to the Cistercian monks at Pontigny. Here Abbot Guichard provided for all his needs. (2560)

* * *

After this very lengthy digression, I must now get back to my narrative, as I am unwilling to distort my history. I resume at the point when St Thomas fled from Northampton and will continue my story by telling how the king reacted to this. (2565)

On hearing that the archbishop had taken flight, King Henry was exceedingly angry, as were all his advisers also. They had a close watch kept on all the ports both day and night to prevent Thomas crossing the Channel in any merchant ship, full or empty. It was in vain, however, since God had already led him to safety. (2570)

When they failed to find him anywhere in England – and they would not be able to find him, short of going over to Sens to look for him – the king unleashed and gave vent to his anger: he declared all-out war on St Thomas's relatives by having them all driven out of the entire country. (2575)

Men, women, daughters, sons, babes in arms, beneficed clerks, townsfolk and knights, he had them all expelled, seizing everything they owned, lands, churches, livestock and other belongings, corn, revenue and money. (2580)

He even seized the whole of the archbishopric, its revenues, fiefs and other sources of wealth. He handed it all over for Ranulf de Broc to control, who collected all of its income for the royal coffers. From all this St Thomas could not recoup as much as a halfpenny. (2585)

The holy man could have no legal recovery for anything. Not a single one of his clerks dared go back there. None of his kin had anything to eat or drink: having first driven them all out of the country, the king confiscated everything for himself, right down to the last penny. (2590)

This is how St Thomas's relatives were driven away. Sad, miserable and woebegone they went abroad, carrying their children with them, together with their robes and clothing. How true the peasants' proverb is: the higher the rise the greater the fall. Yesterday they were living off the fat of the land, and now today they go hungry. (2595)

One day as the archbishop sat at table, his marshal arrived with the news that the king had had all of his relations exiled. Within a few days more than a hundred of them would turn up on his doorstep. In the name of God he begged him not to take it badly. (2600)

"William," said Thomas, "were I to see my servants cut to pieces for this cause, my relatives, sisters and nephews, flayed alive, I would not take fright, for I would be absolutely certain that God in his mercy would have saved them." (2605)

He was completely impervious to the Devil, even though this same Devil had succeeded in depriving him of his position of power and having him exiled from his country, and was now attempting to cause him distress by exploiting his own flesh and blood. But the Devil was quite incapable of undermining his resolve. No one can tell you all the suffering Thomas endured. (2610)

When the holy man saw his relatives coming to him as refugees, the young infants hanging on their mothers' breasts, and realized that the king had banished both him and his family members, he would rather have died, so utterly downcast was he. Yet he found comfort in God and the Scriptures. (2615)

He thought in particular of Abraham, whom God ordered to leave the country where he was living. He did so, taking his wife with him but leaving his friends behind. So beautiful did the pharaoh find her that he stole Abraham's wife from him and took her off. God returned her to him safe and sound and greatly exalted him. (2620)

He remembered Joseph, whose nine brothers sold him for money, telling their father that he had been eaten by a wild beast. Then in Egypt he came to be more powerful even than an emperor and saved his family from the great famine. (2625)

He brought to mind also the infant Jesus, whom the heavenly angel sent off to Egypt for fear of Herod. Herod then had all the two-year-olds beheaded, intending in this way to kill God. But among these children he was not able to find the Deity. (2630)

Thomas found great consolation in examples such as these, but this did not prevent him from being profoundly distressed at the thought of his family being exiled on his account, especially as he himself did not have a large income or other rents that he could give them. This made him feel all the more bereft. (2635)

The exile, however, turned out quite well for him, in that King Louis gave him his full support and provided everything he and his kinsfolk needed. The French barons in their turn offered their assistance, and this enabled him to provide adequately for those family members who had come to stay with him. (2640)

When King Henry heard that the pope was writing to summon the bishops, he had his council assemble at Clarendon. He wished to make the bishops swear that none of them would ever go overseas to lodge any appeal, (2645) and that they would never obey any instructions from Pope Alexander nor carry out any of his orders, nor henceforth take delivery of any of his letters, nor offer any assistance whatever to Thomas or to his family members. Though they did not actually swear an oath, they did give their assent. (2650)

All the laymen, on the other hand, were made to swear an oath to this effect. Rome in any case had relocated to York, so very rich had Roger of Pont-l'Evêque become. Having Lord Gold at his side was now as good as having Rome on his doorstep! England may well be surrounded by sea and wind, but it needs more than a little storm to put the fear of God into Roger!* (2655)

The king had also ordered by proclamation that if any clerk in the entire kingdom were rash enough to appeal to Rome, all his belongings should immediately be seized for King Henry's benefit, and the clerk imprisoned like some criminal of ill repute. (2660)

All appeals were henceforth made to the king and pleaded in his court. There was no talk of Church law, however, in the royal court, as no poor clerk could get fair treatment there, and it was the rich who could pick and choose whatever church they wanted to have. I can vouch for the truth of what I hear and see for myself. (2665)

At that time St Peter's Pence were withheld also and handed over to the Exchequer. The coasts were closely watched and guarded. Anyone seen arriving from Rome with a letter was immediately arrested and hanged. (2670)

Several people did, however, get through secretly on the instructions of Pope Alexander, carrying letters of reprimand, suspension or condemnation to those prelates who had behaved particularly badly. (2675)

It was at this time that St Thomas summoned his bishops one by one, but none of them was willing to come except the earl's son Robert of Worcester. He immediately crossed the Channel without asking for the sheriff's permission. He alone did not dishonour his prelate or Holy Church. His exile lasted seven years. He earned good interest from his investment.* (2680)

Listen now to the ordinances that the king sent to the country's sheriffs. They were delivered by Walter of Grimsby, named in the document, and Wimer the Chaplain who accompanied him. It will not take me long to tell you what was written in the documents. (2685)

If anyone brought into the country a letter from the pope, or one that Archbishop Thomas had sent, forbidding or prohibiting any religious practice, he was to be immediately arrested and placed under guard until it was known what King Henry wanted to do with him.

If any clerk, monk, canon or lay brother were to cross the Channel, he was required to take a justice's letter of permission with him. Anyone wanting to come back into England needed a letter from the king indicating that he had no objection to his making the crossing. Otherwise he would be arrested and imprisoned.

No written order sent to England from the pope or from Archbishop Thomas was to be obeyed or carried out, nor should their orders be brought into the country by anyone. Any clerk or layman found in possession of such a letter was to be arrested immediately and put into prison.

Any bishop or abbot, indeed any cleric or layman, carrying out a sentence of interdict passed by the pope or by the archbishop was to flee the country together with all his family members. Not one of them should remain behind, and they were not to take any of their belongings with them; these should all revert to the king.

Clerks having any income or property in a particular county were to be issued with three summonses. If they wished to return to their properties or their houses, they were to come back within three lunar months. If not, they were to remain forever in poverty:

the king was to have all their possessions down to the last penny. What prompted him to make this proclamation was the fact that St Thomas's clerks were too afraid to return home, and this summons was intended to ensure they stayed away and was designed to make them permanent outlaws and exiles.

The document also made provision for the bishops of London and Norwich to be summoned to appear in court before particular justices chosen by the king, to explain why Earl Hugh Bigod had been placed under interdict by them, contrary to the laws that the king had established in his kingdom.

Just see what suffering, what death, what punishment Holy Mother Church suffered at that time, not daring to do what was right and dispense its justice. Had it done so, revenge would have been exacted. The son staked his life to preserve his mother's rights.

There was another ordinance that I shall mention, in which the king actually gave written instructions that Peter's Pence were be collected from everyone in England and scrupulously kept to one side until such time as he gave further orders.

The English have a great advantage here that was put in place by the Danish king Cnut: the money is levied annually from every household at a unit rate the equivalent of five shillings' worth of livestock. In a number of localities it is set at 30 pence.* (2735)

This money used to go to the pope, in exchange for which the English enjoyed some significant special treatment: atoning for a sin did not involve them leaving the country, and they could do all the penance they had to do in their own homes. It was this money that the king appropriated and stashed away. (2740)

To my mind he was quite entitled to do so, seeing as he considered himself to be not only archbishop and legate but pope as well! If the pope or the archbishop placed his country under interdict, the king simply granted a dispensation – without even having to put on a stole or make the sign of the cross! It was not possible for Holy Church to have any right comparable to this one. (2745)

It was during this time that King Henry had his son sworn in as king and had him crowned.* Roger archbishop of York, unwilling to decline the king's invitation, had anointed him. The thought should never even have crossed his mind, because the duty of consecrating all the kings of England belongs to the archbishop of Canterbury. (2750)

The archbishop of York was joined by two others: Gilbert Foliot bishop of London and Jocelin bishop of Salisbury, as well as several others whose names are not given here. These were the three who did the deed and who carried the burden of what they did. (2755)

It was these three imposters who anointed the child – may God increase his years, his virtue and his honour! – but this was not within their competence; they acted like thieves. The words of consecration are no less valid for that, however, nor is the child any the less consecrated. May God grant him his love! (2760)

They unjustly encroached on someone else's rights in order to carry out someone else's task, but they paid dearly for it. They were accordingly summoned to Rome, but they did not go, and the pope relieved them of their functions. Fear of the king had made them turn their back on God. (2765)

God, what a tragedy it is when prelates fail to act as their duty requires! They obscure the light that enlightens the world; they are the rotting body that corrupts the spirit. Like dumb dogs that do not bark, they hang around under the bench on their leash; they wag their tails at thieves and are their accomplices in crime. (2770)

These three were in every respect unconditional supporters of the king and unwilling to do anything at all for God. Three in one they formed a false Trinity, absolutely silent when it came to telling the truth, only too willing to turn custom into law. (2775)

They made no attempt to modify the king's behaviour; indeed, they encouraged him to take legal proceedings against Holy Church, and went to considerable trouble to pore over the documents to see if they could unearth or discover anything that might advance the king's cause. (2780)

10 Letters

They were closer even than uncle and nephew and kept writing joint letters to St Thomas telling him that he was wrong to be so hard on the king. The king is lord and head of all the churches, and all the churches are part of the royal fiefs. (2785)

Prelates ought to be in every way obedient to kings, and kings must be allowed to preserve their customs. Since no one was ever able to take their customs away from their ancestors, there is no question of their being given up on account of anyone living today. Both clerk and layman have the duty of being very tolerant towards their lord. (2790)

This is the sort of letter they sent overseas to the saint – in addition to many others about which I have no information – in order to please the king as well as to express their own point of view. Thomas wrote replies to demolish their arguments and to strengthen his own case, and these he had sent to them. (2795)

Thomas replied to their letters in measured tones and would provide confirmation of his statements by referring to the Scriptures. None of them could possibly refute in any way anything he wrote. The Holy Spirit was truly in him and spoke through him, and this gave him added confidence in himself. (2800)

In temporal matters it is right and proper to obey temporal lords, but if their intention is to take anything away from Holy Church, this should not be tolerated. And even if they are spared and allowed to go unpunished for the time being, they will not be able to escape once God is willing and ready for them to be chastised. (2805)

Prelates are the servants of God, and it is the king's duty to cherish them. They are the kings' superiors, and the king must yield to them. God is the prelates' superior, and in order to maintain his law, they must bare their necks and be ready to face death. God suffered death on the cross in order to emancipate his Church. (2810)

Kings hold their land from God and from Holy Church. They owe honour and service to the Church and its clergy, since it was the Church that gave them not only their crown but also the power to enact laws. It is entirely right that the Church and its clergy should enjoy the freedom that our Lord gained for it by his death. (2815)

Those fine ancestors of ours who founded and first established churches at their own expense, who enriched and endowed them by their charitable donations, exempted them from all these customs, and from others besides, and thereafter never criticized this in any way.* (2820)

For anyone making a charitable grant has to ensure that it is completely enfranchised, and should be ready to maintain and defend it in all circumstances against everyone. He should not retain lordship or anything else over it, for it is not a charitable donation if he treats it as his own property. Once he has given it to God, he cannot have it back again. (2825)

And should the king, whose duty it is to protect and defend the Church in every way, seek to do anything to harm it, the bishops should criticize him in no uncertain terms and should not pay any attention to his own personal wishes in the matter. But today's bishops, like reeds, are not strong enough to stand up to the storm. (2830)

Barons, knights, men-at-arms and vassals who, except for the fief of their ancestors, hold no land from anyone often fight battles for their temporal lord in which they suffer great loss, pain, maiming and death for no other reason than that they do not wish to be thought disloyal. (2835)

All the more reason, then, for prelates to wage war against all those who seek to oppose Holy Church, for they enjoy positions of power, honour and respect at God's table. God raises up the son of a low-born man to the point where he is awarded a bishopric and far higher office still. (2840)

Prelates should have their sights firmly fixed on spiritual matters and not falter and slip from their high position. Those who come down from the mountain into the valley are like golden rings in the snouts of swine, harlots in every sense:* no longer men of God but worshippers of Baal. (2845)

* * *

Enough, now, of this sort of talk. Instead I shall give you an account of the letters that the good archbishop sent to the king and the bishops about how they should preserve the peace of Holy Church, and the replies that were sent back to him.* (2850)

To Henry, the noble king of England, count of Anjou, duke of Normandy and of Aquitaine, his lord and friend, from archbishop Thomas, who was formerly in his service but is now his in God, greetings – and may he act in such a way that he forsake and make amends for all the wrongs that he has done in this life. (2855)

I have been waiting for the moment when God was ready to visit you, when you were ready to turn away from the path of evil and once and for all dismiss your wicked counsellors from around you. They will, I fear, plunge you into such deep trouble that you will never again be able to climb back out of it. (2860)

I have endured a great deal in silence in the hope that someone might say to me: "The king, your lord and son, who was lost and dead, is found and is alive again. He had been led astray by the counsel of the wicked. He has returned now to Holy Church to see that justice is done. (2865)

"For a long time he has been in conflict with Holy Church, but henceforth he will turn his energy to setting it free. God's compassion has brought him to see the error of his ways." Daily during the sacrament we pray for you that through his mercy God may set you on the right path. (2870)

Why I say this is because you have sent me into exile and forced me to leave the country, I whose duty it is, under the authority of God, to protect the kingdom's Church and to eradicate the wrongs done to it. You have mistreated Holy Church and its duly appointed members. This I have tolerated without seeking any redress. (2875)

All the many wrongs you have done to Holy Mother Church and its duly appointed members grieve me profoundly, for I myself have contributed to it by failing to ensure that justice was done. A judge who has to pass judgement but does not take his task seriously is every bit as guilty as the offender. (2880)

Holy Scripture says as much and attests to the fact that someone who consents to an offence shares responsibility for it, all the more so if that person should and can punish it but fails to do so. It is clear that someone who is unwilling to take a stand against what is obviously an act of folly is complicit in the offence. (2885)

My wish, your Majesty, is to make you fully mend your ways, and this is why I have been sending you so many letters. In the same way as a little township cannot bring down the honour of the whole kingdom, so you, my king, should not modify or diminish the rights of Holy Church by imposing harsh conditions on it. (2890)

Only priests can pass proper judgement on priests. A bishop is established by God, and whatever sort of person he may be, and even if he should, as a man, lapse into great sin, as long as his intention is to maintain religion and its clergy, he should not be brought down by any secular power. (2895)

A devout prince whose heart is set on doing good should build new churches, enrich and restore those that have fallen into ruin, honour God's priests and clerics, and defend them unreservedly if anyone seeks to harm them. (2900)

You should consider good Prince Constantine, for example. When some clerks accused of criminal behaviour were brought before him, he acquitted them all. "The Lord God alone," he said, "can pass judgement on you. You cannot be judged by a secular prince." (2905)

As Holy Scripture and learned theologians show, the apostles and their successors stipulate, in the name of God, that none of those who labour in God's field should be ejected or driven away from their holding, for they are the servants and stewards of Jesus Christ. (2910)

In canon law, priests are masters, fathers and pastors of all those who live in the Christian faith. God hates anyone who seeks to subjugate his father, and anyone who beats his master puts himself in the wrong, all the more so if the master himself holds the iron collar and the rod as a priest. (2915)

If, as we sincerely believe and wish, you are a good Christian and desire to keep your faith, I should call you a son, and not a bishop, of the Church. It is not for you to teach or lead priests; you needs must follow them, and they must be in front of you. (2920)

You have your own privileges, laws and power. Do not take anything away from the order of religion against its wishes. If it is bad advice that has made you transgress, fall to your knees in humility lest God let loose his arrows at you. Unless you repent immediately, he will already be preparing his bow. (2925)

Whatever the people who betray you and God may say, consider it an honour, not a disgrace, to humble yourself utterly before our mighty Lord, who brings down the proud and places the humble on the higher seat. It is entirely right for kings and princes to fear him.

He can take revenge on anyone. Who can resist him? You would do well to recall and remember, your Majesty, in what particular circumstances God found you, how he raised you up, caused you to prosper and enriched you, and strengthened your kingdom. You are the envy of everyone, your enemies as well as your peers.

You are the chosen one of God, as everyone, high or low, declares. For all the benefits he has showered on you, what are you going to offer him in return? Are you going to destroy his churches and persecute its clerks on the advice of the wicked individuals you surround yourself with, and who urge you act contrary to God and Holy Church?

God is calling out and speaking to the ordained when he says: "He who despises you despises me; he who hates you hates me and is in revolt against me" – so says our ever constant God; "he who strikes you strikes me, strikes me right in the pupil of my eye." Anyone who harms clerks God hates and brings to book.

Even if you had distributed the whole world to the poor, and taken the cross and followed Jesus Christ, you would still not have repaid God for everything he has done for you. Saul, God's chosen one, perished together with his household and family for having abandoned God.

King Uzziah, renowned for having so frequently conquered his enemies, grew inordinately proud and self-satisfied. He omitted to give thanks to God who had helped him in everything he did, and so arrogant was he that he took on the functions of a priest,

and was presumptuous enough to bring holy incense into the temple. In his anger God struck him down with leprosy. God's properly appointed priests ejected him from the temple. He never recovered his health, and he remained a wretched leper for the remainder of his days.

If you were willing, dear king, to search the scriptures, you would find that several of the kings chosen by God, having risen and become revered in the world, failed to carry out their functions as they should and acted contrary to God. God cast them back again into oblivion and into poverty.

Ahaz similarly took it upon himself to be a minister of religion: he burned incense *in domo Domini* as if he were a high priest. He was already a king, but wanted also to be a high priest. God grew angry with him, and covered him with leprosy, and as a leper he became an outcast. His pride led to his downfall.

The ark of our Lord was one day placed, under cover, on a chariot. The oxen became restless and stopped suddenly. The ark was on the point of falling when Uzza stretched out his hand to steady it. God's wrath struck him down dead on the spot: this was a task that only priests could perform. (2975)

There is a proverb, your Majesty, that you must have heard quoted in many different circumstances: "It is a pleasant lesson to learn by others' mistakes." The Church, your Majesty, is governed by ordained men, and God did not entrust it to any secular powers. All believers come under the jurisdiction of the Church, and the Church has lordship over them. (2980)

Leave other people's rights alone, and everything that belongs to other people. Do not quarrel with what God himself has established. You have both your crown and your power from God, not from any earthly prince or by virtue of secular law, since consecration, like ordination, belongs to the prelates. (2985)

Secular law must be subordinate to ecclesiastical laws. No one but clerks should try actions in Church matters, nor must secular law take precedence over that of the clergy. It is customary for Christian kings to obey Holy Church. The layman ought not to oppress the clerk, but should cherish him. (2990)

There are two things that rule the world: the holy power of kings and the holy power of bishops. When the day of judgement comes for everyone, the prelates will answer for the crowned kings, so much greater and so very much heavier is their burden. (2995)

In the past many bishops excommunicated kings and emperors, expelling them from the Church. Pope Innocent deprived the emperor Arcadius of Church membership – he was unwilling to make an exception even for him – for having ordered the exile of St Chrysostome. (3000)

Bishop St Ambrose actually excommunicated Emperor Theodosius, cutting him off from the Church for another albeit much less serious offence. But the emperor finished by making appropriate amends, received absolution and was reconciled with God. (3005)

David, king and prophet, committed adultery with someone else's wife and had her husband, a fine knight of his, killed. God sent Nathan to punish him. David did not consider it shameful to humble himself at Nathan's feet and to beg for mercy. (3010)

And because he begged for mercy, God forgave him his sin, having found him to be a good person, humble and prepared to eschew evil. Your

Majesty should follow that good king's example without delay: come back to God, set down the grievous burden of your sins. You have committed a large number of other offences which I forbear, for the moment, to mention. (3015)

I have written you this letter, sire, at this time – and I have omitted many other things about which I prefer to remain silent – to see whether you are willing to treat your sin with the contempt it deserves, so that people might say to me: "Your son who was dead is alive again." My wish is for God to imbue you with his Holy Spirit. (3020)

And if you are unwilling to hear me or grant my requests, I, who am in the habit of praying to God for you before God's body, shall pray God to take urgent vengeance on the woes, injustices and gross insult that you and your people are inflicting and from which you are not willing to desist. (3025)

I will, I promise you, pray to the almighty Lord: "Avenge, oh God, the blood of your people that has been shed and their countless afflictions. The arrogance of your enemies, of those who hate both you and those close to you, has so increased that I can no longer stay silent." (3030)

Whoever actually does what is done, it will be seen as your handiwork, your Majesty, since whoever encourages the offence inflicts the damage himself. Unless you leave Holy Church and its clerks alone, God will swiftly wreak vengeance. His hand is already on his rod. The time has come for him, in all equity, to execute justice. (3035)

He is well able to take the lives of princes and has the power to bring kings low. No individual can escape him. May the grace of God help you find salvation, if you are willing to repent immediately and in true humility. May you in this way find the sort of salvation that you are never able to depart from! (3040)

* * *

Thomas sent to the king, who was at Chinon, the following letter without any greetings, requesting him in eloquent terms to be allowed to return home in peace, and asking him to restore and transfer his property to Holy Mother Church, both his own and that of his family. (3045)

It will not take me long to tell you what was written down and recorded in this letter, if you would be good enough to listen. Sire, – he wrote to him – my fervent wish has been to meet and see you at least once and to speak to you face to face. (3050)

I wished it very much for my own sake, but even more so for your sake. For my sake because, were you to see me, you would, I believe, recall how loyally and how faithfully I served you – so help me God at the frightful day of judgement when he will reward each one individually for what he has done – (3055)

so that you might have mercy and take pity on me, a beggar in a foreign country. But, thanks be to God! my everyday needs are amply provided for, and I have found great consolation in the apostle Paul, having discovered, on reading his epistles, (3060)

that all those who wish to lead a righteous life in God must suffer hardships and torments. David the psalmist also tells us that he never saw anyone who lives a life faithful to God abandoned, or any of his descendants reduced to begging for bread. (3065)

There are three reasons why I have fervently wished to speak to you for your own sake, as I shall explain: you are my lord, and it is therefore my duty as well as my wish to offer you advice; you are my king, and I should therefore cherish you; you are my son in God, and so I must chastise you. (3070)

Just consider how a father chastises his child, speaking very kindly to him one moment and then strictly and harshly the next, and beating him time and time again with a stinging rod. This he does when he sees him doing wrong in order to bring him back to virtuous ways either by remonstrating with him or by giving him a painful beating. (3075)

It was the grace of God that had you anointed and crowned, and this is why you should do all you can to take yourself in hand and show self-control, and make good behaviour the hallmark of all aspects of your life, so that you may serve as a good example to others, since everyone pays close attention to what you do. (3080)

There are people to whom you should be kind and gentle because you have been anointed and consecrated, whereas to most other people you should act ruthlessly, since the sword that you wear was given to you from within Holy Church in order that you might conquer and slaughter the enemies of God. (3085)

When kings are anointed, as you are well aware, it is done on three places: the head, the chest and the arms, since they should have within them great glory, knowledge and power. And glory, strength and wisdom are three things that you should use in order to do good. (3090)

You should consider those kings of antiquity who were unwilling to keep God's commandments: Nebuchadnezzar, Solomon the wise and Saul found God to be a most severe judge, for he took everything away from them when they withdrew their love from him. (3095)

When Hezekiah, David and numerous others had committed crimes against God their Creator, they humbled themselves before him, were contrite and sincerely repentant. In his grace the King of Heaven granted them in return great glory, intelligence and valour. (3100)

God founded and established Holy Church, and with his own blood he delivered and set it free. He was spat at, beaten and then suffered death for doing so. He left an example to us all, so that we may follow in his footsteps. (3105)

Anyone wishing to share in the glory of heaven must, for the love of God, suffer physical martyrdom and forsake the desires of the flesh and bodily comforts. As St Paul said: "If we want to live with God, we must also die for God and suffer death for his sake." (3110)

Holy Church consists of two orders: it comprises the people and the clergy. It finds lawful unity in the following way: the prelates have acquired the task of caring for the people on behalf of God, and this care is to involve undertaking the salvation of souls. (3115)

For God, I know only too well, said to St Peter and to the clergy: "You are Peter, and on this rock I will make my church and build my house, and through it I will destroy the gates of Hell." Clerics have this power, and laymen do not. (3120)

Kings and the baronage belong to the order of the people. The laity are subordinate to them and under their guardianship, and the power of secular law has been vested in them. But their duty is to conduct their business in such a way that the peace and unity of Holy Church are preserved. (3125)

It is in Holy Church that the power of kings originates, but the Church's own power does not derive from any of your kings. It comes from God, its spouse, who obtained it for the Church. It follows that you have no power to instruct prelates either to exercise or to cease exercising ecclesiastical justice. (3130)

It is not for you to issue orders or prohibitions to prelates either to acquit someone or find them guilty, nor to drag ordained clerks – no, not a single one – before your courts and subject them to secular law, nor to institute proceedings against anyone in any matters concerning our churches or tithes. (3135)

It is not for you to forbid prelates to conduct their trials in matters concerning contraventions of the law, perjury, crimes and false oaths, as well as pleas concerning those customs which your ancestor observed in the past. (3140)

Our Lord God said: "Keep my laws." The prophet in his turn said: "Woe unto you who establish unrighteous laws and enshrine wrongs and injustices in writing; woe unto you also who oppress God's poor and treat the lowly with violence!" (3145)

Accept, sire, the advice and counsel of someone who is truly faithful to you. Listen to your father's well-intentioned rebuke, and to your archbishop's admonition. Have nothing further to do with the enemies of the Church. (3150)

It is almost universally acknowledged that you have treated the pope with the greatest possible honour and have done much to maintain and advance the Church of Rome. The pope and the whole of Holy Church have shown that they hold you in great affection. They have complied with your requests as far as was reasonable. (3155)

If, sire, you wish to save your soul, do not deprive Holy Church of anything that belongs to it, and do not for any reason act contrary to the law. Leave all the liberties of Holy Church intact, as happens everywhere else in kingdoms abroad. (3160)

You should bear in mind the vows that you professed and presented at the altar when you were anointed, and the pledge you made to God in his house: you gave your protection to God's spouse and granted it the gift of all its liberties. (3165)

Re-establish, sire, the Holy Mother church of Holy Trinity from which you received your crown and your power. Re-establish it in all the dignity, the status and the integrity which were handed down from its ancestors and which it had by virtue of its history. (3170)

Give back to our clergy and laity and re-establish unconditionally all its properties and other holdings, towns, castles, fiefs and other possessions, all of which you appropriated then distributed and gave away as you saw fit. (3175)

Allow us to return home freely and in peace, and we will serve you loyally as our lord and king insofar as it is appropriate for us. If you do not do so, you can be certain that you will feel the full impact of God's vengeance. (3180)

* * *

The bishop of London sent a letter to St Thomas while he was overseas. He did not, however, sign it in his own name, but drafted it in the name of the country's bishops and other persons, none of whom he named. He sent his greetings, submission and love. (3185)

Father, your precipitate departure from the kingdom immediately caused great consternation here. Our hope was, however, that, thanks to your humility and your intelligence, and through the grace of almighty God, the country would return to the peace that it had known previously. (3190)

Right at the start we were able to take comfort and rejoice when we heard the news spread over the whole kingdom that you had crossed the Channel, and had no intention of instituting proceedings against the king, or of confronting him in such a haughty manner, or causing harm or hatching a plot within the kingdom. (3195)

We understood, on the contrary, that you were quite willing to bear the burden of poverty, devote yourself completely to prayer and study, and make amends, by repenting, repeatedly fasting and spending the night in prayer, for the wrong and damage done by your crossing the Channel, so that you might win back the love of our heavenly King. (3200)

This was the right sort of behaviour for restoring peace. We thought that in this way you might have been able to find favour with the king again, and that he might have been willing to set aside his anger towards you and overlook the wrongs you had done him in leaving the country without permission and crossing the Channel. (3205)

Even those who wished you well and supported you were able to be admitted to the king's presence and talk to him. And when they asked him to bring about a reconciliation between the two of you, and re-establish peace and friendship between you, he would sometimes listen to them favourably. (3210)

But now we are hearing a different story, and this is causing us great distress. You have sent the king a letter, without any formal greetings, in which you have failed to ask for or beg his forgiveness. We can see no trace of friendship in such a letter, and in it you even threaten him with excommunication. (3215)

If you persist in following this course of action, as you have affirmed you will, all the instability and all these disputes in the country will never be replaced by harmony and love. Indeed the result will be an everlasting hatred which no man living will bring to an end. (3220)

A wise man has to be someone who, when he begins something, gives most serious consideration to how he can bring it to a successful conclusion. You must accordingly use all your intelligence to discover whether, by behaving as you are, you will be able to manage what you have undertaken so as to reach the goal you have set yourself. (3225)

Your great temerity in threatening the king dashes the hopes we all had for a good outcome, for we do not see how you are ever going to make peace. Attacking him, as you have, with a drawn sword means that there is no suitable opportunity for anyone to intercede on your behalf. (3230)

This is why we advise you, in love and in all good faith, not to heap one wrong on another, so as not to further aggravate the situation. Entrust your case to God the Creator, leave off your threats, be tolerant towards your lord. Your humility will earn his compassion. (3235)

In this way you will be able to win his love and affection. Your threats have got you nowhere. Your humility will bring you better results. You would do better to suffer poverty voluntarily than to hold a great honour from him grudgingly. (3240)

It is common knowledge that he has shown you great honour, and that it was he who raised you to a high position from the lowly one in which he found you. He handed over to you all the power of the realm, so that anyone you looked favourably on would then have considered himself extremely fortunate. (3245)

He promoted you, from lowly beginnings, to greatness and did you great honour. It was quite against the advice of his mother, who did not recommend the appointment, that he obtained for you the honourable position you now hold; it was against the wishes of the entire kingdom that disapproved of you, and against the wishes of Holy Church that heaved a heavy sigh. (3250)

His belief was that you would not have sought to frustrate him, but rather look to the interests of the kingdom and promote them in every way you could. Trying to bring him down rather than counselling him as you should is no way to show your gratitude for all the good he has done you. People everywhere are able to use this to discredit you. (3255)

Do not risk your reputation because of this, or your honour. The way to overcome your lord the king is by love. If you are unwilling to accept the advice that so many people are giving you, then follow the pope's advice and trust in the affection he has for you. Place your trust in the Church of Rome, for that is rock-solid. (3260)

You need to be told not to do anything that could put Holy Church, which for a long time now has been distressed and tearful, in an even more painful situation. The cost of this should not be borne by people who have done nothing wrong, and who are suffering the consequences of someone else's crime. (3265)

What would you say if the king of this realm, who rules over both its clergy and its laity, should break off relations with the pope and refuse to obey him anymore, on account of the anguish you are causing, and because the pope, out of love for you, takes your side against King Henry? (3270)

Just see how people are begging him to do just this, and with what gifts they are enticing him! But he has not the slightest intention of doing so, however much they promise. He is as immovable as a rock battered by the storm. However, what I fear, my lord, is that this man, whom no one can possibly move or tempt, could – God forbid! – change his mind. (3275)

If this were to happen because of you, you will have to cope with it, even though the whole of your face will be covered in tears. That is why you should decide on a course of action that could not possibly damage the pope, or seriously harm the Church of Rome and yourself. (3280)

But this is something to which your wise clerks will not agree. They urge you to try everything you can to put on a show of power before the king and his advisers. This power, however, is something the wrong-doer and the person who is unwilling to make amends has much to fear from.* (3285)

That is not to say that the king himself has not done anything wrong, but in all circumstances he is always ready to make amends. His duty is to keep the peace in the realm; that is why God has put him there. The reason he wished to re-affirm the laws and customs established in the kingdom was to enable him to keep the peace in the country more effectively. (3290)

In cases where you and the king have quarrelled, the pope has frequently raised questions about it with him, and the prelates of the realm have taken him to task over it. Henry says that if he has in any way harmed the Church or one of its members, he is prepared to stand trial according to the law of his country's Church. (3295)

He is ready, if asked, to make reparation, and do more even, and if he sins against God, he is happy to be punished. If he humbles himself before the Church and God, there is no law or decree or anything else that could place him under interdict, no ecclesiastical sword that could maim or kill him. (3300)

Put away your sword, and use your judgement instead. All of us beg you not to act without restraint, not to kill on the spur of the moment. Look after the flock that is in your care; see to it that they are kept safe and in peace. (3305)

One thing in particular that you have done causes us great distress: you have excommunicated Jocelin bishop of Salisbury and his dean, John of Oxford, as well. Before passing judgement, however, one needs to have full knowledge of the case, and to hear and examine the arguments. (3310)

And so that you do not act in the same way towards the king and the kingdom, towards the churches and parishes under our care, wrongfully and falsely excommunicating them all, to the detriment of the pope and of yourself, in my view, we are making a formal appeal to secure redress and find shelter from distress. (3315)

We set the day of the appeal at Ascension, May 18th. In the meantime, all of us beg you to reconsider your decision: spare yourself such a tiring journey to Rome, and do not put your sons to such expense.* We pray for your salvation in God our Lord. (3320)

* * *

Without a moment's delay, St Thomas wrote back to the bishop of London in similar terms. Instead of a formal greeting, he started his letter on an amiable note by wishing that Gilbert might pass beyond temporal possessions in such a way as not to lose the joy of things spiritual. (3325)

It is astounding – he wrote – that a wise and learned man, and someone who wears the holy habit of a religious order, should so disregard the fear of God as to deny the truth, fail to distinguish good from bad, and be willing to bring down Holy Church and those who have been appointed to it. (3330)

Holy Church is capable of breaking down the gates of Hell, so anyone who wishes to overthrow it is not acting wisely, just like someone who tries to pull down a mountain with a rope. No one should be so angry or so full of hatred that he outrageously offends a bishop or a brother in the Lord God's ministry. (3335)

But from your letter I can both feel and see that it is impossible for me to gather grapes from thorns, or figs from brambles.* For anyone listening to your letter, its beginning and its ending are like the scorpion – its face welcoming but a sting in its tail. (3340)

You start by protesting obedience and submission, and then announce a formal appeal in order to get released from both. You turn your "yes" into a "no" in less than no time. As the apostle Paul asked, am I not the sort of man for whom "yes" means "yes" and "no" means "no"? In the mouth of an honest man there should be only one of these words at any one time.*

We know that God gave his disciples the power to trample serpents and scorpions underfoot. Ezekiel still dwells among the wicked. What sort of remedy could your appeal possibly bring you? You maintain that you are following God, but we can see no sign of this.

Jesus Christ gave us a remedy for all ills, and that is obedience. He set an excellent example of this himself, for he remained obedient to God the Creator right up until he died the death on the cross. What you term remedy actually means a lot of trouble.

Do you imagine that the pope will be willing to support you in your wish not to have to obey your master? Twice already you have asked him, and he was unwilling to listen to you, for he has the heavy responsibility of upholding authority and ensuring that holy obedience is everywhere enforced.

The first request you made was by word of mouth, and thereafter by a letter full of ingratiating blandishments. The vicar of St Peter, however, set as he is on a living foundation, is firmer than a rock, and, as you are well aware, what I write is no hot air. Neither gift, present or entreaty moves or deceives the pope.

Try him out for a third time, so that his triumph is complete at the third attack! And then to make my suffering worse, you have set the date of your appeal at almost a whole year's distance from now. Have you no pity for me in my exile?

Have you no pity for Holy Mother Church, which our Lord God won with his own blood, and which is enduring so much pain and mortal torment? Have you paid no heed to the fact that, by what you have said, you have promised obedience to our lord the king?

As long as he continues behaving as he does towards us and Holy Church, which it is his duty to honour, he will not be able to go confidently into battle, or live either in peace or in war, without fearing for his soul, which he is placing in such danger.

I wish now to respond to what you said in your letter, namely that my departure from the country caused turmoil and anxiety throughout the whole kingdom. All those who had sought to bring it about, and were in favour of it, might well be afraid of becoming themselves victims of such turmoil. (3385)

You heap praise on me for the good beginning I have made. No wise man, as I see it, fails to attach importance to his reputation, but for that he should not count on the judgement of others more than he does on his own. You severely blame me for the wrongs I have done to the king, but as you do not list any, I do not know which one I should respond to. (3390)

You express astonishment at the fact that I dared threaten our lord the king with excommunication. But who is it who refuses to speak up when he sees his own son committing acts of great folly? By not wanting to reprimand him is he not refusing to do what is good for him? Punishing him is preferable to seeing him hacked to death. (3395)

I quite realize that the king is willing to accept being reprimanded, but he has no desire to fall under excommunication. God will not allow what he has planted to wither and die. You see the boat out of control, listing all over the place in the storm; I am at the helm, and you are telling me to go to sleep! (3400)

You remind me of all the acts of kindness that the king has done for me, and that, from almost nothing, he has brought me to a high position of prominence. My answer to this is a simple, childish one: I was not as poor as you maintain when our lord king made me his high administrator. (3405)

At that time I had the archdeaconry of Canterbury, the provostship of Beverley, several benefices and churches in different parts of the country, properties, income and other sorts of wealth. I was not at all as insubstantial a figure as you have made me out to be. (3410)

And if you want to talk about my humble family origins, I was indeed born into a modest family of citizens of London who spent the whole of their lives in the same neighbourhood without ever being the object of any complaint, never coveting what belonged to other people, and doing no harm to anyone. They were not of such low birth as you say they were. (3415)

To anyone willing to look at things honestly and reasonably it is clear that it is better to come from humble origins, to be a moral person and to rise in the world than to be of noble family and go to Hell. We should, the apostle tells us, pay greater respect to those members who are less honourable and cover them with greater honour. (3420)

No Christian should say such a thing, especially a learned one, a member of a religious order and a bishop. But perhaps you are really reproaching me for having been endowed with so little intelligence. Anyone who brings shame on his father commits a sin, as you know. God himself says: "Honour your father, so that your days be longer." (3425)

You have no need to remind me of the king's favours to me. I am able to call upon God as my witness when I say that in the whole world there was no one I could possibly have loved more than him – provided that he had left the rights of Holy Church alone. Unless he does so, he will not be able to reign in safety. (3430)

No one could enumerate all the favours he has done me, but even if these were a hundred times more numerous than they have been, this would still be no reason for me to ignore the rights of God. In this I have no intention of making you or anyone else an exception. I would not even exempt an angel from Heaven – if ever one were to sin in this regard. (3435)

And if anyone were to argue with me about this, I would immediately say to him: "Get you behind me, Satan! Your mouth denies God." The Lord God forbid that I ever so take leave of my senses that I should bargain with the body of Jesus Christ, or that my lord the king should be found doing anything similar! (3440)

When I was elected archbishop, and raised to this high office by God, you say that the whole kingdom protested, that the king's mother advised against it, and that Holy Church heaved such sighs as were seemly. But far from opposing my appointment, the kingdom called on me to take it on. (3445)

If the king's mother wished to be obstructive, she never did so openly and raised no objection beforehand. The only members of Holy Church I heard sigh were those who sought the honour for themselves and were not able to get it. These are the same people who ever since have not stopped trying to stir up trouble between the king and me. (3450)

Perhaps that was their way of taking revenge on me since they were unable to fulfill their aspirations. Ever since then they have been continually opposing me. They are the cause and the advocates of all this conflict. Woe to the person who provokes scandals that lead to calamity! (3455)

They have frequently come up with a large number of ruses designed to harm me, but the power of God, who has raised me up to the high office I now hold, is greater than theirs. It is God also, the God of justice, who calls on me and orders me not to turn my back on him for any reason whatsoever. (3460)

I am not going to remain silent about your seeking to damage my cause and thereby justify the king. You say that he is, and always has been, ready to make amends. But what sort of amends is it when he continually makes matters worse and is unwilling ever actually to make any reparation? (3465)

You see innocent people, orphans and widows being driven into exile, blameless people hounded out of the country, numerous people deprived of their possessions and vilely abused, my own vassals imprisoned and kept in chains, and clerks made exiles, and yet you are unwilling to come to their assistance. (3470)

You see your own Mother Church plundered and its goods and properties stolen, and yet you are unwilling to defend it. You saw me, your father to whom you owe unfailing allegiance, having my life threatened by swords hanging over my head, and from which I only managed to escape with great difficulty, and yet you remained unmoved and unshakable. (3475)

But you are behaving even more badly, and making a far graver mistake, by collaborating with those who seek to harm me, and by declaring war not only against me but against the Lord God and his Church also. You do not do so secretly or in an underhand way; you act shamelessly, and shame is something you have turned your back on. (3480)

Does making amends, then, consist of restoring nothing and of constantly behaving more and more badly? Or you are perhaps saying the opposite: that making amends consists of being the willing servant of the ungodly! That would be making one's arrows drunk with the blood of the righteous. (3485)

You could reply, on the other hand, by telling what is obviously the truth: that you wish to protect your coat, and this is why you have no sword. You won't be in a hurry to sell your coat for a sword, if you can help it! You're not like St Peter who cut off the prince's servant's ear with a blow of his sword.* (3490)

You say that the king is quite willing to make amends according to the judgement of the kingdom. I cannot agree. No one can judge the will of God. It is quite possible to settle secular matters by legal trials, but divine matters must necessarily be left to God. (3495)

You should have been continually urging the king to concentrate on preserving the peace of Holy Church. Things that do not concern him he should have left well alone. He should have turned his mind to honouring God's priests. He should pay attention not to who they are, but to whom they belong. (3500)

You have spared a thought for the two people whom, you say, I have wrongfully (but quite legitimately, in my view) separated from the company of other Christians. Someone seeing his neighbour's house on fire has fears for his own house. If I had my own way, you should already have been removed from the bad position in which you have placed yourself. (3505)

Let the king be in no doubt – and it is up to you to tell him so – that he who rules over both angels and men established two powers under him on earth. The one, the duty of which is to serve God, consists of priests, spiritual people, deserving of respect. (3510)

The second one consists of princes, and their power is exclusively secular. Lords, both domestic and foreign, are subordinate to them. Heathens as well as Christians ought to fear their princes. Anyone who deprives either of these orders of its ancient rights is undoing what the King of Heaven has ordained. (3515)

The king should not consider it beneath him to honour those whom God in Scripture designates as gods. It is in the Psalter that we find God calling them gods.* God raised the prophet above Pharaoh. God demands that people do not even speak ill of clerks. (3520)

A Jew who swore an oath "by Moses" was brought before the priests for sinning, for the King of Mercy says: "Take him before the gods!" Priests are referred to as gods after the name of God because they are consecrated in God's place, above other people. (3525)

The king has no power to judge those whose duty and right it is actually to judge him. The priest's lips are the guardians of knowledge, and the priest himself is God's messenger. As the ever truthful Paul says: "We shall judge the angels and the people also."* (3530)

God was never willing to hand over the keys of Heaven, with their power to bind and to unbind, to a secular prince. This power he entrusts to ordained priests. You would be well advised to explain to the king the highly praiseworthy action of Constantine's. (3535)

An accusation against some priests was laid before King Constantine. The documents detailing the crime were brought to him, and the priests admitted to his presence. Before their eyes the king threw the document into the blazing fire. "I neither judge nor condemn you," he said. (3540)

"You are gods. Judge your cases as you see fit. It is not right for any man to pass sentence on a god." Constantine was a good emperor. He received God's grace, he is praised by Holy Church, he sees God face to face. King Henry ought to follow his example and behave as he did. (3545)

Otherwise the threat of God will be a constant source of fear for him. "Any man so presumptuous as to be unwilling to obey his priest and his judge will have to die."* God has the king appointed to rule over the kingdom in order that he should maintain the peace which is sent to us by God. (3550)

If not, it is not possible for the king to achieve salvation, however great his strength and power might be, and even if he alone ruled over all the kingdoms on earth. The answers I have given to you by means of this letter are directed also at all those who have taken your side. (3555)

And now, my brothers, I beg and entreat you all in equal measure not to allow jealousy, dissent or deception to arise between us. May we have between us one heart and one soul in God, and may we listen to God when he tells us to die for the sake of justice. He has already entered the battle on our side against our enemies. (3560)

Let us not forget, brothers, that God is the true judge. When, at the end of this world and on the Day of Judgement, both the righteous and the sinners come before him, he will judge the whole world. No king, prince or mighty emperor will have the power, then, to intimidate him.* (3565)

* * *

The prelates whose duty it was to defend Holy Church sent St Thomas, when he was abroad, letters to the effect that they wished to see the customs of the kingdom established within Holy Church. The most holy archbishop, however, continually opposed this in order to safeguard the freedom of the Church. (3570)

That custom is not law is very easy to understand, since any powerful man who does not live under the fear of God could impose whatever customs he likes on his people – one here and another, completely different, there. It is not custom that God loves but conventions that are founded on truth. (3575)

What is more, man's life (poor wretch that he is) is extremely short: hot one minute, cold the next – just like tepid water. This is why anyone who establishes a custom that is burdensome or causes anyone harm commits a sin, for even if it were to break his heart, he cannot take it away again. (3580)

If King Henry wishes to revive the customs of his ancestors, then I would like to know which of these laws he would rather establish in his kingdom: those of William Rufus, a man of little wisdom, or those of Henry I, a very powerful king? (3585)

Rufus left the Church with nothing. He confiscated its gold, its silver, its possessions, its income, and he held clerks to ransom. God took his revenge for this: he was killed when out hunting and died in sin. While his body has rotted away, his soul is in continual torment.

If King Henry has adopted Rufus's customs and seeks to wage war on Holy Church and its clerics, vengeance will come down on him before he realizes it, for it is certain that God has already placed the arrow in his bow. His justice is ferocious, and he kills both body and soul.

King Henry I used to take other men's wives, and prevented their lawful husbands from having anything to do with them. He had men killed for the sake of dumb animals, and he frequently committed crimes against Holy Church. If his grandson follows him down the same path, he will have to answer personally to God.

Old King Henry had a priest hanged who was (there is no point in our denying it) an out-and-out criminal. He did this to deter those who were unwilling to give up their evil ways. If a custom can be put in place in error, then bad customs and bad usages are to be abandoned.

Let us say no more for the moment about customs, or about the three prelates whom I mentioned earlier. I have no wish to discuss their behaviour any more. I would now like to tell you about the holy archbishop and of his six-year exile overseas.

11 Pontigny—Sens

The holy man stayed at Pontigny for two years, but kept the sort of life he led there hidden from everyone, both clerical and lay, and as far as he was able he even concealed his way of life from his closest associates. He shunned and rejected all bodily comforts, and took pains to serve God both by day and by night.

He then began to severely mistreat his body and to eat only coarse food such as cabbage and turnips. He had the fine dishes discreetly set to one side and carried off to the poor in the town. Had they known this, his clerks would certainly have criticized him.

They often reproached him with the sort of life he led, for he was weak in the extreme and mortified his flesh excessively. They said that he was cutting off his own people's heads. They had been exiled because of him, and if he were to die, not one of them would ever be able to get back home again.

There was a stream that ran between two of the abbey's storerooms, and every evening Thomas used to bathe in it to cool down his physical ardour. One evening he took William de Capes with him as an attendant. "Lord," William said, "you're going to break all our hearts!" Because of this criticism, Thomas never again took William with him. (3630)

But then one of his cheeks became infected and festered, and this spread to the whole of the inside of his mouth and his teeth. This made him very ill and he suffered from it for a long time. William cured him by extracting two growths. I myself heard this information given; it was recalled so that other people could get to know about it.* (3635)

One night, when he had exhausted himself by praying, he fell asleep and had a dream. He and the king, who hated him for no reason, were pleading in a trial before the pope and arguing. All of the cardinals were railing against him. (3640)

He had the feeling that they were intending to gouge out his eyes and dig them out of his head with their fingers. Only the pope, who knew all the details of his case, was willing to support him. But the pope could not hear him, because all the shouting from other people and the pandemonium had made Thomas hoarse. (3645)

Suddenly he found himself alone, without another living soul, in the courtroom. Then some evil assassins were brought in, and he felt as if they were slicing off his tonsure with their swords. This was God's promise to him that he would be killed for the sake of Holy Church while still pleading his case. (3650)

One of the monastery's lay brothers (I was not given his name) was seriously ill, suffering from a severely swollen stomach as a result of dropsy. All winter and summer long he had been praying to the Mother of God to beg her son to restore him to health. (3655)

So fervently did he pray to the Creator's Mother, night and day, for her to bring relief to his suffering that one night the Lady of Sweetness came to him. She told him to go immediately to Thomas and to have the whole area of his stomach massaged by him. (3660)

The next day the brother went to the holy man, whom he found in his study. He requested and begged him, in the name of God's pity, to massage his stomach with his hand. The brother took Thomas's hand and guided it all over the area. (3665)

Thomas gave him something to drink – exactly what, I am not certain. Almost immediately the brother fell to the ground and vomited a surprisingly large amount of poisonous pus. He stayed on the ground for a long time before finally getting up, and when he did so, he was thin again. He had been cured of his illness by the holy man's hands. (3670)

Thomas cured many sick people with the left-overs from his table. A rich man's daughter who had had a fever for many long weeks recovered her health in this way. There was no one in the region who, however debilitated by fever, would not regain perfect health by virtue of his left-overs. (3675)

* * *

When King Henry understood that Thomas could stay at Pontigny indefinitely, that he and his people had everything they needed there, and that he enjoyed the friendship of King Louis and the French, he said to himself that he would oust him from that nest just as quickly as he could. (3680)

It is an ancient custom, I have heard, for all Cistercian abbots, both from this side of the Channel and from abroad, to foregather at Cîteaux every third year, for all Cistercians must pay homage to the abbot of Cîteaux and follow his advice in all matters concerning their order. (3685)

During the second year of his exile, when Thomas had been at Pontigny for almost two years, King Henry still had him on his mind and still continued to loathe him. He sent a letter to the abbot I have been talking about, in which he reminded him that he was in fact giving refuge to his deadly enemy. (3690)

He assured him – and he was to be in no doubt about this – that if he persisted in harbouring his enemy any longer, and if Thomas were to find refuge anywhere else within the order, he would send over to him each and every Cistercian monk and abbot in the country, and not a single one of them would be allowed to remain in England. (3695)

When this letter was read out in front of the assembled abbots, they all fell at the feet of the abbot of Cîteaux, each one begging for mercy for himself and for his brethren, and imploring him not to allow them to be expelled and lose everything they had worked for on account of one man. (3700)

They talked it over among themselves and came to a decision: they would not tolerate such a loss being inflicted on them, being deprived of their possessions and monasteries, being forced to flee the country, seeing the places that they won for God being destroyed. It was preferable for one individual to be made to suffer rather than the whole community. (3705)

They would rather provide for everything Thomas and his people needed somewhere else, further away. My conviction is that the king had made it clear to them that he would expel them all from his country unless they sent Becket away. (3710)

When Abbot Garin heard that their decision was to send the archbishop away from Pontigny, his response to the abbot of Cîteaux was a sharp one: "Our holy order makes it quite impossible," he said, "for us to drive away God's ally from our community for such a reason as this. (3715)

"He was commended to us by Pope Alexander. In the two years or so that he has been with us we have seen no reason to complain of any burden being placed on us by him or by his people. There has been no extra cost in wine or corn; in fact never before, in a comparable period, has so little been used. (3720)

"The reason King Henry made him flee the country was because Thomas was seeking to defend Christianity. Our order was established for no other reason than to aid and support people in need. Our duty therefore is not to let this man down under any circumstances." (3725)

Master Garin's intervention, however, was not sufficient to prevent them carrying out the decision they had taken in common council. Guichard, incidentally, who had been abbot before Garin, had subsequently been made archbishop of Lyon on St Thomas's personal recommendation to the pope. (3730)

Through Master Garin, the abbot of Cîteaux let Thomas know all the contents of the letter, namely that the king was threatening to destroy their entire order. He begged him, in the name of God, to advise him to find a solution that would be satisfactory to both sides. (3735)

All this had already been reported to the archbishop, since his informants had been present at the chapter meeting and heard the decision. "It would be a great sin," Thomas replied to the abbot, "if so many worthy men were made destitute just because of me. (3740)

"May Jesus Christ in his mercy show his gratitude to you for everything that you and your people have done for me and mine! We have never lacked anything, food or clothes. God will advise me; he is ever at my side, he brings low the proud, and the poor he raises from the dunghill." (3745)

"My lord," replied the abbot, "do not worry yourself about it. You will not be sent away on account of the king's ultimatum without you and your people being provided for, in everything you need, even more liberally than you have been up until now." "May God in his mercy," replied Thomas, "show you his gratitude for that!" (3750)

Someone had informed the king of France of this affair and told him how Henry had driven Thomas out of Pontigny. On hearing this, Louis gave thanks to God for having provided him with the opportunity of giving to the archbishop, if he were willing to accept, everything he had previously offered him on many occasions. (3755)

After Thomas had first fled from England, the king of France several times invited him, either directly or through other clerics and friends, to stay with him in the kingdom of St Denis. He would not have to go cap in hand for anything he needed. (3760)

Thomas had not taken up the king's offers at that time, because he was very much afraid that Henry might react aggressively and say that Thomas had entered into an alliance with Louis with the intention of waging war on him. Now, however, he would no longer be reluctant to accept his offer. (3765)

When, therefore, the king of France learnt that they were forcing him to leave, and that he could now give him hospitality, he joined his hands in prayer and lifted them up in thanks to God, who rules the world. "I believe," he added, "that there are going to be some angels coming to grief." He was referring to the monks and to how they had behaved in this matter. (3770)

Then King Louis mounted his horse and, together with his men, rode off to Pontigny. He went with the archbishop into the meeting in the chapter house, and there he thanked the abbot and the monks most warmly for having received Thomas so honourably among them. (3775)

They had, he explained, done France a very great honour in giving shelter to the good archbishop. But he had no desire to see them now incur the enmity of King Henry, who was threatening them with destruction because of their love of Thomas. His wish now was that the archbishop would henceforth stay with him. (3780)

He explained that he would take him with him to Sens, and there he and his people would have their every need seen to, whatever was required. When the monks heard that he was to leave, they were nearly all moved to tears. (3785)

The king then sent his men on to Sens, to Sainte-Colombe, to arrange for accommodation for the holy man to stay in. He summoned servants and butlers to go there in order to provide, from the king's purse, everything he could need. (3790)

When King Louis was sure that Thomas was going to be his guest, he returned to his own kingdom of France. The archbishop prepared for his journey and then, together with his household, went to Sainte-Colombe. For as long as he stayed there, he was treated with great honour. (3795)

The abbey of Sainte-Colombe, in the vicinity of Sens, is an establishment of Benedictine monks. The good archbishop, placing his trust in God alone, stayed there for four years. His way of life remained the same as it had been, and the abbot and the monks found his company very agreeable. (3800)

* * *

When King Henry understood that it was possible for Thomas to remain in France, now that King Louis was providing everything he and his people needed out of his own personal income, he was, I can assure you, exceedingly unhappy. If he had anything to do with it, he would not stay there for long. He did everything in his power to see to that. (3805)

His next step was to send his son Henry to France to see the king, and there he became the vassal of the king's son Philippe, holding land across the Channel from him just as if he was one of his barons.* You should have seen them exchanging costly gifts, presenting hounds to each other and bringing along hunting hawks! (3810)

In addition, King Henry was so generous to the French barons that his lavish gifts earned him the friendship of each and every one. He believed that in this way he could win over the entire council of the kingdom. The kings then arranged to hold a meeting at Saint-Léger-en-Yvelines. (3815)

There they pledged and undertook to be henceforth the firmest of friends, and swore a joint oath that in future neither would allow any enemy of the other to stay in their kingdom. After which they left. (3820)

They agreed to have a second meeting at Tours, but this time the French did not attend. King Louis had been advised not to go because he had no castle or stronghold in that part of the country, and no one knew what the real intentions of the king of England were. (3825)

King Henry then invoked the agreement they had come to, and accused Louis of not keeping his word by continuing to give shelter for such a long time to his deadly enemy, a criminal and a traitor to the whole kingdom.

Louis replied by saying that this was something that had never been discussed. (3830)

He had not broken the agreement, he said, because the archbishop had not been mentioned in the agreement. This stipulated that it was only if someone was a convicted criminal and had been sentenced to leave the country that he was to be refused refuge anywhere in either of their lands. (3835)

When the archbishop learnt that King Henry was attempting to have him expelled from France and going to such lengths, he had a letter written telling him not to waste his time and energy: the king would never deprive him of sustenance, since God would find more than enough for him and never let him down. (3840)

He had derived much comfort from a visit he had had from a man who promised to supply everything he needed, even if he were to take on twenty more men than he had at present. In addition he would give him £500 in cash, which he could use for all his other personal needs. (3845)

There was another also who promised to do him equal honour, and never to let him down on account of any man. He feared neither the English nor the French king, neither German nor Teuton, neither duke nor emperor.* But it was the good king of France who actually saw to his subsistence. (3850)

One day when Thomas had been hard at prayer and was lying prostrate before the altar in great devotion, as was his custom, God appeared to him in a true vision, calling him twice by his own name, Thomas. (3855)

"In your blood you will exalt my Church," he said to him. "Who are you, Lord, that you should appear to me here?" "I am Jesus, your brother. You will glorify my Church by your blood, and you yourself will be exalted." Thomas replied: "So be it. I am willing." (3860)

He dreamt a second dream at Sainte-Colombe, and the person to whom he told it assured me that his was an authentic account.* Thomas dreamt that he was being tried in a consistory court. He was defending himself against the king of England, and the king was making grave accusations against him. (3865)

Hilary of Chichester and Gilbert Foliot of London were pressing serious charges against him. The cardinals were making common cause with the king, with the result that he had no support in the entire court except Pope Alexander, his sole ally. (3870)

But he had been shouting so much at them, and they at him, that he had become completely hoarse with all the uproar and the shouting. Hilary of Chichester fell silent in the course of the trial. All the bishop of London's flesh turned putrid, and his whole body crumbled into little pieces and collapsed. (3875)

Immediately after this the king had Thomas seized. His head was skinned all round with blades, but he felt no anguish or pain. In fact he laughed, and this provoked the king's anger. Whereupon Thomas woke up in terror. (3880)

What we see here is the power of the pope diminishing in the course of the trial, since he was incapable of supporting the archbishop against all the others. We see Hilary of Chichester struck dumb and repenting for all the harm he had caused the martyr. As for the bishop of London, let him beware now of falling to pieces! (3885)

But I think I know what this disintegration really means. Little by little he has come to the point of repentance, hence the crumbling away of his flesh little by little. But he still needs to see to it that he makes full and proper amends. Otherwise God will take vengeance as justice demands. (3890)

The holy man lived in this foreign country for six years, leading a harsh and painful life which he succeeded in hiding even from those closest to him. There were very few people, learned or lay, to whom he revealed the sort of life he led – only two or three in fact. (3895)

When he got up in the morning, he did not have his servants woken up to put on his clothes or his boots. His first task was to go to church to serve the Lord God with all the honour due to him. This was something he never deliberately neglected in favour of anything else. (3900)

He celebrated mass every day round about noon. He was assiduous in every possible way in serving his Lord. Most of the rest of the day he would spend in a small room in one or the other of his oratories where he performed the tasks he had to do. Although he would keep his door closed, it was never in order to take a break from work. (3905)

When he was inside, he would lie down on the ground to pray and shed copious tears of supplication. No one but God knew the torture he inflicted on himself or how much he suffered. The noble archbishop would remain deep in contemplation. (3910)

He would leave the room at mealtimes. He ate, however, not to fill his stomach or gain weight, but to keep his household happy, to see the poor and hungry and to minister to them. His prime concern always was to conceal his own way of life from others. (3915)

He used to drink the best wine that was to be found, but drank in order to warm his stomach, for he suffered from a chill on the stomach. Indeed he suffered very much from the cold all over his body, and used to eat ginger and cloves by the handful. But he always used to drink his wine diluted with water. (3920)

When the holy man got up from table, he was not interested in listening to any song or story or anything else unless it were something truthful. He preferred to hear about the Heavenly King and consult writings whose value was eternal. (3925)

And when day sank into darkness, St Thomas's bed was prepared, on a leather-padded bedstead set on a scattering of straw, with an embroidered quilt and expensive white bedclothes in finely woven linen. (3930)

Archbishop Thomas remained prostrate in prayer until he was exhausted, then he lay down to sleep on the bare ground in the same clothes as he had worn during the day, for his habit was not to change them. No one, high or low, realized quite what sort of life he led. (3935)

He wore rough goat-hair underwear that was coarse and itched, and the rest of his body, including his arms to below the elbows, his stomach and his back, was completely covered in a hair-shirt. Patches of this were crawling with masses of lice and fleas which never gave his flesh a moment's respite. (3940)

But he inflicted even worse punishments on his body: every night he mortified the flesh by having himself beaten with sharp scourges that cut right into him. Robert of Merton, who did not dare disobey the request of his religious superior, can bear witness to this. (3945)

Robert of Merton was his chaplain, and on very intimate terms with him. He slept in the same room as Thomas. It was only when he was in dire straits and on the point of death that he made this revelation. He had promised Thomas that he would never disclose his private life as long as he lived.* (3950)

Even when his chaplain had gone to bed and should have been resting, Thomas, so he said, continued his self-humiliation, and he would go on for a good third of the night. He would then come over to Robert, get him out of bed and hand him the whips so that he would resume mortifying his flesh. (3955)

Having beaten him so much until Robert himself was exhausted and sweating from pain, he was moved by pity and would throw the whips with their knotted ends down onto the floor, saying: "Wretch that I am, why was

I ever born? Of all the wretched people in the world, there is no one worse off than me!" (3960)

But even when the chaplain went back to bed, St Thomas would still not stop, and he would begin to tear at his own body and to hack at his flesh with his own hands. Flesh was of no consequence to him, so thoroughly chaste were his thoughts. (3965)

And when Robert was about to make his last confession, he revealed that the saint had never been at peace with himself, day or night, since the time he had taken on the burden of being consecrated archbishop: every day he would have himself beaten four or five times – or three at the very least. He was never willing to make an exception. (3970)

This was the sort of life that our Lord's vassal led. He did, however, take a bath every forty days. He also changed his hair-shirt on account of the fleas and the sweat, only to replace it with another which he had put by. For the sake of God he continually suffered discomfort and pain. (3975)

This is how the holy man lived, and this was the suffering he endured. To no one in the world did he reveal or admit this, except, as I have heard, to Brun, his valet, whose service consisted of washing his underwear, and to his chaplain Robert whose task it was to administer the nightly beatings. (3980)

12 Negotiations

But in the meantime, Louis, the noble king of France, was making strenuous efforts to bring about a reconciliation between King Henry and St Thomas. The pope sent frequent letters when the meetings took place that they had arranged in order to solve the conflict. (3985)

A conference was scheduled to take place at Pontoise, which the pope, who had come from Paris, attended, as did the archbishop for whom it had been convened. But once King Henry was sure that the pope would be coming, he turned back. (3990)

A meeting was then organized at Nogent-le-Rotrou between King Henry and King Louis. King Henry had arranged it in order to see to his own business. The king of Saint-Denis brought the archbishop along to see if it might be possible to reconcile him with Henry.* (3995)

The king of England, however, had no interest in reconciliation, and he asked the king of France to drop the subject of Archbishop Thomas and to stop talking about him. If he did so, Henry would be ready to agree to all of Louis' requests. "I'd be only too pleased to," answered the noble Louis. (4000)

"I've no cause to complain about him or his people, and I'm extremely happy to keep him with me. My kingdom gains in distinction from his great intelligence, whereas yours is that much more diminished by his absence. You would certainly need him more than I do." (4005)

When the noble king of France came back to Thomas, he told him: "Previously I had always hoped you would be reconciled with the king, but from now on I have no confidence that you will. The king of England is so arrogant, I find, that he is unwilling to listen to me on this subject either in private or in public. (4010)

"I once asked, indeed begged you, to stay in the kingdom of Saint-Denis. Now today I put my kingdom and my country at your disposal, Etampes, Orléans, Chartres, Paris. Everything you need to live here can be taken from my possessions and my revenue." (4015)

A conference was then arranged for Montmirail, and this time two cardinals, William of Pavia and Master John of Naples, arrived from Rome. They approached King Henry and pledged him their total support. They would have been quite willing to betray the archbishop. (4020)

The king told them that he was willing to humble himself to the extent of doing whatever they saw fit in the matter of the archbishop and whatever would be acceptable to Holy Church, provided it met with the approval of the archbishop. "He will approve," they replied. "He has no choice." (4025)

St Thomas spent the night before the meeting at Chartres, together with the people he had brought along with him. God sent him a dream that made it absolutely clear to him what the outcome of the following day's negotiations would be, and he revealed this to his closest associates. (4030)

He dreamt he was in the same place as the king, and that Henry handed him a very beautiful golden, or gilded, goblet full of wine, and invited him to drink from it. He took a look at the wine, and saw that it was so cloudy that he dared not touch or drink it. (4035)

He was horrified to find the wine so cloudy, and as he was carefully examining the goblet from all sides, he saw two spiders emerge from the bottom in precisely the same way. They came to rest on the rim, one on one side, and one on the other. "Take it away!" he said. "I'm not going to drink that revolting stuff!" (4040)

Next morning he called together his clerks and his closest advisers and told them the dream he had had the previous night. "I know precisely how these talks will go," he said. "The king will make us some very fine offers, but I will turn them down because it's a trap. (4045)

"The beautiful gilt goblet that he was ready to offer me were the fine offers that I do not want to accept, the cloudy wine is the trap he is laying, and the two huge spiders are the two rascally cardinals who intend, if they can, to entrap us." (4050)

When he came to the meeting, he found the cardinals already there. The king declared that he would be happy to put the matter in the hands of these two, and was ready to accept whatever judgement they might make and whatever decisions Holy Church might come to. Thomas fully realized the trap they were laying and took the necessary precautions. (4055)

The cardinals were attempting to ensnare him by insisting that it was not possible for him to object to the judgement they would come to or the decisions that Holy Church would take. To this he replied that it was not his intention to oppose Holy Church, and that he was making no demands on the king other than that he should do what was right. (4060)

He did not wish, however, – he said – to start proceedings or make his case until the king had fully restored and formally returned to him and his people everything that belonged to them, in the same state as they had left it, on the day the king made them leave England. (4065)

He had no intention of pleading his case as long as he remained dispossessed. The king was unwilling to agree to this, and insisted on Thomas submitting to the judgement of the two cardinals. The archbishop was unwilling to accept their judgement, so, not able to make any headway, he left. (4070)

* * *

There was another meeting at Montmirail arranged by papal letter. Good King Louis attended along with the French, and King Henry came with a group of very powerful barons. Prominent clergy were there also in number, and many barons of renown. (4075)

Also present, from Rome and representing the pope, were Master Bernard de la Coudre, a holy man of great virtue, and Simon prior of Mont-Dieu, a most upright man, as well as archbishops, bishops, priors and abbots – all there to bring about the peace and trying their utmost to do so. (4080)

St Thomas's demands were for the rights of Holy Church to be observed and the restitution of the properties and revenue that the king had confiscated. The king, on the other hand, demanded that the established customs of the kingdom be observed. There was no way that Henry would abandon these customs, and St Thomas replied that he was not prepared to make the great mistake of accepting them. (4085)

There was so much to-ing and fro-ing between clerks and laymen all day that the king finally declared that he asked nothing more than that his honour be respected. Let the archbishop simply behave towards him as his predecessors had done towards his people. It was necessary for the king's subjects to fear him, and this is why he gave the appearance of being haughty and inflexible. (4090)

Many of the people he had to rule over were disruptive, and this was the reason why he had to seem very severe. But if the archbishop were willing to agree to the same conditions as his predecessors, Lanfranc and St Anselm, had been willing to observe for his ancestors, he would make no further demands. (4095)

To this Thomas replied that God forbid that he should ever agree to observe something without knowing exactly what it was. It was entirely right that he should emulate his predecessors when they acted correctly, but when they made mistakes he was not obliged to follow in their footsteps. There is no one in the world who does not sometimes make an error. (4100)

St Peter the apostle, whom God honoured by granting him power in Heaven as well as on earth, denied his lord Jesus Christ three times. Thomas would never accede to Henry's demand for anything in the world, or observe any custom that was unlawful. (4105)

He could not think of a single custom, he added, that his predecessors had had to observe at a king's request. The king replied that he would produce knights and priests ready to swear to the existence of two hundred such customs. To which Thomas replied that, while Henry might well find a considerable number of people ready to swear to that, (4110)

never would he succeed in putting Holy Church on oath in that way. "My lords," answered the king, "he is not interested in peace. Just see how kind I am being to him and how accommodating!" Then everyone, clergy and laity, joined together in jeering the archbishop and reproaching him with being far too inflexible. (4115)

When the archbishop saw that he was under attack from all quarters, and that there was no one now willing to take his side, he heaved a heartfelt sigh and began to weep tears. He prayed to Jesus Christ, worshiped by Holy Church, to keep him from being guilty of reaching an agreement against God. (4120)

King Henry then declared that he would place the matter in the hands of three bishops of France whom Thomas could himself choose, and that he would accept whatever decision they might come to. Everyone shouted out that he was going far enough. Thomas replied that there were many upright men in France, (4125)

and that he was quite willing to accept whatever their decision might be. He would be willing to observe the customs – saving his order. The king swore that this phrase had to be dropped. It was, he said, an attempt to trick him with sophistry. On every side everyone agreed that Thomas should drop this phrase. (4130)

The holy archbishop then agreed to observe the customs saving the faith he owed God. The king swore by God's eyes that that phrase would not do, since it was, in his view, sophistry and deceit. However there can never be deceit in faith in God. (4135)

Thomas then declared that he would do everything for him that any archbishop ought to do for his king. The king swore by God's eyes that that phrase would not do, since it was, in his view, trickery and deceit. However someone who is ready to do his duty cannot be resorting to deceit. (4140)

The king said that all he was asking was for was that Becket respect his honour. Let Thomas do for him what his predecessors did for their kings, what the best amongst them had done for the worst of kings. All the wisest and most prominent men declared that the king was doing enough to show that he wanted peace and was offering friendship. (4145)

When the archbishop saw that Simon prior of Mont-Dieu, Bernard de la Coudre, and even the king of France, in whom he had the greatest trust, were all taking the king's side, his fine eyes filled with tears, and lost in thought he fell silent. Eventually he said to them: "My lords, I agree to what he wants." (4150)

When the archbishop had made all these concessions to the king, and the two sides had reached agreement, he removed his hat, and Henry did likewise. Then they went up to each other to exchange the kiss of peace in true friendship. (4155)

Then the archbishop, to whom God was always so close, said: "Sire, I kiss you in God's honour and in yours." Whereupon archdeacon Geoffrey Ridel said: "There's sophistry here in plenty!" "Indeed," said the king, "by

God's eyes, he's got no interest in peace." He turned his horse round, spurred it on and galloped off. (4160)

When they saw the king of England ride away like this, both clerks and lay people began to hurl insults at Thomas, telling him he was wrong not to have kept to the agreement, and no one could blame the king. Never had they seen the chance of peace thrown away for something so trivial. (4165)

On that day St Thomas lost the support of all the French. Throughout the whole country he was considered to be in the wrong and a traitor. Our Lord's vassal went back to his lodgings. His clerks were dejected and angry with him, saying that he had condemned them all to death without any means of escape. (4170)

"You are totally wrong," he said. "You must all be blind, I think. Our Lord God has today saved us from being put to great shame. In the past the king used to reproach us with arguing endlessly with him, calling us individually malicious and treacherous. Now he has released us from such charges and exonerated us. (4175)

"All he asks from us now is that his honour be respected, and that we observe the customs just as our predecessors did. This we have agreed to do. But it will never ever come to this, whatever anyone might do.* Thanks to God our Creator, we have been spared such a terrible disgrace." (4180)

He then had a letter written informing the pope of all the concessions he had made to the king in the interests of reaching agreement, and the reason why the king had refused and withdrawn, having wilfully excluded God from the kiss of peace. Thomas begged the pope to let him know how he wished to proceed. (4185)

The king stayed the night at La Ferté-Bernard. He brought Geoffrey Ridel out in front of his closest advisers and said: "I want all of you to honour this man. Today he has proved his worth to be greater than gold seven times refined. I was saved by his intelligence, and that criminal archbishop did not succeed in deceiving me." (4190)

When he went to bed and thought over the concessions that the archbishop had made him, and how he had rejected them on account of a single phrase, he said to himself that he had miscalculated and done the wrong thing, since he had actually got what he wanted from the archbishop. (4195)

He swore by the eyes of God and readily admitted that he would never be able to get back to that point again. He immediately woke all his servants up, and had John bishop of Poitiers sent for, ordering him to come straightaway to speak with him. This he did without delay. (4200)

He arrived at midnight and went to speak to Henry. "You must go to the archbishop," the king said. "I was wrong not to go through with the kiss of peace because he had in fact met all my demands. By God's eyes, I will never be able to get back to that position again. (4205)

"Go after him, and be quick about it! Tell him I now accept everything he offered me yesterday." The bishop mounted without a moment's delay and sent on ahead to announce his arrival. When St Thomas heard this, he had his personal belongings loaded up, (4210)

and, without waiting for the bishop, he set out. The bishop galloped off after him, and when he caught up with him, Thomas said that no one could ever get him to go back to the point they had reached the day before, since it was an unreasonable thing to ask. (4215)

* * *

King Henry went one day to pray at Saint-Denis-en-France, and, in order to speak to him, King Louis also came to Saint-Denis. In the name of the saints whom he had come to visit in pilgrimage, Louis asked for efforts to be made to bring about a reconciliation between him and the archbishop. (4220)

Subsequently the two kings met at Montmartre, where they discussed some business which they had completed at Saint-Léger-en-Yvelines. Afterwards the king of France tactfully brought up the question of Archbishop Thomas and the need for there to be a reconciliation between them. (4225)

The king of England replied: "If all the wrongs he has done me and my fief holders were to be redressed, then it is quite possible, with your approval, that there could be peace between us." The good king of France replied: "If each side were to keep bringing up past grievances, there would never be any settlement. (4230)

"It is deplorable that there should be such great enmity between you. Let both sides agree to drop all charges, and let neither of you make any demands on the other." To this the king of England replied: "I place myself in the hands of the clergy." Thereupon the clerks were sent for from Paris. (4235)

The king was informed when they arrived, but the king of England refused to say anything to them. The good king of France, however, did not leave him in peace, and told Henry that he was guilty of bad behaviour towards God by not showing his archbishop affection and fidelity. (4240)

The good king kept arguing with him and pestering him so much that the king of England finally agreed to give back to St Thomas and his people half of all the income he had confiscated. For the other half he would leave it up to the court at Rome to decide. (4245)

He formally promised to let Thomas and his people have this money without fail. They would have it as and when they needed it, and as soon as they were ready to return to England. They would have peace and friendship from him and his successor. King Louis said: "I will inform him of this." (4250)

And this the king did, and both parties came to an agreement on these terms. Then the king of France said: "If it is friendship you want, all that now remains to do is to exchange the kiss of peace." "That is something," said King Henry, "that I will not agree to. (4255)

"I have sworn," he said, "never to kiss him, but I will have my son give him a hundred kisses on my behalf. I will keep him and his people in peace and friendship. I will return their property and income to them, and will not cherish them any the less because of this." (4260)

Good King Louis then went to inform the archbishop of this. St Thomas responded by saying that he cared very little about the kiss, as long as Henry was willing to grant him peace and friendship, and that he henceforth show himself to be sincere and trustworthy. They then agreed on another meeting to confirm the settlement. (4265)

The meeting to conclude the peace was scheduled to take place near Fréteval over in the direction of La Beauce.* Good King Louis was there with his French, King Henry with his magnates, and the cream of the clergy of both countries. (4270)

But in the evening, when they returned to their lodgings, Thomas's clerks blamed and heavily criticized him for not taking pity on them and for not yet having made peace with the king. Master Gunter in particular made these sorts of accusations against him, to which the holy man replied: (4275)

"Master Gunter, you are extremely anxious to go back to England. I don't find this at all surprising, but I'll tell you one thing for sure: you would not have been there a full forty days before you would be wanting not to be there any more, even if someone offered you 500 marks of silver to stay." (4280)

The archbishop let the pope know how things had gone with the king and what the result had been. He appealed to his holy kindness and asked him to be good enough to inform King Henry that all his sins would be forgiven him if only he were to kiss the archbishop as a guarantee of peace. (4285)

The noble archbishop was asking the pope, in his usual shrewd way, to order the king, in the name of holy obedience, to come to see Thomas and give him the kiss of peace. He gave the letter to Madoc, who hurriedly set out. He handed it over to the pope when he was admitted to his presence. (4290)

The pope immediately had his letter written, informing King Henry, sovereign lord of England, that he should give the kiss of peace to Archbishop Thomas of Canterbury, and to set aside completely the anger and spite he had towards him in order that Jesus Christ might heal him of all his sins. (4295)

Let him also restore, to Thomas and his people, all the property that they are able to itemize, and let nothing be omitted. The pope had the power and the right to place his land under interdict – not one part of it only but his entire empire. He can never again refuse to administer justice on account of anyone. (4300)

In the name of Holy obedience he informed St Thomas that, if it were possible to make peace, he was not to refuse. Let him not hold back but make every effort he can, for the pope was thoroughly tired of this conflict, and besides he had not received even the smallest payment from the whole of England. (4305)

13 Truce

In order to draw up the settlement, the pope then sent to King Henry Archbishop Guillaume de Sens, a most noble man without peer in France as far as virtue and honour were concerned, as well as Bernard bishop of Nevers and several others whose names are unknown to me. (4310)

King Henry agreed and promised that he would be happy to do as they advised and to follow the instructions of the pope. They finally reached an agreement and decided to reconvene over in the direction of La Beauce. (4315)

Archbishop Thomas arrived with his group, as did King Louis with a large number of magnates, and the king of England with a powerful contingent, archbishop, bishops and highly learned clerks, in order to conclude this peace settlement, if that was what God had determined. (4320)

King Louis together with the archbishop, bishops and other clergy put such pressure on King Henry that he declared that he would do everything that they advised him to. He was afraid of the pope because of the threats he had made against him. "Only one thing is missing," they said; "you have not given him the kiss of peace." (4325)

The king replied that no one in the world could persuade him to kiss Thomas: he could not and ought not do it, and he had sworn an oath to that effect. He refused to do it even for his overlord, King Louis. But in lieu of that one kiss, he added, the honour he would do Thomas before leaving there would be worth a hundred kisses. (4330)

Each side, good King Louis and the bishops and abbots, took such pains over the agreement that the king and St Thomas did finally meet together. As soon as they saw each other, each came up to the other: King Henry greeted Thomas, and Thomas Henry. (4335)

Everyone on each side, clerks and knights, thought that the king would then be willing to give Thomas the kiss of genuine peace, but instead he said: "My lord archbishop, I should like to confer in private with you." He took him into the middle of the field off the beaten track. They did not call for anyone to join them, so people kept their distance. (4340)

The king and St Thomas spent a long time talking of one thing and another, sometimes raising their voices, sometimes whispering – so long in fact that people on both sides grew tired of waiting for them. Twice, even, they got down from their well-fed horses, and twice remounted. Everyone said: "They must be joking!" (4345)

The king held Thomas's stirrup for him when he remounted, and when Thomas made as if to refuse, the king said to him: "I will not take no for an answer this time. You are my father in God, and it is my duty to honour you." Everyone who saw this thought it a very fine gesture. (4350)

During his conversation on horseback with the king, St Thomas kept changing the position of his thighs, leaving one on the saddle and the other hanging free. This was because his goat's-hair underclothes were causing him so much discomfort. The people who did not know better thought this a very insulting thing to do. (4355)

St Thomas and the king stayed a long time on their own in the middle of the field in secret talks, without ever calling out for any of their retinue. My knowledge of what they talked about is limited, but I shall tell you as much of the truth as I know. (4360)

Having brought him, on his own, to the middle of the field, the king said to him: "My lord archbishop, I've been very much looking forward to seeing you again. Since I've been without your advice, others have been giving me advice that has proved detrimental. Far from getting anything out of it, I've wasted a great deal of my own money." (4365)

Thomas replied sternly like the true priest he was: "Sire, give up this sort of advice, and from now on choose different counsellors, the sort who will tell you things you do not want to hear, and not utter a single word of what you want them to say." (4370)

"I shall not in future," said the king, "pay attention to any advice except yours, and I will now rely on that. I will even entrust the whole of my kingdom to you, and the care of my son Henry. I've hardly any land of my own left, so I'll have to go and get myself some." (4375)

"Really?" replied St Thomas. "Do you really want people to believe that you would leave your kingdom that is so dear to you, and your young children who need you, go off to other lands and challenge other people's rights? That is something I would not approve of and would not advise you to do." (4380)

"By God's eyes!" Henry said, "I shall give it all up and entrust both my son and my kingdom to you." "What is certain," replied St Thomas, "is that I shall never administer the land. I shall have nothing to do with worldly honours any more, since I already find the responsibility I have very burdensome. (4385)

"But if your intention is to give up the land and the kingdom in the service of God, and if you are willing to become a crusader, my advice to you would be to entrust your kingdom and your son to that loyal knight Hugh de Beauchamp, in which case I will help them take care of the country." (4390)

They discussed a large number of other things, about which I have not as yet been informed and which I have not ascertained, nor is it, in any case, possible for me to mention everything that happened in my book. The king took Thomas to task about many matters, and Thomas made some angry accusations against him: (4395)

of having driven him and his clerks into exile, of not having left them an inch of their rentable property, of having ill-treated his men by arresting them and putting them in chains, of even having expelled little children together with their parents; he had acted heartlessly. (4400)

King Henry replied: "The fault is yours for having wrongfully run off out of my kingdom like a fugitive without anyone having done you the least harm. That is why I sent your family and your people after you. However, when you come back home, everything will be put right again." (4405)

The archbishop replied: "Sire, and what about your son, then? You had him anointed and crowned king with unseemly haste and to no advantage, simply in order to cause trouble for me." "That was, I see now, quite wrong," said the king, "but should it be necessary for me to make amends, I shall do so handsomely." (4410)

Thomas answered: "And what have you got to say about the three prelates who crowned him? To do your bidding, they usurped the rights of the Holy Mother Church of the Holy Trinity, whose long established privilege it has always been to anoint kings." (4415)

To this Henry replied: "I shall never again interfere with you or the bishops; henceforth I shall hold my peace. I leave you free to demand whatever reparation you think necessary." Both sides said that the two of them had reached a peaceful agreement, since the king was behaving in a consistently friendly manner towards Thomas. (4420)

When the king and the archbishop had finished their lengthy conversation, the king arranged for them to meet again at Tours. There, so he said, the matter would be settled and appropriate amends made. There the archbishop would obtain the sort of written document he wished to have. Then, in peace and friendship, each of them went on his way. (4425)

When Thomas mounted, the king held his stirrup for him. People everywhere then begged to king to give Thomas the kiss of peace. But he replied that he would not do so. He did not want to kiss him there and then; he had sworn an oath to that effect. He would kiss him when he came to Tours. (4430)

Then Arnulf bishop of Lisieux went up to Thomas and said: "My lord archbishop, listen to me if you please. God in his grace has brought about a reconciliation between you and the king. Geoffrey Ridel is present here: he has fallen out with you, and we would now like to ask you to forgive him." (4435)

"My lord bishop," Thomas replied, "I am aware that he is suspended. I will accept if he is willing to make amends for the wrong he has done, and after that I will do whatever it is my duty to do with regard to him." To which Geoffrey replied: "I'm terribly sorry, but if he hates me, then

I shall hate him – but if he is willing to love me, then I will love him." (4440)

* * *

The day before the meeting was due to take place at three leagues from Tours, as had been agreed, Thomas stayed the night at Tours with his closest advisers. He chose to do so on the advice of Archbishop Rotrou of Rouen in order to put the king's real intentions to the test. (4445)

For outwardly the king behaved in an extremely friendly fashion towards him, so much so that everyone, high or low, said that the king would never hate him again for as long as he lived. The reason St Thomas went to Tours the night before the meeting was to see whether he could get confirmation of what everyone was saying. (4450)

He spent that night in Tours in order to find out whether the king would be willing to give him the kiss of peace there. He had gone there, however, without a penny to his name, and he had either to redeem his pledges or forfeit them. He got no kiss of peace from the king, nor did the king redeem his pledges for him. (4455)

The vassal of our Lord became extremely worried at this. At daybreak he loaded his pack horses and ordered everyone to leave and go back. The king was standing at an upstairs window in his grand palace and saw his archbishop's men ride off at speed (4460)

and Thomas following behind them at a furious pace. The king immediately sent someone after him with instructions to wait because he wished to speak to him. But Thomas had ridden a whole league before he was ready to stop, at a time when he turned off the road in order to sing the canonical hour. (4465)

Without getting down from their horses they sang their service on a piece of open ground, and there they waited for the king. The king came up to him the moment he saw him. The king and the archbishop approached each other and exchanged greetings. (4470)

"In the name of the Trinity," he said, "there are three of us present here." St Thomas was, in fact, accompanied by the archbishop of Rouen – Rotrou was his name, I think – so there were actually three of them, those two and the king. Their clerks stayed in the background in a huddle. (4475)

"Your manners, your Majesty, are wanting," said St Thomas. "You are not the same person that you used to be when I was employed by you. You are a very different man. I was obliged to forfeit my pledges in your city of Tours, and King Louis would never have acted as you did, even if he would have had to mortgage his fiefs."

At this the king smiled, though I have no idea whether or not it was a genuine smile. "My lord archbishop," he said, "I see that you are very angry. But be patient for the moment. Things will work out. Other business has been taking up so much of my attention that I was unable to see to you – even at the cost of having to mortgage a piece of land or a fief!"

When they had conversed for as long as they wished, they mounted their horses and rode off. The king went back the way he had come, while Thomas and his people pressed ahead. But they met up again the next day at Amboise, and there they reached an agreement – at least to judge from their behaviour and from what was said.

It was there that all the conditions were spelled out, and the king gave his approval for all to hear. He issued Thomas with a letter to which he affixed his seal, and copies of it were sent to the justices and to the king's son. Richard Malban and Hugh the Clerk delivered them.

If you would like to hear what this letter contained, I can tell you word for word just as the king had it composed and written out.* "Henry, lord of the English and duke of the Normans, sends greetings to his dear son Henry, king of the empire. Know that Thomas archbishop of Canterbury

"has made his peace with me in full accordance with my wishes. I therefore command that he and all his people, clerics and laity, who left the country on his account be allowed to live in peace, and that they have full access to all their property throughout my kingdom without any financial deductions.

"I also command that the archbishop and his people should have possession, in peace and honour, of the lands, churches and other holdings in the same state as they held them most recently, three months before he and his people left England.

"Have the oldest and the most senior knights that you can find in the Saltwood fief brought together. See to it that whatever they declare, on oath, to belong to the archbishop within the whole of this fief is made over and delivered to him.

"When you have read this letter, keep it to yourselves." However, the holy archbishop, a very intelligent man, gave orders for the letter to be copied out and shown not only to those close to the king but more widely to outsiders as well, for he thought the words "keep it" particularly significant. (4520)

The letter was issued to St Thomas at Amboise, but was given to his people only later at Chinon. Archbishop Rotrou, who held the see of Rouen, was named in it as witness. By every means at his disposal, the king kept delaying and holding them up as long as he could. (4525)

After Amboise he made St Thomas go back into the French kingdom as if he were a messenger sent on the king's business. The two were to meet up at Rouen, and the king would have five hundred marks brought to him there to enable Thomas then to pay his debts. (4530)

It had been formally agreed that the king was to pay back to him the equivalent in value of whatever he had taken from him and his people, and St Thomas had no desire to see this sum reduced. But the first repayment was still a long time coming; the king kept delaying time and time again. (4535)

The king had at least thirty thousand pounds from the archbishopric in addition to everything he had appropriated from the revenues of those who had been driven out of the country. And the people from the archbishop's fief had had to pay extremely high ransom costs, and the archbishop's woods had been stripped bare and sold off. (4540)

Thomas's men crossed over to England to deliver the old king's letter to the Young King. They had numerous copies of it made, and showed it everywhere. They brought together the most prominent men of the district and took them along with them to appear before the king and the justices. (4545)

When they had been brought before the king, they should have spoken up in support of the archbishop, but instead they went and sat down, unwilling to open their mouths. None of them was willing to stand up for his lord in a court of law. They saw bad faith all around them, so their own bad faith matched everyone else's. (4550)

The king's justices dragged things out endlessly, and this led to the whole of the archbishopric remaining in a state of poverty. Before the two archbishop's men got possession of the manors, there was nothing at all left – not an ox or cow, capon or hen, horse, pig or sheep, not even a decent bushel of corn. (4555)

The archbishop and the king had made peace on the feast of St Mary Magdalene on the 22nd of July, and it was not until the feast of St Martin on the 11th of November that Thomas, having been kept waiting by a lengthy adjournment, finally got possession of his property, by which time Ranulf de Broc had either appropriated or destroyed everything. (4560)

Which of the two, Ranulf or the king, will be accountable, on the Day of Judgement, for what he got out of this? That is the day when those that covet will be damned and die an eternal death. The one will not be able to shelter behind the other. No amends were ever made for all Ranulf did.

All-knowing and all-seeing God will right all wrongs. So just is God that he can do only justice. He hates all wickedness and will see to it that it is punished. Itinerant justices will have little success when that time comes. They themselves will all be judged by someone whom none of them can deceive.

Oh God! How many men are blinded by this world where there is no love, no faith, no peace, no charity! If I were to obtain all the possessions there are in the world in such a way as my son could inherit them after my life is spent, I would not be better received when summoned before God.

Were I to buy abbeys or mighty bishoprics which would raise me in stature and give me an exalted position in this world, I would be severely called to account for it before God, and none of my relations would be of any assistance to me. There is a high price to pay for an honour that condemns you to death.

14 Return

As soon as St Thomas had made peace with the king, his thoughts turned to his flock: they were of little faith, having been led astray by their lord king's arrogant behaviour. He sent his holy messenger ahead of him to England in an attempt to sweep away all the mess and clear the way for him.

He sent John of Salisbury, who held a plenary synod of the clergy and, speaking on the archbishop's behalf, declared that he absolved them all, both clerks and laymen, for the sin of having had dealings with people who were excommunicated.

This Thomas did to avoid having to give the kiss of peace to any clerk or layman who might have come into contact with de Broc's people. At the same time he absolved those monks of the monastery who may have had connections with them. He wanted to be able to give the kiss of peace to his own people without any prohibition.

When St Thomas was ready to cross over to England, King Henry was to have met him at Rouen, as he had promised, to have the money handed over to him. But instead he had a letter delivered to him there, which I can read to you if you would be kind enough to listen:* (4600)

"Henry king of the English, duke and lord of the Normans, greetings to Thomas archbishop of Canterbury. King Louis of France, I am reliably informed, has mobilized his entire army from every part of his kingdom. His intention is to go to Auvergne to crush my troops. (4605)

"He seeks to wipe out my men and ravage my land. My allies in France have given me this news, and in Auvergne the local inhabitants have asked me to go to their assistance. I was to meet you at Rouen as you returned home, but have to tell you that I am unable to be there. (4610)

"Accordingly I am sending you a clerk of mine who is one of my close confidants, John of Oxford, with orders to escort you back to England. Through him I have informed the young king of England, my eldest son Henry, that you are to have your property back without any interference. (4615)

"If anything were to go wrong as far as your business is concerned, my son will see to it that you obtain redress. Both I and my son have heard a lot of talk about your delaying your return – all lies, I daresay. For this reason you would, in my opinion, be well advised to hurry up." (4620)

This letter, in the form presented here, was written at Loches and witnessed by King Henry himself. When St Thomas read it, he made preparations for his departure and, taking leave of the French, left for England with John of Oxford as his guide and escort. (4625)

The three prelates who showed such animosity to the archbishop were very afraid on learning that he was to return. They went to Canterbury to have secret talks with Lord Ranulf de Broc and encourage him to teach Thomas and his people a lesson they would not forget. (4630)

They had de Broc's knights and men-at-arms put on their armour and took them along with them to the coast at Dover. They had all the ports on the way searched, closely watched and placed under guard. If the archbishop were to land there, they had instructions to intercept him, to be ready to give him a hostile reception, (4635)

steal his men's belongings, go through their baggage and confiscate all the letters that he might have obtained from Rome, and not let him keep a single one. This was why these three prelates had the ports closely watched. Their aim was to prepare an uncomfortable welcome for their father. (4640)

And to strengthen their hand in this criminal enterprise they took Lord Reginald de Warenne along with them, with Gervase of Cornhill, no friend of Thomas's at that particular time, and Ranulf de Broc. All three swore by the son of the Virgin Mary that if they encountered the archbishop, he was a dead man. (4645)

This was all reported to the archbishop by his friends and allies, who informed him of what they had heard. He was not at all alarmed, however, by any of this, though he was moved and felt sorry for his country and for the French people who had helped him during his exile. (4650)

He very much wanted to see his country again and to take back with him his family members, whom King Henry had had exiled for six years, and make provision for them. He came to Wissant, where he walked along the beach to see what the weather was like and to relax. (4655)

Then the dean of Boulogne, one Milon, I understand, arrived with a message for him. "My lord," he said, "I'm not here to ask you for any landing-fee but to bring you a message from my lord, Mathieu count of Boulogne, whose envoy I am. (4660)

"He advises you to be on your guard. You have many enemies. They are armed and are keeping a very close watch for you at all the ports over the Channel. If you land there, you will be thrown in prison, locked away in some fortress or other, or even torn limb from limb." (4665)

"My dear son," replied St Thomas, "I can assure you that even if I were to end up completely dismembered, nothing, neither fear of death nor any other deterrent, would stop me from going through with the journey I have begun. From this point on, no danger or suffering can possibly dissuade me. (4670)

"Day and night for seven years, it seems to me, my church has been in constant mourning for its pastor. And now, if I am suddenly taken from this world and unable to complete the journey alive, I request my people, if ever they valued my friendship, to carry me back to my church. (4675)

"Have my books taken back with me also. If I have failed so far to do anything for my people that they could be pleased about, let them at least honour me for donating some of my possessions to them. When it comes to the final reckoning, no one can give a better present to anyone than to be willing to grant what he himself treasures the most."* (4680)

When the archbishop understood that the three people who had been his most consistent enemies were at Dover, as he had been told, he entrusted the papal letter suspending and restraining the three to a messenger with orders for him to cross the Channel. The messenger left at once. (4685)

When he arrived at Dover, he found the three, who had just finished their canonical hours, waiting for him. He addressed the archbishop of York: "My lord," he said, "the pope, whose messenger I am, sends you, through me, such greetings as you deserve. Here, read this letter that he has sent you. (4690)

"Pray, be quick. You are holding up the business of Rome. You are suspended from your priestly functions, and no appeal is possible." Turning to the two others he said: "Look, my lords, I have a copy of the letter! There's no escaping it: you've been expelled from the Church community." (4695)

He handed the letter over to them. On discovering that they had indeed been relieved of their functions, they turned livid with anger and were mortified. Ranulf de Broc came close to killing the messenger, but God had removed him from the scene and Ranulf could not get him. (4700)

Robert the treasurer of Canterbury also landed in Dover. He was arrested for not having a letter from the king with him and for having entered England without permission. He explained that he was the archbishop's envoy and was in a hurry to bring him his cross in time for his arrival. (4705)

"So he's coming, is he?" they asked. "Oh yes, indeed," said Robert. "In that case, you should have planned your arrival better, and got the permission of a different lord." They quickly released the treasurer, making him promise to go back again on the next tide if the wind was favourable. (4710)

St Thomas had King Henry's formal permission to return to England and to recover what was his by right. If, however, such permission had been unambiguous and authentic, Thomas's people would not have suffered any injustice or humiliation. As it was, it quickly became apparent what the catch was with the permission. (4715)

St Thomas set sail the next day. God granted him good wind, and he came ashore at Sandwich, avoiding landing at Dover, which was heavily guarded. Sandwich was part of his territory, and he took lodgings there. A huge crowd of his people came to meet him there. (4720)

When they learned that he had landed, the three king's men were overjoyed. They took their arms, just as the three prelates had advised them to, and set out for Sandwich, where the archbishop was. (4725)

When John of Oxford saw them approaching the archbishop fully armed, he was extremely worried, for he knew very well that their minds were set on mischief and on doing something stupid, and he fully realized that the king would be severely blamed if St Thomas came to any harm there. (4730)

So without a moment's hesitation he went up to them and informed them of the agreement between the king and Thomas. Speaking on behalf of the king, he gave them specific orders to do no harm to him or his people, otherwise the king himself would be accused of treacherous behaviour. (4735)

They were to put down their arms, he told them, before approaching Thomas. When this was explained to them, they complied, then came up to the archbishop and spoke to him. They told him that he had brought an enemy of the king with him, thereby contravening the king's ordinance. (4740)

This was on account of Simon, a native of Sens and an archdeacon there, a high-ranking, virtuous and well-born man who had crossed over with Thomas to visit his family. The king's men wanted to make him swear that he would take their king's side against everyone else. (4745)

They made no exception for anyone, not even for the pope. But St Thomas did not want him to pledge his word for fear that all the clergy in the country might have to do the same thing. The king's men could not do anything that Thomas did not agree to, in view of the large crowd of his followers that had gathered round him there. (4750)

As he was unwilling to do as they asked, they went away. As for the holy archbishop, he proceeded to his own town of Canterbury, very happy to do so, since he had long been yearning to go back. The monks and the people welcomed him with great warmth, forming a large procession to come and meet him. (4755)

For the rest of his days he lived a holy life, endeavouring to serve his Lord to the best of his ability. He provided for widows, orphans and the poor, giving them clothing, shoes, food and money. In his view, too few needy people actually came to get help from him. (4760)

No one could succeed in deflecting him in his quest for justice. He went as far as to take those churches away from the king's clerks that they had illegally appropriated, and to give them back to those who had lost them. He steadfastly did what was just and right in the full knowledge that he would eventually have to die for the sake of justice. (4765)

* * *

Soon after he returned from overseas, he made up his mind not to stay any longer in his diocese without going to speak to the country's king. First, however, he sent a monk with a message from him, one Richard, prior of St Martin's Dover. (4770)

He found the Young King at Winchester. A council had been called there on the advice of the three excommunicated prelates together with Geoffrey the Married Cleric.* It consisted of the country's magnates, deans, archdeacons, abbots and beneficed clergy. (4775)

Six of the country's dioceses were without bishops, and this is why a council of these people, together with princes, earls and numerous magnates, had been called for that day in order to elect and designate bishops to this high function. After this, they were to cross the Channel without delay.* (4780)

At Winchester the new bishops were presented and invested on the advice of the four dignitaries named above. They had, however, been unwilling to invite the archbishop and primate, nor did they invite a number of bishops who they knew would have remained loyal to Thomas, and whose names I will not omit to mention. (4785)

Henry bishop of Winchester was among those they had not invited, as was Bartholomew bishop of Exeter, Roger of Worcester, a noble and virtuous bishop, and Nigel bishop of Ely, who had in any case no wish to attend. No self-respecting bishop should have officiated at this particular consecration ceremony. (4790)

Under no circumstances should any bishop be ordained without the approval of the primate, however many other bishops may be present. This is what is stipulated in canon law. It is possible, should the need arise, for three bishops to carry out the consecration, but in that case there can be no formal promotion unless it be on the primate's orders. (4795)

If a bishop is to be ordained in a particular part of the country, all the bishops in the kingdom are to be summoned, and any who cannot attend the council must send a messenger with a letter stating whether or not they approve of the consecration. (4800)

If ever a bishop, priest or deacon is elected and promoted by a prince, he is to be stripped of his office. And if anyone achieves high ecclesiastical office by dint of having been in a position of secular power, he must be excluded from the community and definitively removed from office. (4805)

At the present time I see no one, clerk or layman, adhering to canon law. In fact clerics are the worst of all. They have succumbed entirely to secular power out of fear of losing their positions. From whatever direction the wind happens to blow, they bend and accommodate.

These are no sons of Jesus, just degenerate offspring, unlikely in the immediate future to be laying down their lives on the cross for God! Once they've got their hands on something, they would be loath indeed to let it go. They were not born in heaven, and their gaze is not directed upwards. They are made from the dust of the earth, and they hang their heads to the ground.

The duty of bishops is to give moral guidance to everyone, hence the need for them to be upright people, good clerics, of legitimate birth. Putting good graft onto good stock ensures good fruit, and in my experience good graft on bad stock leads to bad fruit. He who grows a bad tree must needs eat bad fruit.

The Devil has deprived kings and princes of the use of their eyes. Having a bad father means receiving a bad inheritance, and having a weak master means being frequently beaten. When a son beats his father, the world is turned upside down: heaven is underground, and the stars are extinguished.

When the king appoints a pastor, he should choose someone he can trust body and soul. If he deliberately opts for someone who is indecisive, it is like setting a pure emerald in lead, and he alone, in my view, can be asked to justify such a decision.

A king should give Holy Church an honest pastor, one so upright that people can bow their head to him with honour. Holy Church is the bride of the sovereign Lord. To give the bride a bad steward is to bring dishonour not only on the bride but on God also.

* * *

The archbishop's messenger arrived at Winchester to find the door of the meeting room firmly shut in his face. Both clergy and laymen were afraid that he might bring an official letter announcing the formal suspension of any number of them.

He assured them, very skilfully, that he was not the bearer of bad news, and that the primate had a sincere affection for both the king and those close to him. He finally managed to be admitted to the Young King's presence. With a low bow, he spoke to him with great respect: (4845)

"Thomas archbishop of Canterbury," he began, "legate of the see of Rome, primate of the whole empire, to King Henry, lord of England, greetings. You will already have heard this news from others often enough, but I have nonetheless had it written down for you in this letter, (4850)

"because I want you to hear it directly from me. God in his goodness has, by his grace, brought about a reconciliation between your father, who was very annoyed with me, and myself, and has brought us together again in harmony, peace and love. Several people, however, are unhappy about this, as I see it, (4855)

"and wish to harm me in your eyes, cause us to fall out, and undo and destroy the love and peace between us. They even say I want to take away your crown from you! But, so help me God, Lord of us all – and may God in time grant me a life of heavenly joy – (4860)

"I would have liked personally to have won for you many other kingdoms in addition to the one you already have, even at the cost of shedding some of my own blood, though without incurring any blame from God – and may the Holy Trinity help me in my last hours! (4865)

"Why therefore would I seek to harm or dishonour you, seeing that I acknowledge you, as I should, to be lord and king, heir and successor to the whole kingdom, someone for whom I have more love and loyal affection than anyone else – saving only my lord King Henry who raised me to the office I now hold? (4870)

"One thing, however, that I feel profoundly bitter about is that I was not the one who placed the golden crown on your head in accordance with the privilege conferred on Holy Mother Church. This is the reason I have written you this letter requesting you to be good enough to allow me to discuss this misunderstanding and other matters with you." (4875)

Richard delivered his message most commendably, but the Young King's counsellors advised him not to speak with the archbishop on this occasion. Lord Geoffrey Ridel swore that King Henry had given him his views on the matter, (4880)

namely that he did not see why his son should speak with Thomas, whose aim was, if he could, to deprive him of his inheritance rights and to remove his crown from his head. The Young King then dispatched two knights to the archbishop, one of whom, I am informed, was called Thomas de Tournebu. (4885)

Jocelin of Louvain was the other envoy from the king, and he debarred Thomas from entering any of the king's properties, towns, burghs or castles. Woe betide him if he were ever to be seen there! The archbishop had already left for London, where he would speak to the king, and his journey had come to an end at Southwark.

"What's this?" said St Thomas. "Have you renounced your allegiance to me?" "No," replied Jocelin, "but the king has sent us to tell you that you have behaved extremely badly towards him, seeking to abolish the laws and customs of his realm, and to remove the Young King's crown.

"You lead armed knights all over his territory, you bring foreign clerks into his country, you have suspended his bishops from their office. King Henry demands that you now grant them absolution, for in this, as in other matters, you have gravely wronged him."

To this Thomas, who could no longer restrain himself, replied: "It is not right, nor do I ever hear anyone say it is, that an inferior should undo what a superior does. All the more so when the pope is involved: no one subordinate to him can legitimately rescind anything that he does, has done for him, or confirms."

In reply they shouted at him like lunatics: "Unless you do as the king demands, he will obtain full justice – and he'll make you pay for it!" This whole scheme had been prepared and carried out by the three prelates who had been suspended from office.

To this Thomas replied, with great composure, that, if the bishops of London and Salisbury were to come to him and be willing to swear to stand trial according to canon law and recognize the peace treaty, he would be willing to take on himself the weighty responsibility

of treating them in the kindest possible way and with benevolence in honour of the pope, since they were people of whom he was very fond. This he would do on the advice of the king, if he were willing to lend his support, and of Roger bishop of Worcester and the other bishops with whom it was his duty to consult.

Jocelin replied: "Since you persist in refusing to absolve the king's prelates, the king hereby debars you from entering any of the royal strongholds, castles, towns and burghs, and woe betide you if you do! Go and get on with your business in Canterbury!"

"If I am not able," replied St Thomas, "to visit my province and give advice in the parishes and their churches and look after them, then I cannot carry out my work or discharge my responsibilities." The envoys' message left Thomas in no doubt that in the very near future he was to die a martyr's death. (4930)

Having commended London and its inhabitants to God, our Lord and Saviour, he continued on his journey. Every time he stopped, God performed numerous miracles for him: the blind, the lame, the deaf, the mute, lepers – all found renewed health and strength. (4935)

He commended himself to God and continued his journey. As he went, making what progress he could, he confirmed children in the burghs and towns, dismounting every time any were brought to him. Never did he consider serving God in any way burdensome. (4940)

It was a pleasure for him to serve God. There is no need for me to enlighten you on all the places where he stopped to confirm children. We can easily locate the chapels that were built there. In such places God gives sight to the blind, hearing to the deaf, speech to the dumb, healing to the lepers, life to the dead who can rise and walk again. (4945)

In this way St Thomas returned to his see, and thereafter remained in his archbishopric for the rest of his life. He took pity on the poor whenever he saw them, and laboured day and night in God's service. He was well aware that he would die a martyr, and had indeed predicted it. (4950)

But after his sermon on Christmas Day he expelled Robert de Broc from Holy Church together with others who had done him wrong. On the previous day de Broc had committed a disgraceful outrage against him by cutting the tail of his packhorse in his presence.* (4955)

He also told the congregation about the bishop of London and Jocelin bishop of Salisbury, as well as the archbishop of York who, on his own authority, had usurped the church of Holy Trinity's unique privilege of anointing kings. (4960)

He told them also about Ranulf de Broc, who had harmed him in many ways and on many occasions had thrown a large number of his men into prison. The archbishop proceeded to curse all those who had been instrumental in his quarrel with the king, those troublemakers who in the past had put him on bad terms with his lord and would do so again in the future. (4965)

"May they all, each and every one, be cursed by Jesus Christ!" he said, before throwing the candle down on the stone floor and breaking it, to indicate that the memory of them should be erased from the written record, and they themselves banished from the kingdom to which the good are called.* (4970)

15 Plot

When Roger de Pont-L'Evêque realized and fully understood that he had been excommunicated and placed under interdict, he was unwilling to go to the Church court and beg for mercy because in his heart he was a wicked person, arrogant and overweening. The Devil had set up house within him. (4975)

The two other prelates, on the other hand, his colleagues Gilbert Foliot and Jocelin, were willing to make amends and do what was right and just as regards their archbishop. Both fully acknowledged just how wrong they had been. (4980)

But Roger de Pont-L'Evêque led them astray, directing them to act unreasonably and against God. He wanted them as accomplices in hatching his wicked plot. "Don't, I beg you, go down that path," he said, "for fear that Thomas might downgrade your religious status.* (4985)

"He is capable at any moment of making you change your mind and of tricking you. I have £10,000 in my treasury, and I can guarantee you that I will be willing to spend every penny to see Thomas's pride well and truly punctured! He won't be able to offer me much resistance. (4990)

"We'll cross the Channel now and go to see the king who is over there. Up until now he has supported us and our cause against Thomas, and will continue to do so. He'll see it through to the end as long as you don't prevent him. Do you know what he will do if you desert him, (4995)

"if you change your mind and go over to his enemy? For as long as you live, you will never benefit from his friendship, you will never get back into favour with him. He will say that you are acting unreasonably and illegally, and if he takes you to court, you will lose everything you own. (5000)

"What will you be able to do then? Where will you go to beg? If, on the other hand, you remain an ally of the king's, how can Thomas harass you more than he does now? He has already passed sentence on you, though this cannot be binding since it has no basis in truth." (5005)

So successfully did he talk them round that he convinced them to go with him. They reached the boat and put to sea. But Roger de Pont-L'Evêque was incapable of hiding his feelings at that moment. "Thomas, Thomas," he said, "you will regret forcing this journey on me! I'm going to see to it that you don't sleep soundly in your bed!"* (5010)

No sooner had they landed than they sent ahead to the king the papal letter removing them from office. On seeing it, the king grew very angry. He banged his hands together, and his moans and cries of grief were heartfelt. (5015)

He went off into his private quarters, pale and furious, saying that he had taken into his care and looked after unworthy people, that he had wasted his time feeding such worthless individuals. No one among those close to him, he said, shared in his grief. He thoroughly frightened everyone around him when they heard him speak like that. (5020)

"What's making the king so terribly upset?" they asked. "Even if he were to see his sons and his wife dead and buried, and the whole of his land go up in flames, he shouldn't show such grief as this. If he has heard some terrible news or other, he should have said something about it. (5025)

"Besides, you shouldn't think everything you hear is true. We are quite prepared to carry out all his orders, to attack and demolish castles and strongholds, put our lives in danger and our souls in jeopardy. He is wrong to complain about us and yet not reveal what the trouble is." (5030)

The king replied: "A man who has eaten bread at my table, a man who came to my court in poverty, this is the man I have raised to high office only for him to lift up his heel and kick me in the teeth! He has put the whole of my lineage and my kingdom to shame. It grieves me and breaks my heart, and no one has taken revenge for what he has done to me."* (5035)

The whole court was immediately in turmoil; they began to blame themselves pitilessly and to utter violent threats against the holy archbishop. Several of them began grouping together and swearing on oath to take immediate revenge for the shameful disgrace which had been brought on the king. (5040)

When the three bishops had crossed the Channel, they made straight for Bur-le-Roi where they found the king. They fell at his feet and begged him to take pity on them. They showed how deeply upset they were by lamenting and shedding copious tears of grief and sorrow. (5045)

The king's expression changed completely. He asked them to get to their feet and to stay standing, and instructed them to tell him the cause of their unhappiness. Archbishop Roger, who was very adept at making all sorts of mischief, spoke up: (5050)

"My lord king," he said, "we have every reason to be upset. I am at least in a position to talk about it, but not so my two colleagues here: no one can speak to them without falling under the same sanction as Thomas imposed on them after he came back from overseas. (5055)

"Thomas has excommunicated all those who attended your son at his coronation, as well as those who gave their consent to it." The king's immediate reply was: "So I'm no exception, by God's eyes, since I also freely gave my consent." (5060)

"Sire," said Archbishop Roger, "your having to share in the suffering along with us will make it easier for us to bear. Thomas is expelling your noblemen from Holy Church and placing your bishops under excommunication, but he has no intention of stopping there. (5065)

"Ever since he came back to England, he has been riding around the country at the head of an enlarged retinue consisting of fully armed knights and soldiers. He is afraid of being exiled a second time, so he is looking all over the place for recruits to increase his strength. (5070)

"We have devoted a great deal of hard work to serving you as loyally as we have, and this has led to our spending and using up a large amount of our own money. We do not mind this and are not sorry, as long as we manage to retain your friendship. (5075)

"What we do complain about is the fact that he has treated us so unjustly, shaming and slandering us as if we were common criminals. If you were now to try a different tactic, no one would blame you. Wait, however, until he feels more secure, and then you will be able to get proper revenge without any sort of fuss." (5080)

The papal letter suspending the three prelates from office was produced and read out aloud to the assembled company. Everyone listened carefully, then anger erupted from every direction as insults and threats were hurled at St Thomas. (5085)

That particular year Christmas Day fell on a Friday, and it was on Christmas Eve, the Thursday, that this council of God's enemies met and swore to bring about the death of God's beloved Thomas. Their intention was to rid themselves of him, but in the event they themselves ended up in dishonour and disgrace. (5090)

Swearing on holy relics, they pledged themselves to tear his tongue out down over his chin and to gouge both of his eyes out of his head wherever in the world they might find him. They would take no notice of where or when: be it in church or before the altar, whatever the day or whatever the time. (5095)

Curiously, the hall at Bur-le-Roi seems destined to be a place where, time and time again, very bad news has been heard. It was here that Rainild* was promised in marriage to King Harold, here also that the pledge to make war against England was made by William the Bastard, here also that St Thomas's death was sworn and sealed. (5100)

The most prominent members of the court all swore to one another to carry out and complete this brutal act. I will, however, neither give nor record their names in my book. Since they have made amends and been forgiven by God, they will not be put to shame in the eyes of the world through my book. (5105)

This is how the most prominent, the most worthy and the wisest members of the court, both English and Norman, were bewitched by the treacherous Devil. They set off for different ports, some to Dieppe or Winchelsea, others to Barfleur and Wissant.* (5110)

They would all have liked to cross the Channel, had they been able, to guard and keep a close watch on all the English ports to prevent anyone going over to England who could warn the archbishop of what was afoot, thus enabling him to take evasive action or flee. (5115)

If they had succeeded in crossing the Channel at that particular time, perhaps they would have acted differently from how they subsequently did, but on this occasion the wind and the weather were against them. God did not hate them to the extent of letting them do as they wished, and the Devil did not have sufficient power over them. (5120)

Nevertheless the four traitors and enemies of God, who hated them for the evil lives they led, did leave the court. They were: Hugh de Morville, William de Tracy, Reginald fitz Urse, and, lastly, Richard Brito. (5125)

Roger de Pont-L'Evêque went part of the way with them, frantically urging them on to commit the dastardly crime. Thomas, he declared, was a disruptive force in the kingdom, on which he was also inflicting damage. With him dead, he said, peace would be restored throughout the country. Any sins they might commit in bringing this about, Roger personally would assume responsibility for. (5130)

He drew up the charge against Thomas, and told them, word for word, exactly what it consisted of, and these are the same words they subsequently used in the archbishop's apartments in Canterbury. Roger gave each one of them sixty marks.* Thus was the blood of a righteous man bought and sold. And the covetous Judas went off to the Jews. (5135)

These are those ones who had St Thomas hacked down and killed, whereas their duty should have been to give the king better advice on how to do good, to set him on the right path and guide and direct him away from evil. They are, therefore, all the more blameworthy and should be brought to trial, and the king ought clearly to distance himself from them. (5140)

If he is sincerely sorry for what he has done, he should not go anywhere near them, for their advice has severely damaged him, and he is much to be blamed for continuing to listen to them. They have always given him the sort of advice he wanted. It is dishonest to tell people what they want to hear. (5145)

Two of the four crossed over at Dover, the other two at Winchelsea.* Neither the boat, nor the crossing, nor the wind or weather caused them any difficulty. Everything went smoothly, and they met up at Saltwood. (5150)

Lord Ranulf de Broc came out to greet them, and led them to the castle where they took lodgings. They put out all the candles that had been lit there, and spent the entire night conferring. The only people allowed in were those privy to what was being discussed. (5155)

At daybreak the knights in the vicinity were summoned to come along fully armed and equipped, ready to do the king's business. Lord Ranulf de Broc had given the orders earlier, and the proclamation now went out for them to join those in the castle. (5160)

16 Hostilities

All these people arrived in Canterbury just as people had finished eating. It was the fifth day of Christmas, the day after the feast of the Holy Innocents whom Herod in his great cruelty had killed, in the belief that he could murder the Godhead by murdering all the children. (5165)

The knights and soldiers in the vicinity had been summoned to avenge the shame suffered by the king of England. If anyone were to seek to hide the archbishop, they said, or spirit him away, they would be ready to besiege the church the day after, set fire to it and raze it to the ground. (5170)

The governor of the town had a general proclamation issued to the effect that no one, great or small, should be rash enough to offer any opposition, whatever they might see or hear others say. Anyone who cared about his own life and possessions should hold himself ready to help the king carry out his business. (5175)

In their frenzy the four galloped into the archbishop's courtyard and dismounted directly in front of the great hall.* By this time the archbishop, having finished his meal, was sitting in his private apartment with his inner circle of clerics. Even the servants had already got up from the table. (5180)

The four entered the hall unaccompanied except for an archer of Ranulf de Broc's whom they had brought with them. But the first person they encountered was the steward, who had come down to the foot of the steps to greet them. As a greeting he kissed them, and they returned the greeting. (5185)

The steward, William fitz Neal, was a local-born man, a fine, handsome knight and a rich landowner. He had already served at the table before eating himself. Then he had come into the archbishop's apartment and said: "My lord, please listen to me a moment. (5190)

"I wish, my lord, with your agreement to go to our king's court and stay there. You are not on very good terms with the king and his people, and because of this I do not dare stay in your company in case the king should take a dislike to me and bring some charge against me." (5195)

"William," Thomas had replied, "of course you have my permission. I have no wish to keep you here if you want to go." At this point he had left the archbishop and come down the steps, and that is where he encountered the four king's men. They ordered him to go back to the archbishop's apartment. (5200)

"My lord," he said, "there are four young men outside. They're the king's knights and wish to speak to you on the king's behalf." He did not give their names. "Show them in," the archbishop replied, and William immediately went to fetch them. (5205)

The four of them had a plan that they all agreed on. They sat down in front of St Thomas, right at his feet in fact, while the archer sat on the floor behind them. But they said no word of greeting to St Thomas and did not speak to him. Nor did the archbishop, who was busy having a discussion with his clerks, greet or speak to them. (5210)

I have no idea whether Thomas deliberately failed to greet them immediately they came in, whether it was because they made no attempt to let him know what they wanted, or because he himself was so busy discussing with his monks and clerks. (5215)

Leaning on the arm of one of the monks, Thomas sat upright and looked the knights in the eye, but he did so with great compassion. He is reported to have greeted only one of the four, William de Tracy, whom he called by his name. (5220)

The four madmen looked at the ground, neither acknowledging nor returning his greeting. Their leader hated the very idea that their souls might be saved.* They then looked at one another, but remained silent, which the archbishop found very surprising. (5225)

Some say that, while the other three did not break their silence, Reginald fitz Urse spoke up with an ironic "So help you God!" At this the holy man, well aware that the words were meant contemptuously, grew red in the face, redder than the brightest and choicest scarlet cloth. (5230)

"The king," continued Reginald with some irritation, "has, through us, sent you a message from overseas, and it is his exact words we bring you. Tell us if you wish to hear the message in private, or do you want all your people to hear it too?" The good archbishop replied: "Just as you wish." (5235)

"No, as you wish," they replied. "No, as you wish," was Thomas's rejoinder. A contest followed as to which side could outdo the other. It ended with Thomas deciding to bring all of his people back into the room until he had finished listening to the message – all, that is, except one who was to stand guard at the door. (5240)

Then St Thomas said: "Don't worry about the door! There is no need for the message I am going to hear to stay secret. Have each and every one of my clerks brought back in here.* I don't want any of them to be excluded from my privy council." They were then brought back in, but I am not able to record all their names. (5245)

Had they not come back as quickly as they did, and if the scoundrels had had weapons or knives on them, between them they would have killed him, as they themselves admitted some time later. They very nearly struck him down and killed him with the shaft of his own cross, but God took it out of their hands. (5250)

"The king," Reginald continued, "has sent you the following message from overseas: he had made peace with you and pardoned you. You had done likewise, but you have failed to keep your word. Instead of returning to his kingdom in a sensible manner, you passed through his fortified towns with your vassals fully armed. (5255)

"What is more, you have excommunicated and cut off from God those of the king's men who attended his son's coronation, and an archbishop of his whose duty it was to be present, as well as two of his bishops whom he needed to consult. You are attempting to suppress and abolish the customs of the kingdom. (5260)

"You also intend to deprive the Young King of his crown. The king now demands to know whether you are willing to appear before him in his court to stand trial and accept the verdict." "I have fulfilled all my obligations to the king," Thomas replied, "and I cannot recall there being any outstanding business. (5265)

"I deny wanting to deprive the Young King of his crown; indeed if it were legally possible, I would help him to obtain three crowns! I came back into this country with his full permission, and my lord has no cause for complaint if I was escorted by my men and those that hold land from me. (5270)

"I am quite prepared to stand trial in his court or anywhere else, if I have done any wrong. But he has forbidden me access to his burghs and citadels, towns and castles: woe betide me if I am ever found in any of them! The king has waived the rights of Holy Church! (5275)

"The suspension is none of my doing; it comes from Pope Alexander on account of their having anointed the Young King – God's blessing on him! – which it was wrong and illegal of them to do, and also because they have been unwilling to make amends for it." (5280)

Reginald replied: "But it was you who instigated the excommunication of all three of the king's prelates. This is why the king wants their sanction to be lifted and requires you to absolve them without any delay, since it was you who had them suspended and penalized." (5285)

"I do not deny," said Thomas, "that I instigated it, but they are not to expect any help or comfort from me. Let all three of them go immediately to our pontiff. They fell foul of him for straightforward legal reasons. I simply obey the pope and carry out his orders." (5290)

"You're blustering!" said Satan's sons.* "From now on we'll keep you under stricter control than you've been used to. You won't get away from us as you did last time." St Thomas remained unmoved and showed no fear. He replied: "I will never again be driven out by anyone. (5295)

"I will never be expelled from the country on account of any man." "What?" they replied, "even if that man were the king?" "No," said Thomas, "you won't find me overseas again. I will never leave on account of any man. Here is where you'll always find me." This made the knights' tempers really flare. (5300)

"You had no business bringing me a message like this," Thomas said, "and my lord the king is so trustworthy and honest that he would never have wanted me spoken to in this way. He won't be willing to guarantee or confirm what you've said." "Oh yes he will," they said. "We're confident we're reporting his very words." (5305)

St Thomas replied: "His men are giving me much cause for complaint, sinfully using force to occupy our churches, beating my men, docking my horse's tail, forcibly making off with my barrels and the wine that my lord the king had sent me." (5310)

"If my lord the king's men," said Reginald, "have done you any wrong or misbehaved, why would you not have notified the king in the first instance? He would have acted on the advice of his barons and put things right." Looking up, the saint replied: (5315)

"Were it necessary for me to call witnesses, I would remind you, Reginald, that you yourself and two hundred knights were present when the king granted me permission to obtain satisfaction for the wrongs inflicted on Holy Church. I'll see to it myself that there is redress. I am the one who has to do it; that is part of my function." (5320)

This caused the knights to go red in the face and to flare up. "What!" they answered, "Was it the king who handed over to you all those involved in his son's coronation? As you well know, everything they did was at the king's behest. You are as good as calling the king a traitor before our very eyes! (5325)

"You have already dishonoured him before, and you are doing so again." "No, that's not so," said St Thomas. "He is no traitor in my opinion, nor is it my wish to put him to shame. In fact I wish him all possible honour. But on the day when God re-established harmony and friendship between us, he granted me permission to see to it that they faced justice. (5330)

"I had registered a formal complaint against the three prelates in question, and in front of two hundred witnesses he gave me permission to subject them to the full force of the law. What I or my clerks do is no concern of his. I personally shall administer justice, as is my right. (5335)

"It is not possible for me to go running off to court every time an offence occurs. As a priest, I shall administer God's justice to those who commit offences against Holy Mother Church." "That sounds like a threat," they said. "Unless you absolve those who are under sentence, you will pay a high price." (5340)

Thomas replied: "If you really are the king's messengers, you will not make people more afraid of you by threatening them. It would be easy for you to stab me here in my unprotected neck with a tinpot knife; no one will stop you." He put his hand to his neck. The knights left the room. (5345)

"There's more to it than just threatening!" they shouted out in a shameful act of defiance against the holy archbishop. In the king's name they issued a proclamation ordering everyone to leave at once. Anyone caught dawdling would pay dearly for it. (5350)

In the name of the king also, they ordered the monks they found in the room to detain and keep a close eye on the archbishop, for if ever he got away, they would be called to account, and have to pay compensation. The saint heard and understood that they were defying him. He got to his feet. (5355)

Realising just what their defiance meant, he followed the knights to the door and shouted out to Hugh de Morville: "What did you say? Say it again!" Without responding, they immediately left. Thomas would have preferred them to have killed him there and then. (5360)

St Thomas came back and sat down on his bed. He looked as if he had suddenly gone into an ecstasy. John of Salisbury then said to him: "My lord, you have never followed our advice except when it coincided with what you had set your own heart on." (5365)

"What, Master John," said the good archbishop, "do you want me to do?" John replied: "You should have summoned your council when the knights first came in to talk to you. All they want is an excuse to kill you, but no one can save you from your own stubbornness." (5370)

To this the saint replied: "We must all of us die, and you will never see me stray from the path of justice for fear of dying. I am willing to suffer death for the love of God. I have set my heart on suffering martyrdom, and am no less ready to do so than they are to strike me." (5375)

Master John replied: "At present we are not yet willing to lay down our lives, since we are wretches languishing in a state of sin. Apart from you I see no one dying of his own free will." "Then may God's will now be done!" replied St Thomas. (5380)

* * *

Outside, meanwhile, the knights, each of whom had arrived on his warhorse with all his armour on, had removed their surcoats and taken up their arms, girding on their steel swords. In no time at all, they were ready to carry out their evil deed. There were plenty of people around to report this to the archbishop. (5385)

"Go into the church, my lord," the monks said to him. "They're singing vespers now, and you should not have missed the service. These knights intend to get hold of you and slaughter you." "That won't frighten me," he replied, "as you will see. I shall wait here for whatever judgement God sees fit to pronounce on me."

Once armed, the four young men came to the hall doors. They could not, however, gain entry because the doors had been securely barred behind them earlier. They then started to batter the doors violently, for their intention was to seize the saint and hack him to pieces.

As they were unable to break down the doors by brute force, Robert de Broc, a very skilled operator when it came to dark deeds, said: "My lords, noble knights, follow me! I know another way of getting you in." Crossing in front of the kitchen, they came into the orchard.

A covered porch, giving directly onto the orchard, had been constructed over the door to the living quarters. It had been there a long time, and the stairs leading up to it needed repairing and had been dismantled. The carpenters had gone off to eat. The knights made their way to this porch.

It was by this route that Robert de Broc broke into the living quarters, and he got the knights to follow him up by using the carpenters' ladders. They brought with them the tools that the workmen were using to repair the stairs, hatchets and a two-edged axe, to break down the doors, should any be found to be locked.

When St Thomas's people heard them coming, they began to take to their heels like sheep before wolves, just like the apostles when they saw Pontius Pilate's men seize Jesus, who had come into the world to die establishing his Church.

Of all of his servants not a single one stayed behind, except a handful of his clerks, some of whom were very brave, Master Edward Grim and a number of monks – I do not know how many. They took hold of St Thomas, who was still sitting there waiting for the end of his days and death.

Since his return from exile over the Channel, several people told me that they had heard him say that he was more or less sure he would die within the year. And now there were only two days left before the end of the year, and the one before that, the day that was to see him die, was nearing its end.

He had said as much on Christmas Day in front of the many people who had come to listen to his sermon. "I have come here," he said, "to die among you." The day had now arrived when this was to come to pass. His death was that of a great martyr, as was his life. (5430)

At the end of his sermon he said, prophetically, to one of his clerks, Alexander of Wales – and many of his people heard it as well: "There has already been one martyr here in Canterbury, St Alphege, and if it please God, in our days you will have another." (5435)

The reason he waited where he was and refused to flee was not only because he felt safe there, but also because he was quite prepared for death. He believed that no one would have dared attack him inside the church, and as he had no intention of avoiding death, he stood waiting where he was. God, however, wanted him to fall in a more fitting place. (5440)

His people then began to take him into the church, but in fact they had to carry him there forcibly. You should have seen them: some pulling, others pushing. But to get there, they would have had to go through some locked doors as well as through the solid wall! (5445)

There was one particular room built on to the living quarters which provided a less public way through to the cloister, but at that time the door was shut and heavily bolted. The monks were greatly dismayed to find their way blocked on all sides. (5450)

Coming up to the door, one of the monks grasped the bolt in both hands, whereupon God performed a miracle: when the monk tried to release the bolt, it came off in his hand just as if it had been stuck on with a bit of glue. The monk opened the door and hurried everyone through. (5455)

They then took the archbishop through towards the church despite his reluctance, for it looked as if he would have preferred to stay to await death where he was. Some pulled him, others pushed him, and they rapidly reached the cloister. They had, however, to stop twice on the way through, (5460)

for as soon as the saint was able to touch the ground and plant both of his feet on the floor, he pushed everyone away from him and started to argue: "What do you think you're doing," he asked, "tugging at me like that and dragging me along? Let go of me!" They then took hold of him and carried him into the church. (5465)

17 Murder

The monks had only just got him inside the church when the knights, dressed in their chainmail and with swords in their hands, reached the cloister. They were accompanied by one Hugh, known as Mauclerc, one of Robert de Broc's clerks, an individual bursting with wickedness.

These four, poised to carry out their evil deed, were followed, though at a distance, by four more knights. Hugh went with the first group into the church, but the second group never went in. The murderous fiends met up with them again in the cloister when they came back out.

Some of the monks shut the church doors when they saw the four arriving. St Thomas, who was fully expecting them to enter, said: "Open the doors! I order you in the name of holy obedience. I wish to let these blind and ignorant people do what they want to do. As long as you stand guard at the doors, I will not take a step more.

"The house of God, our true Lord, ought not to be made into a castle, fortress or keep, and we clerics, his ministers and servants, should always be its defenders and use our bodies as shields against the evildoer."

He himself unbolted and opened the doors wide, pushing back the crowds that had gathered there to see what was going on. To the monks he said: "What are you afraid of?" "Just look at the armed knights!" they replied. "I will go to them," he said. "Oh no you won't!" they replied.

They got him to go as far as the steps up to the north aisle in the hope of bringing him under the protection of the holy relics. "My lords," he said, "let me be! You've no business being here. Let God see to this! Go up to the choir to sing your vespers!"

Satan's henchmen had by now come into the church, each one holding a drawn sword in his right hand and a hatchet in his left hand – the fourth had a two-edged axe. They were unable to see the holy archbishop because of a pillar that supported the vaulting.

Three of them went round one side of the pillar, shouting out for the man who had betrayed the king. Reginald fitz Urse, going round the other side, came across a monk and asked him where the archbishop was. Up spoke the saint: "Reginald," he said, "if it's me you're looking for, then you've found me, here."

St Thomas had not responded when he was called a traitor, but on hearing the word "archbishop" he stood still and took notice. He came down the steps towards Reginald. "Reginald," he said, "if it's me you're looking for, then you've found me, here." Reginald caught hold of him by the skirt of this cloak.

"Reginald," said the good priest, "I've done you many favours, so what are you looking for from me now, coming into a sacred church fully armed?" Reginald fitz Urse replied: "You'll know soon enough!" He pulled him towards him, giving him a severe shaking, then said: "You're a traitor to the king. Come over here!"

His intention was to drag him out of the sacred church. I am sure that being shoved around and tugged by Reginald annoyed Thomas a great deal. He gave Reginald such a push that he forced him back and snatched the skirt of his cloak from out of his hand.

"Get out of here, you evil man!" said the holy priest.* "I am no traitor, and should not be accused of being one!" After a moment's thought Reginald said: "Get out of here yourself!" "I will not," said the saint. "This is where you'll find me, and this is where you will carry out your evil crimes."

Thomas made his way towards the north transept. Here, he stopped next to a pillar, and placed his back up against it. The pillar had been constructed between two altars, the upper one dedicated to the Mother of God, the lower consecrated to St Benedict.

The king's demented servants, having driven and pushed him thus far, shouted out: "Absolve those who are under excommunication, and those you have had suspended and banned!" "I will do no more than I have already done," said Thomas. Whereupon all of them, speaking in unison, threatened to kill him.

Thomas replied: "Your threats do not frighten me. I am ready and fully prepared to suffer martyrdom. All I ask is that you let my people go and do not touch them. Do what you have to do to me, and me alone." Even when faced with death, the good priest did not forget his people.

This is exactly what Jesus had done when he went to pray on the Mount of Olives at nightfall, and when those who were looking for him began shouting: "Where is the Nazarene?" "You can find me here," Jesus said to them, "but let all my people go!"

The sons of Satan then began to manhandle Thomas, violently pulling and pushing him with the intention of hauling him onto William de Tracy's shoulders in order to get him out of the church, there to tie him up or kill him. They were unable, however, to pull him away from the pillar.

For the pillar to which he had anchored himself was the same as the one who suffered death on the cross to establish his Church, and no one could separate or remove him from it. But what was needed at present, to save God's people, was the death of a single man next to a church pillar. (5555)

The people whose duty it should have been to protect Holy Church were intent on overthrowing it and its members, and on demolishing the pillar and the head that it supported. The blood shed in this sinful crime needed to be washed clean by more blood; to be able to raise its head again, the Church needed the sacrifice of its chief's head. (5560)

But God was not willing for Thomas to be subjected to shameful treatment. He acted as he did in order to put these evil people to the test, to see whether they would dare behave with such brutality in a church. From here to the Orient there is no one so thoroughly bad that he would not recoil in horror on hearing about such a crime. (5565)

When the knights had attacked, Master Edward Grim had grabbed hold of Thomas, seizing him bodily round the shoulders. He clung on to him fearlessly, and the knights were unable to make him let go. Everyone else, clerks, monks and servants, had taken to their heels, (5570)

but Master Edward kept hold of him as the knights tried to pull him away. "What do you think you're doing?" he said. "Have you taken leave of your senses? Just look at where you are and at what feast it is we are celebrating. Laying a hand on your archbishop is a great sin." But neither the Christmas celebrations nor being in church was enough to stop them. (5575)

It was at this moment that St Thomas understood that his martyrdom was at hand. With hands joined in front of his face, he gave himself over to the Lord God, hurriedly commending himself, the cause of Holy Church and his own cause to the martyr St Denis, patron saint of sweet France, as well as to the patron saints of his own church. (5580)

William de Tracy was the first to step forward – not, however, in order to worship God! To avoid being weighed down, he had decided not to put his hauberk on. He started by shouting out for the person who had betrayed the king. It having proved impossible for them to get the saint out of the church, William proceeded to strike him a violent blow to the head with his sword, (5585)

knocking off his bonnet, cutting deeply into the top part of his scalp and severing it. The sword ended up on St Thomas's left shoulder, cutting through his cloak and the clothing beneath right into the skin. It almost sliced Master Edward Grim's arm completely in two. (5590)

It was this blow that caused Master Edward to loosen his grip. "Hit him! Hit him!" shouted William. Reginald fitz Urse was the next to strike him, but he did not succeed in knocking him to the floor. William de Tracy then struck him a further blow, this time literally sent his brains spilling out, and St Thomas fell. (5595)

How we know it was William de Tracy who wounded Master Edward is because, when the criminals returned to Saltwood that night and were boasting about the horrendous crime they had committed, William asserted that he was the one who had cut off John of Salisbury's right arm. (5600)

Not having any armour on, William had been the first of the four to follow Thomas, and he was easily recognizable from his face and his voice. He was wearing a green tunic under a double-coloured cloak. When he saw Reginald fitz Urse step back, he struck the saint twice on the head, as I said. (5605)

When Richard Brito saw that Thomas had been knocked to the ground and was lying stretched out on the flagstones, he aimed a blow at him that fell slightly to one side of the others, with the result that he broke his sharpened blade in two against the stone. On the spot where the martyr died, people kiss the very fragment that broke off. (5610)

During the whole of the time that these criminals were hitting and slashing at him, and battering him with as much force as they could muster, no moan, no groan, no shout even did Thomas utter. Nor did he lift a finger to protect himself or take a single step back, for he steadfastly placed all of his reliance on God. (5615)

And in the same way as Jesus was, for the sins of man, crucified by the Jews, his own sons, on Calvary where justice righted wrongs, so was this man made a martyr for his clergy by his own sons in a place where sins are taken away and washed clean. (5620)

Hugh de Morville, who had run ahead, was turning back the people who had gathered there. His fear was that the archbishop's body would be taken away. Perhaps he had come to realize what sort of position he was in and was trying in this way to disclaim responsibility for the crime. (5625)

When Herod's soldiers, children of Ishmael, killed Rachel's son Joseph in Jerusalem, they did not completely sever the top of his head. It remained attached to the skin and flesh of his forehead in such a way that you could have seen the brain totally exposed. (5630)

That man Hugh Mauclerc, who had come in after the others, placed his foot on St Thomas's neck and pressed it down. With his sword he then gouged the brains out of his head and onto the ground. He shouted to the others: "Let's be off! He won't be rising again from the dead!" (5635)

Anyone who saw the blood and brains fall to the floor and lie mingled on the flagstones might have called to mind roses and lilies, for he would have seen the red of the blood grow brighter still against the white of the brains, and the white of the brains shine whiter against the red.* (5640)

Then the slaves of wickedness left the scene and went back across the cloister, their swords still drawn and shouting out "king's men!" They were once knights, but now are the lowest of the low and objects of derision. From having been rich and powerful they are now degraded and wretched. (5645)

Oh you abject sinners, what have you done? You did not give a second thought to God or to the church you were in. Stories of your crime will follow your descendants for as long as this world lasts. The king has his eyes closed, the same one who has fine men put to death for the sake of a few game animals.* God is above in heaven while the kingdom below loses its way. (5650)

It was for the Church of the north and in the north transept, with his face turned to the north, that St Thomas suffered death. So mighty and so powerful has God made him through his death that all Christians seek security and consolation in him. It is he who brings to a safe haven those in danger of shipwreck. (5655)

18 Aftermath

While these sons of the Devil were committing this horrendous sacrilege within the sacred church, Robert de Broc, along with several others, had stayed behind in the living quarters to plunder the rooms and break open the coffers. They stole clothes and plate, silver and pure gold, (5660)

they stole Thomas's fine table knife, worth as much as a whole city, and his ring set with a sapphire of outstanding quality – no one ever saw a finer one, and Thomas would not have sold it at any price. They also stole a very valuable hanging of bright purple samite, as well as his books and all his writings, (5665)

and the gold chalice he used for mass – this they repeatedly crushed and broke to pieces on the table –, vestments and clothing, and anything they could lay their hands on: spoons, drinking cups, silver and fine gold goblets, and at least sixty pounds in newly minted silver coin, (5670) and all his jewels which he kept a very close eye on and showed only to a few selected people, charters, privileges – all this they had carried off, as well as many other objects which I cannot give details of, and which none of his men could list for me. (5675)

They looted St Thomas's apartments and rooms, taking every single thing and leaving nothing behind. They took away with them all of St Thomas's horses. Whenever they could find them, they arrested his people and his clerks, confiscated their belongings and threw them into prison. (5680)

There had never before been such brutality in any land where peace reigned and law and order should have prevailed – all the more in a country where the king pardons no one, for in the whole world, near or far, there is no harsher justice than what he metes out. But I will say no more. (5685)

His justice is exceedingly harsh even when dumb animals are at issue, for he has many a fine man sentenced or put to death. But God, who punishes wrongdoing when he sees fit, was not willing to let revenge be taken for a holy martyr killed in a sacred church. (5690)

So profaned and violated was the sacred church that no mass, matins or vespers were sung in it, no service was celebrated and no candle lit. The doors were shut, and the people denied access. For a whole year the sacred church was in solitary confinement, (5695)

a whole year, that is, less ten days, for it was on the fifth day after Christmas that its imprisonment began, and on the fifth day before Christmas that it got its freedom back. Ten days were saved, as was the tithe that people owed the Church,* and the battle between the clerics and the king was brought to a close. (5700)

For the sake of the tonsured clergy, the good tonsured cleric offered his tonsured crown, unarmed, to the knights' arms. The battle that he in his turn fought when he made his crown a shield against the sword was a purely spiritual one, and never did he seek to avoid the blows he received. (5705)

But if he had followed the advice of the monks, he could easily have avoided death on that occasion, for there are innumerable nooks and crannies in that church where he could have hidden. He suffered death of his own free will in God's sacred house, and for this God has granted him high honour in this world. (5710)

Never before in the world had such a foul deed been perpetrated, and never one which turned out to be of so much benefit to the world. Yet however this may be, the cost of it to the world will still be very great. Sooner or later God's anger will be ready to strike, for vengeance in this case is God's and God's alone. (5715)

But God's vengeance does not come immediately; it first requires that amends be made for the guilt incurred. God has no wish or desire to see the soul damned, and the time when crime is discovered and punished within the same week has yet to be seen. (5720)

Normandy is the first victim to suffer damage, for it was here that the saint's death was first plotted, and it was the king, Normandy's legal guardian, who instigated it. He believed that he could close the door on his breach with Thomas, but instead it has opened the way to God's anger. (5725)

But God, I am certain, has turned aside the anger with which he was prepared to strike the kingdom and people of England because King Henry has fully acknowledged his guilt, made amends personally for the crime, and given Holy Church all its liberties back. (5730)

Anyone who saw Thomas's clerks and his men in full flight, his kinsmen and relations going into hiding, changing their good clothes and putting on shabby ones, could have shuddered with pity for them, for each and every one was convinced they were going to die. (5735)

Then Satan's sons went off happy and content, rejoicing at the great wrong they had committed. May God grant them the power to make amends for the crime! Yet never will they be loved and cherished anywhere except by those who took part in the crime with them. (5740)

19 Burial

Everyone, young and old, quaked with fear as news spread that there was a new holy martyr lying dead on the floor of the church. The monks gathered his blood and brains, placing them at his head in jars, which they positioned on the outside of the tomb. (5745)

His holy body was carried up and placed before the high altar, and there the monks and other people kept vigil over it the whole night. The blood that dripped down from the corpse was collected. The next day a nephew of Ranulf de Broc, by the name of Robert, arrived in Canterbury. (5750)

He was well known as the king's usher. None of the gates or doors was kept closed when he entered, because as the king's man people were frightened and afraid of him. He seized two of St Thomas's most valued horses, and confiscated all of those belonging to the clerks. (5755)

St Thomas's clerks and all of his other people had taken refuge in the monastery with their horses and other belongings. But to no avail: de Broc's men simply seized everything in sight that they took a fancy to, even Thomas's clerks and his men, and let nothing out of their clutches. (5760)

"The country," said Robert, "is well rid of the traitor who wanted to deprive his lord of his crown. He should have been treated really shamefully and thrown into a rubbish dump or some even more stinking place." There spoke someone with no fear of God for the moment. (5765)

"It is a very good thing," he said, "that this criminal has been killed. Such a good deed has never before been undertaken. If I had been there and seen St Peter behaving as badly as that towards the king, by St Denis I would have plunged my drawn sword right into his brain." (5770)

He then ordered the monks to take the body and to hide it away so that nobody, fair or dark, would see it. Otherwise he would have it dragged ignominiously out by horses, or irretrievably dismembered or thrown to the dogs and pigs into a rubbish dump. (5775)

Terrified by what they heard, the monks hid the body and buried it in the crypt. But before doing so, they closely examined the clothing and the body. They found there was little fat or flesh on him, and that he was dressed heavily in the saintliest of clothes. (5780)

Over his other clothes he wore a cloak of black clerical material which did up with a black fastener, and which was lined with a white lamb's fleece without edging. Under this he wore a beautifully made and finely woven white surplice, and under this a white lambskin coat. What he did not wear was either miniver or squirrel fur, samite or sandal. (5785)

To all appearances, this was the attire of a regular canon. Under this he wore two short but ample gowns, both made of lambskin. These they removed by cutting them off him with knives. I myself saw them some time later, and knew therefore who had been given them. (5790)

He had always felt very cold in his upper body and the stomach region, and was afflicted by this frequent pain of his in the side. This is why he always dressed warmly, in order not to fall ill from catching cold and to be able to get warm again quickly after scourging. (5795)

Under all this the good archbishop wore a woollen shirt and a monk's cowl, the sleeves and lower parts of which he had had shortened, for he did not want to make a display of his way of life to the outside world. When the monks saw this, they cried out: "Look! He's a proper monk. You can see for yourselves!" (5800)

He wore a hair-shirt next to his skin, arranged in such a way as to stay hidden from view. Against his bare flesh his underpants were also of hair, and over these he had a second pair, made of costly white linen, because he did not want the outside world to know how he really lived. (5805)

This goat-hair underwear was swarming, inside and out, with minute fleas and lice, masses of them all over in large patches, so voraciously attacking his flesh that it was nothing short of a miracle that he was able to tolerate such punishment. (5810)

The martyrdom he suffered when he was alive was much more painful than when he was killed in the church. Whereas in the church he died immediately and was instantaneously transported into the joy of everlasting life, all those vermin to which he was prey tormented him day and night over a number of years. (5815)

The monks were both very sad and very happy for him, sad at seeing him slaughtered but at the same time happy at learning what sort of life he had led. Had they inspected the whole of his naked body, they would have found it torn to shreds by scourging, (5820)

for on the very same day that he was cut down, St Thomas had undergone scourging three times. He was buried, then, with great honour in the crypt for fear that he might have been found by de Broc's people. Now, however, it is St Thomas who is an object of awe and honoured throughout the whole world. (5825)

His first martyrdom was an expiation for the sins he had committed in his past life as a layman: in reparation for the life of luxury that he had led he underwent great suffering. His second martyrdom was by way of sanctification. The first was the means by which he finally reached the second. (5830)

* * *

The de Brocs thereafter took possession of the archbishopric – an unsavoury gang of archbishops for the king to have installed! They set up laws in their own image, forcing the priests to sing mass despite it being formally forbidden. Holy Church had completely gone to rack and ruin. (5835)

Ranulf de Broc was head of the archbishopric. Whatever he did and whatever he undid got everyone's approval. He sent all the money and income to the king. All that money would never be put to good use: it was ill-gotten gains obtained by criminal means. (5840)

When this money is all spent and used up, wasted on wars and dishonest people – a case of badly come by, badly spent – the dice will have turned in a trice from double sixes to double ones. (5845)

No one can count on money they have hoarded. You cannot postpone the final result by hiring Brabant mercenaries, still less Flemings, English, or all the Frenchmen in France, since God holds the scales of justice on his little finger and allows our misdeeds to go unpunished for just as long as he pleases. (5850)

The same thing will happen to de Broc's people as happened to the Jews. They contrived to get sweet Jesus killed for fear of losing their lands and their holy places, and are now all in exile without fiefs or inheritance. The de Brocs' fate will be much worse, and their enemies worse even than that by far. (5855)

* * *

The holy martyr whose story you have been hearing was born before Christmas on St Thomas's night, 21st of December, while vespers were being sung, and after vespers were finished he was baptized and received the name Thomas after St Thomas the Apostle. It was while vespers were being sung that Thomas was borne up to the highest heaven. (5860)

His namesake was killed and buried in the East at a time when Holy Church was expanding. St Thomas, as a defender of the West, was killed in the north for the sake of his Church which was in serious decline. What they shared also, in equal measures, was Christmas and Jerusalem. (5865)

Both of them were killed for the Church on earth, and through their death they both reached the kingdom of heaven. Both devoted all their five senses to the service of God, and they both successfully climbed the five steps that lead to the Lord. Between them they have become the guardians of either side of the whole world. (5870)

The holy man whose story I am telling you was born on a Tuesday.* When he fled from Northampton it was in fact a Tuesday also, and a Tuesday as well when he crossed the Channel. It was again the same day of the week when he returned from exile, and it was on a Tuesday that he suffered martyrdom. (5875)

It is because this new martyr has been given to us so recently that Guernes, the clerk born in Pont-Sainte-Maxence, wishes to let you know the actual date of the martyrdom, namely one thousand one hundred and seventy years since Jesus was born of the Virgin Mary. (5880)

St Thomas has found great favour with God. This is clear to absolutely everyone, and there is no point in trying to find people who dispute this. Since the world began, it has never been known for God to show such great love for any man who has died. Day and night, God performs great miracles for him. (5885)

God is here amongst us on earth for love of his martyr. He brings the dead back to life, gives speech to the dumb, hearing to the deaf, makes the lame healthy again and those suffering from gout and fevers, cures lepers and those with the dropsy, makes the blind see again and the mentally ill recover their senses. (5890)

Many a king comes to seek him in true pilgrimage, princes, magnates, dukes and their retinues, visitors from foreign countries speaking countless different languages, prelates, monks, recluses, many coming all the way on foot, and taking phials back with them as souvenirs of their pilgrimage. (5895)

Pilgrims to Jerusalem bring back palm crosses, those to Rocamadour lead figures of the Virgin, and from Compostela shells cast in lead. And now God has granted to St Thomas a phial that is cherished and honoured throughout the world. (5900)

Mixed with the water within the phials, God has the martyr's blood taken all over the world to cure the sick in the same way as God has his own blood, represented by wine and water, drunk all over the world to save souls. The honour due to the saint is doubled by the cures the phials bring about and by what they stand for. (5905)

20 Penitence

But what is even more extraordinary is that we can see and hear reports of people who used to hate St Thomas like poison becoming his liege vassals in order to obtain forgiveness – the same people who made mischief and soured his relations with King Henry, and plotted and brought about his death. (5910)

Even the king of England, his sworn enemy, who for six years and more had him exiled from his country, and whose spiteful anger caused his men to kill St Thomas, even Henry came in great humility, in the fourth year after the murder, to visit his shrine in order to beg forgiveness for all the wrongs he had done. (5915)

In the fourth year following the martyr's passion, during the seventh month, July, on the twelfth day, a Friday, the king arrived to make amends to the martyr. He really came, however, to the archbishop because he was in dire need of help. (5920)

Near Canterbury there is a lepers' hospital housing many sick, diseased and rejected people. It is about a league from the main church where the holy body lies of the spiritual physician who has restored many a sufferer to health and happiness. (5925)

It was here at Harbledown that the king dismounted. He went into the church and prayed, asking God's forgiveness for all the wrongs that he had done. For love of St Thomas he granted this poverty-stricken house the gift of an income of twenty marks. (5930)

Two or so leagues from there is another hospital housing the poor, and here the king also did what was expected of him by granting this house an annual income of one hundred shillings. God's blessing on him! In this place, God changed him from what he had been previously, and he will yet improve him still further. (5935)

He continued, still on foot, as far as St Dunstan's, the first church that he encountered inside Canterbury. He went in with the prelates who had congregated there, and cleansed his spirit by confession and punished his flesh by scourging. (5940)

He then sent the prior to the monastery, asking him to assemble the monks. He declared himself ready and willing to agree to anything that they might deem appropriate, amongst themselves, for him to do in order to make amends to the martyr. (5945)

Then he immediately had his shoes removed and, with bare feet to mortify the flesh, and wearing nothing but his underwear and a rain cape, he walked up to the town on the stony pathway that he usually rode along. He wished to make peace with God by doing austere penance. (5950)

The usual custom was to welcome kings by having all the bells rung, by forming a procession to go and greet them, and then by leading them into the church with great honour. But this time the king wanted none of such pomp, for his intention was to enter not as a king but as a beggar. (5955)

He approached the door with great humility, fell to his knees and stayed a long time weeping and praying. He entered the church and went up to the scene of the martyrdom, where he said the confession prayer and kissed the marble floor. He then went to the tomb and made his peace with the martyr.

The king spent a long time in prayer, lying prostrated in supplication and shedding tears, with contrite heart and profound devotion, after which the bishop of London preached his sermon in the form of a confession on his own behalf and on that of the king.

"My lords," said the bishop, "listen to me! You see before you our lord the king. He has come to the martyr in all good faith and love. He wishes me, on his authority, to repeat here the full confession which I and several others have already heard him make in private.

"He declares before God and the martyr that he did not have St Thomas killed or murdered, nor did he give orders for him to be beaten or slaughtered. However, he does freely admit to you that he uttered the words that were the reason for the killing and the cause of the murder being carried out.

"He has come to the martyr because, as he himself acknowledges, Thomas was killed because of him. He is the guilty party and the plaintiff, he admits the wrong he has done and confesses his sin. He begs the saint's pity for the wrongs he has done, and he submits entirely to the judgement of you all for the amends he has to make.

"All their holdings he restores to this sacred church, to the archbishop and to the whole monastery likewise, with all the liberties and dignity it enjoyed previously and that any church anywhere in Christendom should properly have.

"The king now asks you all, in the name of God, to pray to the true martyr here among us that he forgive him all the spite and the anger he showed towards him, for he recognizes his crime and acknowledges his guilt, and has come here to make amends.

"And so that he may, through your prayers and petitions and through his own sincere repentance and the amends he makes, earn the love of this most precious of saints, he is granting to this house land with an income of ten pounds a year in addition to the thirty pounds' income he has already given you."

When the bishop had finished his address, King Henry confirmed everything that he had said. The monks forgave him all the resentment they felt against him and agreed to all his other requests. On behalf of the whole monastery, the prior gave him the kiss of peace.

So genuine was King Henry's humility that everyone present was moved to tears. He himself removed his cape in front of the assembled monks, and introducing his head and shoulders into one of the openings of the tomb, offered up his back. (6005)

Since he was not willing to remove his green coat, however, I am not able to say whether he was actually wearing a hair-shirt or deliberately keeping one hidden. He then allowed himself to be scourged, first by the prelates and afterwards by more than eighty monks. You should have seen them: almost all were weeping with emotion! (6010)

The bishop of London, birch in hand, looked first at the saint and then at the king. "St Thomas, true martyr," he said, "hear what I have to say! If you have found such favour with God as people say, and as I firmly believe you have, have mercy on this sinner whom I see before me." (6015)

The ever faithful and loving saint heard him. This was the man who had so often done him harm in the past and was now praying to him on both his own behalf and on someone else's. The martyr saw sincere repentance in both his heart and the king's. Both were redeemed. (6020)

To seal their reconciliation, the king gave St Thomas income to the value of some forty pounds per year in perpetuity and a properly weighed sum of gold to make a shrine for him. But what he attached so much more value to than Anjou, England or France was true repentance. (6025)

The bishop of London struck the king five times, corresponding to the five senses by which Henry had offended God. The bishop of Rochester beat him next, followed by Walter abbot of Boxley who was also present. He then received three strokes from each of the monks. (6030)

When King Henry had finished being beaten and his punishment was over, and when he had been reconciled with God by virtue of the amends he had made, he withdrew his head from the tomb and stood upright. Then, with his feet still dirty, he sat straight down on the ground, without any carpet or cushion, beside a pillar. (6035)

He spent the whole night praying and singing psalms. He forswore his hostility to St Thomas's men. He begged St Thomas's sister, abbess Mary of Barking, to have pity on him, and in compensation gave her a mill, from which she receives an annual income of at least ten marks. (6040)

He stayed awake the whole night praying and never once got up to relieve himself until after matins. Then, getting to his feet, he went to pray at all of the church's altars. He had come to the martyr having eaten and drunk nothing, and he continued fasting. (6045)

At daybreak he had mass sung. He then had his shoes put back on, even though his feet were still covered in mud. He would never allow anyone to wash his feet. It is impossible to imagine a more penitent prince than he was, except that he had to delay coming on his pilgrimage for far too long.

Periods of forty days are needed to wean oneself off sin, but the king was still delaying even after forty months. Had he waited a further forty weeks, and then forty days more on top of that, I can assure you that God would have taken vengeance on him.

And when the forty months had passed, and the forty weeks had started, trouble broke out all over England. If St Thomas had not been able to turn God's gaze away from this, his anger would have erupted in one or other of these three periods.

God has now set aside his anger against the king. On the same day that Henry made amends, Philippe count of Flanders, who had been intending to completely destroy England, decided against crossing the Channel with his army. And the very next day William the Lion, king of Scotland, was captured.

Normandy was on the point of being overthrown and destroyed, and the French army had reached Rouen. The whole of England was heading for disaster. They had turned their backs on heaven and clutched at the clouds. But God in his mercy did not close his eyes to the suffering people.

They did not want to be ruled by such a powerful king, preferring to have a mere suckling amongst them whom they could twist around their little finger like a glove.* By their loyalty to him they had a malevolent influence, and they used the child as a cover for their own treachery.

The child was incapable of governing the kingdom. No one could be a more reliable guardian of it than his father. For any right-minded person, father and son are one. Those who sought to separate son from father wanted to deprive each one of his hereditary rights.

* * *

The advice I now give the king is to restore the rights and liberties of Holy Church, as he had promised, cherish his noblemen, be moderate in justice, not to avenge a few game animals by taking a human life, to grant each individual their rights, to shun covetousness.

I am, however, well aware of the king's character and how his mind works. The people he has to rule over are good-for-nothings.* The prospect of an easy killing spurs them into action: put the whole of the river bank at their disposal and they will empty the moor of all its pigs and sheep. (6090)

If the king were not feared by his Normans, English, Angevins, Bretons, Welsh, Scots and Poitevins, they would lose no time in bringing the whole kingdom down to the poverty line. Whatever impression he might make, the king will manage to die a good death. I once heard Master Feramin tell of a vision that he had had. (6095)

Before St Thomas was killed in the sacred church, Feramin saw a great procession passing next to the bell tower. St Thomas was riding on the left-hand side, and some way off there was a clerk whom he did not recognize. Opposite was the king astride a huge warhorse. (6100)

The person leading the procession held the cross up high, and from it hung a golden crown. There came a voice from on high, shouting that whoever should place jewels and shining gold on the cross would have a golden crown in heaven for ever and ever. (6105)

The voice made itself clearly heard, and St Thomas listened to it. If only, he thought, he could reach the cross in some way or other, for he had a burning desire to have a heavenly crown. He was riding a tall horse, so he rode up to the cross and placed a large number of jewels and a lot of refined gold on it. (6110)

Some time after, it occurred to the king that it would be very shameful for him not to approach the cross. He was also riding a tall horse, so he rode up to the cross and placed a large number of pure jewels and a lot of tried and tested gold on it. He did not, however, put as much as the good priest had. (6115)

Then the clerk came along, trying to work out how he might reach the cross. He managed to ride up to it, and placed a large number of jewels and a lot of shining gold on it. It was a most suitable offering, but he did not put as much as either of the other two who had made their offerings before him. (6120)

While the procession continues, the word goes downhill. Most people take things at a walking pace, for few have their sights set on higher things. May St Thomas the martyr provide us with real help! I can tell you for certain that the day will yet come when the king puts worldly honours behind him for the sake of God. (6125)

No one knows what he has set his heart on, but his kingdom is unstable, and this worries him, as do his children, who are poorly endowed with common sense. Merlin's prophecies frightened him a great deal, and the misguided people who interpret them have done little to turn him against them.

The ill-advised scheme that hampered him so much and almost brought about his downfall did in fact originate in Brittany. Let him see now how the female eagle had laid gold there, having already built her nest more than three times and three. The third nest in England made her heart rejoice,*

and if it please God, she will also rejoice for the others as well as for this one. But there is no need for the king to fear this eagle any more. She will never make her nest somewhere else, since she has lost her feathers and will never hatch anything again. Let him keep his eye on the country, however. It is badly in need of it!

The king should know as well – and I am telling him the absolute truth – that his sons will be honourable, strong and brave. The more they stand by each other, the more powerful they will be. English, Poitevins and Normans will be in great fear of them. Some who are laughing now will end up weeping.

As long as father and son continue to love each other, as long as both love their mother and the king's daughter-in-law,* as long as the children stay as close as brothers should, as long as the king reigns over them, as emperor and as king, then anyone who meddles with the sauce will find it tastes very bitter.

I pray to God, and to the martyr whom I have long served, that he bring peace to the kingdom, sustain the affection between father, son, daughter-in-law and wife, and grant them happiness and long life without any change in sovereignty. And may God encourage them to look favourably on me!

Epilogue

Guernes, the clerk from Pont-Sainte-Maxence, here brings his discourse on St Thomas the martyr and his passion to a close. This is a poem that he has recited many a time at the saint's tomb. Not a single word of what he has written deviates from the truth. May God in his mercy grant him true forgiveness for his sins!

Never has such a good narrative been composed in the French vernacular. It was written and revised at Canterbury. Not a single word of what has been written departs from the truth. Its verse form is five-line stanzas linked by a single rhyme, and my language is good because I am a native of the province of Ile-de-France. (6165)

I first began this work during the year after the saint's murder in his own church, and I have worked extremely hard at it. I learnt the truth from those closest to St Thomas, and in order to eliminate error, I have frequently deleted material that I had already written. I completed it in the course of the fourth year.* (6170)

Everyone who hears this Life should know that what they will hear is the pure truth from beginning to end. And everyone who has written about the saint, whether in French or in Latin, and has not followed the same path as I have, should know that where they differ from me, they are writing untruths. (6175)

Let us now pray to Jesus Christ, son of holy Mary, to grant us his help for the love of St Thomas so that in this mortal life we do not fall into want, and that we so succeed in avoiding the frivolities of this world that, when we die, we are admitted into his company. Amen. (6180)

Here ends the Life of St Thomas the martyr.

Postscript*

The abbess Mary of Barking, St Thomas's sister, to her honour and in honour of the saint, gave me a saddle-horse – even the spurs were thrown in – and some clothing. My luck had certainly not run out when I turned up at her convent. She did the right thing as well, because I will repay her by singing her praises everywhere and to everyone, high or low. (5) No one could find a more benevolent lady anywhere between here and Patras. And the ladies of the convent saw to it that I was well fed, each giving her gifts freely. May God, now and always, provide them with a plentiful supply of bread, wine, meat and fish, and when in time their bodies are lifeless and spent, may God grant their souls true forgiveness! From now on I shall never again bewail my lot, for the lord I have served is a most benevolent one. (10) In return for the tiredness I have frequently felt putting his suffering and death into verse, he repays me generously – I tell you this in all seriousness – by finding me multiple rewards: gold, silver and clothes to fill my bags, horses and other goods and chattels. If anyone asks me: "Guernes, where are you going to?" I reply that I could go anywhere in the wide world. And I can even find only praiseworthy things to say about Judas – at least once he begins his confession. (15)

Odo, the good prior of Holy Trinity Canterbury, and the monastery's monks – may God look favourably upon them! – have been of great assistance to me, frequently giving me what was properly theirs and providing me with board and lodging over a number of years. Wherever my travels take me, however far and wide I roam, I shall always come back to see them, so exceptional is their goodness, for nowhere in Christendom have I ever seen kinder people. (22)

Appendix

Guernes' first draft from ca. 1171–72 survives only as a fragment of 80 lines: London, Society of Antiquaries 716, fols. 5–6v. See Introduction, pp. 6–7. See also Ian Short, "An Early Draft of Guernes' *Vie de saint Thomas Becket*," *Medium Ævum* 46 (1977): 20–34.

... they did not inform the king of this, and that was very naïve of them, for if they had talked to him about it, they would not have proceeded. But the evil Devil so enticed them that they finally reached the Channel. Taking advantage of a favourable wind, they sailed across without mishap and landed at Dogs' Port.

When the king heard that they had left court, he sent after them to have them turned back. His fear was that they might have planned some great act of madness, for he would not, for all the gold in his kingdom, have wanted them to behave as they did.

And when he heard it reported that they had killed the archbishop, he was tormented with grief and sorrow, filled with shame and anger, sad and downcast. He went into his chamber and did not emerge for fully eight days. He firmly rejected food and drink.

This is how he gave vent to his grief: once he had heard news of the holy man's death, he refused to speak to anyone. His own plan had been to put him in prison. No one, however, can avert anything that God has willed. It is clear to us now what a worthy person Thomas was to die as he did.

Just look at the great betrayal these four madmen committed once they had landed! They caused blame and reproach to be heaped on the king. They assembled a large number of knights, maintaining that they were acting on the king's orders.

No one dared argue with the four, for they were well known as being the king's most favoured young knights. They sent for the knights of the neighbourhood, not one of whom refused to come, so afraid were they of the king.

They came directly to Canterbury just as people had finished eating. It was the fifth day of Christmas, the day after the feast of the Holy Innocents, whom

Herod in his great cruelty had beheaded in the belief that he could murder the Godhead by murdering all the children. (35)

So, beside themselves with anger, the four lords rode into the archbishop's courtyard and dismounted directly in front of the great hall. By this time the archbishop, having finished his meal, was sitting in his private apartment with his inner circle of clerics ... (39)

* * *

... as recently as Christmas Day in front of all the people when he reached the end of his sermon: "There has already been one martyr here in Canterbury, St Alphege, and if it please God, in our days you will have another." (43)

The reason he waited there and refused to flee was not only because he felt safe there but also because he was quite prepared for death. He believed that no one would have dared attack him inside the church. The monks then converged on him from all sides and took hold of him. "By God," they said, "in that case you really have to come with us!" (48)

This is how they began to lead him away, whether he wanted to go or not. But it was not possible for them to go through the orchard. They were, nevertheless, close enough to the knights to see them pass by outside. They did not dare open the doors of the hall, for they saw that the courtyard was full of knights. (53)

There was one particular room built on to the living quarters which provided a less public way through to the cloister, but the door had long been shut off and heavily bolted. The monks were greatly dismayed to find their way blocked on all sides. (58)

Coming up to the door of the room, one of the monks grasped the bolt in both hands, whereupon God performed a miracle: when the monk tried to release the bolt, it came off in his hand just as if it had been stuck on with a bit of glue. The monk opened the door, but could not prevent himself shouting out: (63)

"Take him through!" he told them. Whereupon they led him off, forcibly picking him up, despite his reluctance, and carrying him. His foot never touched the floor or the step until they came running into the cloister. They had, however, to stop twice on the way, (68)

for as soon as the saint was able to touch the ground and plant both of his feet on the floor, he pushed everyone away from him and started to argue: "What do you think you're doing," he asked, "tugging at me like that and dragging me along? Let go of me!" They then took hold of him and carried him into the church. (73)

The monks had only just got him inside the church when the knights, dressed in their chainmail and with swords in their hands, reached the cloister. They were accompanied by one Hugh, known as Mauclerc, one of Robert de Broc's clerks, an individual bursting with iniquity. (78)

He was subdeacon, and Thomas had ordained him. He was a repulsive person and terrifying, a lover of everything wicked ... (80)

Notes

1 In common with many medieval clerics, Guernes was particularly fond of proverbs and edifying maxims. The 'truth' of the pseudo-popular dictum of paroemiological discourse is predicated on an unarticulated authority that is supposedly both timeless and universal; see Elisabeth Schulze-Busacker, *Proverbes et expressions proverbiales dans la littérature narrative du moyen âge français* (Paris: Champion, 1985), pp. 15–20. A list of the proverbs used by Guernes can be found in Thomas's edition, vol. 2, pp. 375–79.

15 Although Becket's cult had begun almost immediately after his death, and although John of Salisbury was already treating him as a saint in 1171, his official canonization dates from 21 February 1173.

38 See below lines 1106 ff. for the controversy surrounding secular and ecclesiastical justice.

118 Holy Trinity, officially known as Christ Church Cathedral Priory, was a Benedictine abbey of which the archbishop was abbot and the church was Canterbury Cathedral. The other major abbey of medieval Canterbury, and an earlier foundation, was St Augustine's.

146 The surviving fragment of Guernes' first draft (see our Appendix) shows that he was already using the Latin lives of William of Canterbury and Edward Grim. In his second version this written source material was revised and supplemented by first-hand oral testimony gathered at Canterbury and Barking.

168 Guernes is here using the term *barun* to mean 'worthy man.' Both Becket's parents were Norman immigrants, respectable citizens of London but modest merchants whose status fell far short of the nobility. His father was sheriff of London sometime in the 1130s. Becket himself was born in Cheapside, on the site of the present Mercers' Hall, probably in 1120 or thereabouts. To his contemporaries Becket was known simply as Thomas, Thomas of London, or Archbishop Thomas. When William fitz Stephen describes the murderers entering Canterbury Cathedral shouting "Where is Thomas Beketh, traitor to the king?" the use of the name, in addition to

the absence of any title, were clearly designed to show the knights' contempt for someone of such humble (that is, non-aristocratic) birth. Becket talks about his family origins at lines 3411–15 below.

175 "He who believes in me ... 'out of his heart shall flow rivers of living water'" (John 7:38). A list of Guernes' numerous biblical references will be found on pp. 369–73 of the second volume of Thomas's edition.

258 Clerk Hatchet-Man might be a modern equivalent.

303 Rosamund Clifford was the best known of Henry II's mistresses, but he had several others whose names have survived. Avice of Stafford does not usually figure amongst them. There are records of Henry having at least four illegitimate children, but adding contemporary rumour more than doubles that figure. Ranulf de Broc, whom Guernes sees as one of Becket's bitterest enemies, was King Henry's official whore master ("marscallus custodiendi meretrices de curia domini regis"). Nicholas Vincent, "The Court of Henry II," in *Henry II: New Interpretations*, ed. Christopher Harper-Bill and Nicholas Vincent (Woodbridge, 2007), pp. 278–334, note 2.

478 Guernes derides the intervention of Gilbert Foliot, one of Becket's most implacable critics, by using the rare verb *grenoner*, based on *grenons* 'whiskers,' and meaning 'to mumble into one's beard.'

486 Henry of Blois was apparently well qualified to expatiate on the conflicting demands of the secular and religious worlds; Henry of Huntingdon described him as "a new kind of monster, part pure and part corrupt, part monk and part knight." *Historia Anglorum*, ed. Diana Greenway (Oxford, 1996), pp. 608–10.

493–504 These second thoughts attributed by Guernes to Henry are not corroborated in any other source.

507 We are here in June 1162, when Henry's son was only seven years old (and already married). He was not to be crowned as the Young King until June 1170.

529 Becket was ordained priest on June 2nd, 1162, the day before his consecration as archbishop. In order to make sense, Walberg's text needs to be emended in this line, as it does also below at lines 580, 649, 1140, 1325, 1576, 2907, 3370–75, 3393–94, 3479, 4926. For further details see vol. 2 of Jacques Thomas's edition of the text.

578 One manuscript talks of the prior of Alnwick. The priors of both Kenilworth and Alnwick in 1162 happened to be called Richard.

591–95 Archbishop Stigand was deposed for political motives by the Conqueror in 1070. Ælfsige, consecrated archbishop of Canterbury in 951, died on his journey to Rome to fetch his pallium in 959.

707 Saracen was the conventional literary (epic) term for the infidel, more specifically Muslims.

755 The hide was a unit of fiscal assessment rather than an actual land measurement. Originally it was as much arable land as could be cultivated by one plough in one year (hence its synonym 'carucate'), the modern equivalent of which would be about 50 hectares or 120 acres.

811 According to Grim, the judges ordered Philip "to stand naked before the sheriff [Simon fitz Peter], just as a layman might, and to offer him arms for the injury he had done him." Grim's 'naked' and Guernes' 'undressed' presumably mean that Philip was not to wear clerical clothing.

830 That is, as long as their observing the customs did not in any way involve their infringing canon law, or prejudice their own clerical status, and more generally the clergy and the Church. See also line 4127 below.

863 Two manuscripts have Gloucester, which seems more likely.

1022 A chirograph (or indenture) was a parchment sheet on which the text of an agreement was copied out in duplicate and then cut in half so that each party could retain a copy.

1120 Justice by mutilation, primarily blinding and castration, was a standard feature of the criminal law of 12th-century Britain.

1187 Literally: "They have given the horn into the sinner's hand," a reference to 1 Maccabees 2:48.

1231–35 The first reference is to the Biblical sorcerer Simon Magus, who gave his name to simony, the buying and selling of appointments in the Church. If the bishops are simonists in Guernes' eyes, Henry is presumably the new Nero. In the second allusion Rome must represent the Church in England. Thereafter Moses is Becket, the absent Aaron his silent episcopal brethren, and the Pharaoh is Henry.

1248 The medieval fool's tonsure took the form of his head being shaved in the shape of a cross.

1282 The Latin fables of Avianus, who is thought to have written in the fifth century, were widely used as a medieval schoolbook. The reference here is to Fable 30: *De apro et coco*.

1363 Adam of Charing, who seems to have acted as spokesman for the crew, was perhaps their skipper. He was fined 100 marks by the king, and threatened with excommunication by Becket.

1440 £300, a vast sum, would approximate to something in the region of £200,000 in today's money.

1455 Tropes were short sung embellishments to the mass. A troper was, therefore, an unsuitable substitute for holy writ in oath-taking.

1460 John, King Henry's hereditary marshal, had several sons, the most celebrated of whom was William Marshal, subsequently regent to Henry III.

1568 The fact that all five examples of *empire* in Guernes' poem occur at the rhyme lessens the likelihood that the term is being used in any specifically geo-political sense to designate what modern historians refer to as the Angevin Empire. Other occurrences are at lines 303, 4299, 4499, 4847. At line 6149 Henry is referred to as emperor, but again the word is at the rhyme.

1596 *Humblement*, which can also connote friendliness in Medieval French, is used by Guernes here to describe Thomas's measured and respectful reply under provocation. It reappears in similar contexts at lines 2796 and 4845. Becket replies with composure (*dulcement*) when provoked at line 4911. At line 1390, Guernes had used *humilité* to describe Becket's deliberate (and uncharacteristic) avoidance of public ostentation.

1636 Literally: "... is no game for children" (= child's play).

1724 "in the word of truth," quoted from the Latin Vulgate (2 Corinthians 6:7).

1746–59 Narrative repetition of this sort (there is another example at lines 1806–20 below, and lines 1966–70 repeat 1946–50) is a well-attested literary technique in medieval epic poetry. It need not be attributed, as it has been, to scribal incompetence or to lack of adequate revision by the author.

1890 Becket refuses to acknowledge Henry as his feudal overlord, since the lands he holds, granted in perpetuity, are free of all feudal obligations.

1934 See note to line 4953 below.

1972 Nones, the fourth of the canonical hours, was celebrated at the ninth hour after sunrise, that is early or mid-afternoon depending on the season. Tierce, at line 2041, approximates to nine o'clock in the morning. Vespers was evensong. Compline, at line 1991, was the last service of the day.

2172 "Solomon ... has forsaken me and worshipped Ashtoreth the goddess of the Sidonians" (1 Kings 11:33). After the destruction of Sodom and Gomorrah, when Lot's wife had been turned into a pillar of salt, Lot slept with his two daughters, and "both ... were with child by their father" (Genesis 19:24–36).

2260–63 Despite Guernes' discretion, we know from the Latin biographies that the prelate with the ungrammatical Latin was Hilary of Chichester, and that it was Gilbert Foliot who was reprimanded by the pope for his intemperate language (lines 2262–63).

2368 Becket's Latin must certainly have been competent, though the elegance of his Latin letters was presumably due in large measure to the clerks who drafted them for him. His formal education had, moreover, been unconventional, and Stephen of Rouen (an admittedly hostile witness) even reported that he was "not educated enough to speak Latin." Initially Becket had been counting on his clerks to plead for him (lines 2333–37), and subsequently he gave onlookers the impression of reading from a script prepared for him (line 2364). Given this, his fluency and eloquence as described here do indeed seem to verge on the miraculous. While Becket's vernacular was French, he can be presumed to have been bilingual in English. In his flight from Northampton he took on the dual Anglo-French pseudonym of Dereman/Christian.

2395 The text of the Constitutions of Clarendon, issued in January 1164, can be read in translation in *English Historical Documents: 1042–1189*, ed. David C. Douglas and George W. Greenaway, 2nd ed. (London, 1981), pp. 766–70.

2416–17 Literally: "... should not give pledges to Holy Church to make amends for their offence ..." It is the Latin source that talks of a pledge for future good behaviour.

2421 The Latin original has: "Laymen ought not to be accused save by accredited and lawful accusers and witnesses in the presence of the bishop ..."

2450 England would not qualify as a member of the Church unless the pope were its head.

2455 The contrast is between an ordinary feudal (lay) tenure and a purely ecclesiastical (free-alms) tenure, free of service obligation and granted in perpetuity.

2655 Meaning, presumably, that Roger is quite impervious to the storm of criticism surrounding him.

2680 A literal translation showing Bishop Roger borrowing (or even lending!) at interest is clearly inappropriate in the context, and Guernes can be assumed to be speaking metaphorically.

2735 This seems to mean that, except where the sum due is fixed at 30 pence, the rate is a penny for every five shillings' worth of livestock.

2746 Guernes' narrative seems to jump here from September 1169 to June 1170, but he is following Grim's Latin.

2820 Literally: "and did not thereafter ever stretch out a single finger at anything in this respect." Pointing the finger traditionally implies criticism or accusation.

2845 "Like a gold ring in a swine's snout is a beautiful woman without discretion" (Proverbs 11:22).

2850 The originals of the four Latin letters, all from 1166, that Guernes incorporates into his narrative can be read in *Materials for the History of Thomas Becket*, ed. James Craigie Robertson and J.B. Sheppard (London, 1875–85), vol. 5, pp. 269ff (for our lines 2851–3040), 278ff (for lines 3048–3180), 408–13 (for lines 3181–3320) and 512ff (for lines 3326–3565). Cf. *English Historical Documents*, pp. 793–98.

3284 Gilbert Foliot is reminding Becket that the power he is flaunting is borrowed from God, and that Thomas should beware that this same power can also serve to punish unrepentant sinners – such as himself.

3318 Pope Alexander III returned to Rome in November 1165 after an exile in France that had begun in 1162.

3337 "Are grapes gathered from thorns, or figs from thistles?" (Matthew 7:16).

3345 Compare Becket's own initial 'yes' at Clarendon which, on second thoughts, became a 'no'; lines 981–1010 above.

3487 The Biblical references here are to Peter's betrayal of Jesus: "Let him who has no sword sell his mantle and buy one" (Luke 22:36); "Then Simon Peter, having a sword, drew it and struck the high priest's slave and cut off his right ear" (John 18:10).

3518 "I say, 'You are gods, sons of the Most High, all of you'" (Psalms 82:6).

3530 "Do you not know that we are to judge angels?" (1 Corinthians 6:3).

3546 "The man who acts presumptuously by not obeying the priest ... or the judge, that man shall die" (Deuteronomy 17:12).

3565 What does not follow here is Gilbert Foliot's rejoinder to Becket's letter, known by its opening words *Multiplicem nobis*, which is regarded by some modern critics as a masterly indictment of Becket's performance as archbishop. Others, however, describe it as a furious denunciation and a tissue of half-truths. Becket, at all events, did not pursue the correspondence, and his biographers also preferred silence.

3634 The rare word *osselez* 'little bones' could refer to splinters of tooth or, more likely, bony tissue or tumours. This looks very much like first-hand testimony from William de Capes, Thomas's lay marshal, who was still alive in 1189 and living in Canterbury. Guernes stresses the authenticity of his oral sources during this time at lines 3862, 3894–95, 3944 and 3978. Cf. also 5422, 5674, 5790, 6168.

3807 The homage was actually performed in February 1169, three years after Becket left Pontigny for Sens. The meeting at Saint-Léger-en-Yvelines, mentioned a few lines below, took place in the same month.

3841–49 Of these two putative benefactors, both anonymous, the second looks very much like the pope.

3861–90 This vision, the source of which is William of Canterbury, is a repetition of Grim's version which Guernes had already translated at lines 3630–50.

3950 In Grim the subject of "as long as he lived" is Becket, which would exonerate Robert from breaking his word with his deathbed confession at line 3966.

3994 Saint-Denis was regarded as the capital of the French royal demesne, a relatively small area, in the 1170s, centred on Paris. In line 4011 we learn that "the kingdom of Saint-Denis" comprised Etampes, Orléans and Chartres as well as Paris.

4179 Although at Montmirail Becket had agreed to accept the ancestral customs, in the end the terms on which he returned to England avoided all mention of them. So he was saved from shame.

4266 At least eight months elapsed between the Montmartre and Fréteval meetings. Guernes' narrative of all the various attempts at reconciliation is often at variance with the actual events, as well as being predictably prejudiced in favour of his protagonist.

4498 For the original text of this letter see *Materials for the History of Thomas Becket*, vol. 7, p. 347.

4600 The original text of this letter is to be found in *Materials for the History of Thomas Becket*, vol. 7, p. 400.

4679 Becket's most treasured possessions are his books, and he can think of no finer present to make than to bequeath them to the monks of Canterbury.

4775 Despite being an archdeacon (and later bishop of Ely), Geoffrey Ridel was married. Though clerical marriage was outlawed, celibacy was still not uniformly enforced at the time.

4780 In order to obtain the approval of King Henry, then in the region of Bayeux.

4953 Docking a horse's tail was a recognized insult on a par with pulling or cutting a knight's beard. In the early 13th-century *Roman de Waldef*, messengers are insulted by being beaten and vilified, by having their heads shaved like fools and their horses' tails docked. In addition, *torchaz* are hung around their necks, perhaps the same as the *torgeluns* and the *torges* with which Becket was insultingly pelted at lines 1934 and 1943.

4966–70 Anathema, a sort of definitive excommunication, was a solemn ceremony in which lighted candles were ritualistically thrown to the ground and crushed underfoot once sentence had been passed.

4985 Grim's Latin makes Becket the subject of this sentence: literally, "lest he endanger your religion."

5010 Literally: "I am going to prepare a bad pillow for your head."

5035 William fitz Stephen reports that one of the three bishops had said to the king: "My lord, as long as Thomas lives you will have neither peace nor quiet, nor know good times." As recorded by Grim, Henry's fateful words were: "What idle and faithless wretches have I nourished and promoted in my realm, who allow their lord to be treated so contemptuously and shamefully by a low-born clerk!" William of Canterbury's and Guernes' image of an ungrateful companion lifting his heel against his benefactor has clear Biblical echoes (see John 13:18, Psalms 41:9).

5098 The name Rainild is found only in Guernes; for William's daughters, see David C. Douglas, *William the Conqueror: The Norman Impact upon England* (Berkeley, 1964), pp. 393–95.

5110 Winchelsea must be a scribal error, but all manuscripts preserve the reading.

5126–35 Such active and direct intervention by Roger of Pont-l'Evêque in the plot is not corroborated by any of the Latin biographers. Judas's thirty pieces of silver are here converted into sixty silver marks, that is £40 each. This would represent, at 1160 prices, a small fortune: the equivalent of more than 250 oxen, or a dozen or so warhorses, or the sum needed to keep ten students at university for a year. A modern equivalent – though such comparisons are of very limited value – would be something like £25,000.

5147 In Guernes' first draft (see Appendix, line 5), he makes the four knights land at Dogs' Port, a literal rendering of Grim's *Portu Canum*. Presumably Portsmouth was intended, with a play on words on the second element of Latin *Portesmuta*, in which *mota*, reflecting Anglo-Norman *mute* (Medieval French *muete*), means 'pack of hounds.'

5176 ff. The practicalities of the events leading up to the murder can be summarized as follows. Having occupied the palace gateway, the four knights crossed the courtyard and went through the porch into the great hall. From there they were escorted by the steward into Becket's inner chamber where they were received. After an abortive exchange, Reginald fitz Urse ordered Becket's detention before leaving with his three accomplices. They went back into the courtyard, where some of them put on their armour. They then opened the outer gate to admit the waiting soldiers. Alerted by the ensuing noise, the monks bolted the door between the porch and the hall. Robert de Broc, who knew his way around the palace, reacted by leading some of the soldiers past the kitchen and through the garden to a postern door giving access to the living quarters via the south side of the palace. This entrance was reached by way of an oriel, an upper porch at the top of a flight of stairs. These stairs were being repaired, and using the workmen's ladders and tools, the soldiers broke their way from here into the hall and thence into the chamber. Becket and his attendants had, in the meantime, left via a connecting door, the jammed bolt of which was miraculously freed. They thus found their way into the cloister and from there into the church. The monks began to bar the door behind them, but Becket ordered it to be left open. He then made his way up the stairs leading to the north aisle in the direction of the choir, where vespers were being sung. The four knights had, in the meantime, succeeded in entering the church. Becket stopped by a pillar in the north transept between the altar of St Benedict, in the wall of the eastern apse, and the Lady chapel. It was here that he was attacked, fell and died.

5223 An obscure line. Literally: "He who was leading them hated their salvation/safety," referring perhaps to Henry or to the Devil. There is no doubt a pun on *salut* meaning both 'greeting' and 'salvation.' The actual leader of the group seems to have been Reginald fitz Urse.

5243 An initial decision, present in Grim's Latin, to exclude the clerks seems to have been omitted in Guernes' text.

5291 Guernes' text is probably corrupt here as it omits the knights' explicit announcement of Becket's banishment by the king, present in Grim's Latin. *Belement manaciez!* 'fine threats!' would be more appropriate coming from Becket's mouth after news of the banishment.

5521 Guernes' *malveis hum* is something of a euphemism in relation to Grim's Latin, in which Becket unceremoniously calls Reginald fitz Urse a pimp (*leno*) – presumably a reference to his being an underling of Ranulf de Broc, royal whore master.

5636–40 William fitz Stephen's Latin text reads: "... in the garlands of the Church neither lilies nor roses are lacking, and in the passion of the blessed Thomas both the gleaming white of the brain and the crimson red of the blood ... were sure and certain signs that ... he was destined to receive from the Lord a stole of two colours: white in token of his faithful governance of his archiepiscopal see, and purple in token of the happy consummation of his martyrdom." Cf. Song of Songs 2:1: "I am a rose of Sharon, a lily of the valleys."

5649 Hunting was more or less the monopoly of the king and his men, and Guernes rarely loses an opportunity to criticize the oppressive and widely hated Forest Law that Henry enforced; see lines 3598, 5686, 6084.

5699 An obscure line. Presumably the tithe would not have been payable if the church had remained closed for a whole year.

5871 December 21st fell on a Tuesday in 1115 and 1120, and historians generally prefer the second of these two for Becket's date of birth.

6072 The Young King was five when he was married, fifteen when he was crowned, and nineteen when Guernes was writing in 1174.

6087 Guernes' unflattering characterization of Henry's subjects, specifically, one suspects, the English, as undisciplined louts is conveyed by the term *pautonier*. Its semantic range covers hirelings and vagrants at one end, and all sorts of riff-raff and social inferiors at the other.

6128–35 The female eagle can be identified with Henry's wife Eleanor, imprisoned since March 1173, and the product of the third nest might, or might not, be the future king Richard. Geoffrey of Monmouth wrote the *Prophecies of Merlin* around 1134, and incorporated them into his *History of the Kings of Britain*.

6147 Marguerite, daughter of Louis VII of France and bride of the Young King.

6166–70 Since King Henry's public penance (lines 5906 ff.) took place on 12th July 1174, and since Guernes makes no mention of the great fire that engulfed Canterbury Cathedral on 5th September 1174, we can safely assume that he must have finished the second version of his poem in the course of August 1174. It looks as if he must have started his first draft before he acquired a copy of Grim's Latin Life, which was finished in 1172, since he explicitly claims (line 144) to have taken the best part of four years to complete the work. If, therefore, he started writing in the early months of 1171 (line 6166), he would presumably have finished his first version by the end of 1172 or early in 1173, leaving something like a year and a half during which to revise and rewrite it, and to bring it to the state in which we know it today.

Postscript This survives only in one manuscript: Paris, Bibiothèque nationale de France, nouv. acq. fr. 13513, ff. 98r–v. Marie was appointed abbess of Barking in April 1173. Odo was prior of Christ Church from 1167 until July 1175, when he was elected abbot of Battle Abbey. The postscript is in a different metre from the preceding narrative. The reference to Judas's confession is obscure. If not a simple piece of rhetoric or a contrived rhyme (in the same vein as *Patras*), it probably goes back to the Apocryphal tradition.

Bibliography

A bibliography devoted to Guernes de Pont-Sainte-Maxence is available online at http://www.arlima.net/eh/guernes_de_pont_sainte_maxence.html. Another bibliography, by Serena Modena, "Vent' anni di studi sulla *Vie de saint Thomas Becket ...*," in *Critica del Testo* 15 (2012): 365–77, is also available.

Editions and Translations

Guernes de Pont-Sainte-Maxence. Jean-Guy Gouttebroze and Ambroise Queffélec, trans. *Guernes de Pont-Sainte-Maxence: La Vie de saint Thomas Becket*. Paris: Champion, 1990.

—. Janet Shirley, trans. *Garnier's Becket*. Chichester: Phillimore, 1975.

—. Jacques T.E. Thomas, ed. and trans. *Guernes de Pont-Sainte-Maxence: La Vie de saint Thomas de Canterbury*. 2 vols. Louvain: Peeters, 2002.

—. Emmanuel Walberg, ed. *La Vie de saint Thomas le martyr par Guernes de Pont-Sainte-Maxence, poème historique du XIIe siècle*. Lund: Gleerup, 1922.

—. Emmanuel Walberg, ed. *La Vie de saint Thomas Becket*. Paris: Champion, 1936; repr. 1964.

Sources

The Life and Death of Thomas Becket, Chancellor of England and Archbishop of Canterbury, Based on the Account of William fitzStephen, His Clerk, with Additions from Other Contemporary Sources. Ed. and trans. George Greenaway. London: Folio Society, 1961.

The Lives of Thomas Becket. Ed. and trans. Michael Staunton. Manchester: Manchester University Press, 2001.

Materials for the History of Thomas Becket, Archbishop of Canterbury (Canonized by Pope Alexander III., A.D. 1173), ed. James Craigie Robertson and J.B. Sheppard. 7 vols. Rolls Series 67. London: Longman, 1875–85. For William of

Canterbury see 1: 1–136; for Edward Grim see 2: 353–450; for William fitz Stephen see 3: 1–154.

Selected Studies

Boutet, Dominique. "Hagiographie et historiographie: la *Vie de saint Thomas Becket* de Guernes de Pont-Sainte-Maxence et la *Vie de saint Louis* de Joinville." *Le Moyen Age* 106 (2000): 277–93.

Chaurand, Jacques. "«Mis languages est bons, car en France fui nez», ou l'avantage d'être né sur le continent au XIIème siècle." *Carnets d'atelier de sociolinguistique* 2 (2007): 3–27.

Löfstedt, Leena. "La Loi canonique, les Plantagenêts et saint Thomas Becket." *Medioevo romanzo* 15 (1990): 3–16.

—. "La *Vie de s. Thomas Becket* par Garnier de Pont-Sainte-Maxence et la traduction en ancien français du *Décret* de Gratien." *Neuphilologische Mitteilungen* 98 (1997): 161–77.

Perrot, Jean-Pierre. "Violence et sacré: du meurtre au sacrifice dans la *Vie de saint Thomas Becket* de Guernes de Pont-Sainte-Maxence." *Senefiance* 36 (1994): 399–412.

Peters, Timothy. "Elements of the chanson de geste in an Old French Life of Becket ... ." *Olifant* 18 (1993–94): 278–88.

—. "An Ecclesiastical Epic: Garnier de Pont-Sainte-Maxence's *Vie de saint Thomas le martyr*." *Mediaevistik* 7 (1994): 181–202.

Robertson, Duncan. *The Medieval Saints' Lives: Spiritual Renewal and Old French Literature*. Lexington, KY: French Forum, 1995. See especially pp. 182–98.

Roques, Gilles. "Les Régionalismes dans la *Vie de Thomas Becket*." In *A l'Ouest d'oïl, des mots et des choses: Actes du VIIe colloque international de dialectologie ... (Caen ... 1999)*, ed. Catherine Bougy, Stéphane Laîné, and Pierre Boissel, pp. 187–200. Caen: Presses universitaires de Caen, 2003.

Schmidt, Gerhard. "Die *Thomas Becket Vita* des Garnier de Pont-Sainte-Maxence als Pilgerpredigt." In *Stimmen der Romania: Festschrift für W. Theodor Elwert*, ed. Gerhard Schmidt and Manfred Tietz, pp. 377–88. Wiesbaden: Heymann, 1980.

Schulze-Busacker, Elisabeth. "Écrire au goût de son temps: Guernes de Pont-Sainte-Maxence, *La Vie de saint Thomas le Martyr*." In *Studi di filologia romanza offerti a Valeria Bertolucci Pizzorusso*, ed. Pietro G. Beltrami, Maria Grazia Capusso, Fabrizio Cigni, and Sergio Vatteroni, 2: 1443–61. Pisa: Pacini, 2006.

Varvaro, Alberto. "«Ja mais ne resurdra!» : glossa a Guernes de Pont-Sainte-Maxence v. 5635." *Medioevo romanzo* 20 (1996): 161–69.

Other Works

Barking Abbey and Medieval Literary Culture: Authorship and Authority in a Female Community. Ed. Jennifer N. Brown and Donna Alfano Bussell. Woodbridge: York Medieval Press, 2012.

Barlow, Frank. *Thomas Becket*. London: Weidenfeld, 1986; 3rd ed. 2002.

Bryant, Arthur. *Makers of the Realm*. London: Collins, 1953.

Careri, Maria, Christine Ruby, and Ian Short. *Livres et écritures en français et en occitan au XIIe siècle: Catalogue illustré.* Rome: Viella, 2011.

Clanchy, M.T. *From Memory to Written Record: England 1066–1307*. 2nd ed. Oxford: Blackwell, 1993.

A Companion to the Anglo-Norman World. Ed. Christopher Harper-Bill and Elisabeth van Houts. Woodbridge: Boydell & Brewer, 2003.

Damian-Grint, Peter. *The New Historians of the 12th-Century Renaissance: Inventing Vernacular Authority.* Woodbridge: Boydell, 1999.

Dean, Ruth J., with Maureen Boulton. *Anglo-Norman Literature: A Guide to Texts and Manuscripts*. Anglo-Norman Text Society. London: Birkbeck College, 1999.

Douglas, David C. *William the Conqueror: The Norman Impact upon England.* Berkeley: University of California Press, 1964.

Duggan, Anne. *Becket*. London: Arnold, 2004.

English Historical Documents: 1042–1189. Ed. David C. Douglas and George W. Greenaway. 2nd ed. London: Methuen, 1981.

Fragments d'une Vie de saint Thomas de Cantorbery. Ed. Paul Meyer. Société des anciens textes français. Paris: Didot, 1885.

Gransden, Antonia. *Historical Writing in England, c. 550 to c. 1307.* London: Routledge, 1974.

Guy, John. *Thomas Becket: Warrior, Priest, Rebel, Victim: A 900-Year-Old Story Retold*. London: Viking, 2012.

Henry of Huntingdon. *Historia Anglorum.* Ed. Diana Greenway. Oxford: Clarendon Press, 1996.

Kay, Sarah. *Courtly Contradictions: The Emergence of the Literary Object in the Twelfth Century.* Stanford: Stanford University Press, 2001.

Laurent, Françoise. *Plaire et édifier: les récits hagiographiques composés en Angleterre aux XIIe et XIIIe siècles.* Paris: Champion, 1998.

Legge, Mary Dominica. *Anglo-Norman in the Cloisters.* Edinburgh: Edinburgh University Press, 1950.
—. *Anglo-Norman Literature and Its Background.* Oxford: Clarendon Press, 1963.
Schulze-Busacker, Elisabeth. *Proverbes et expressions proverbiales dans la littérature narrative du moyen âge français.* Paris: Champion, 1985.
Short, Ian. "An Early Draft of Guernes' *Vie de saint Thomas Becket.*" *Medium Ævum* 46 (1977): 20–34.
—. "Patrons and Polyglots: French literature in 12th-century England." *Anglo-Norman Studies* 14 (1992): 229–49.
—. Review of G.M. Spiegel, *Romancing the Past*, in *Romance Philology* 51 (1997–98): 97–99.
—. "Denis Piramus and the Truth of Marie's Lais." *Cultura Neolatina* 67 (2007): 319–40.
Thomas Saga Erkibyskups: A Life of Archbishop Thomas Becket in Icelandic. Ed. and trans. Eiríkr Magnússon. 2 vols. Rolls Series 65. London: Longman, 1875–85. Repr. Cambridge: Cambridge University Press, 2012.
La Vie de Thomas Becket par Beneit. Ed. Börje Schlyter. Études romanes de Lund. Lund: Gleerup, 1941.
Vincent, Nicholas. "The Court of Henry II." In *Henry II: New Interpretations*, ed. Christopher Harper-Bill and Nicholas Vincent, pp. 278–334. Woodbridge: Boydell, 2007.
Warren, W.L. *Henry II.* Berkeley: University of California Press, 1973.
Wogan-Browne, Jocelyn. "*Clerc u lai, muine u dame*: Women and Anglo-Norman Hagiography in the Twelfth and Thirteenth Centuries." In *Women and Literature in Britain 1150–1500*, ed. Carole M. Meale, pp. 61–85. Cambridge: Cambridge University Press, 1993.
—. *Saints' Lives and Women's Literary Culture: c. 1150–1300: Virginity and Its Authorizations.* Oxford: Oxford University Press, 2001.

Index

All references in this index, including those to the Postscript (pp. 176–77) and to the Appendix (pp. 178–80), are to line numbers.